A Christian
Approach to
Education

A Christian Approach to Education

H. W. BYRNE

A Mott Media Book

BAKER BOOK HOUSE
Grand Rapids, Michigan 49516

Library of Congress Cataloging in Publication Data

Byrne, Herbert W   1917-
    A Christian approach to education.

Bibliography: p.
    Includes index.
    1. Byrne, Herbert W   1917-   2. Education—
Philosophy. I. Title.
LB885.B9   1977   370.1   76-56229
ISBN 0-915134-20-9

To
My Wife
With Love and Gratitude

CONTENTS*

Foreword by Charles G. Schauffele

Preface

SECTION ONE

The Foundations of a Christian Approach to Education

SECTION TWO

The Implications for a Christian Philosophy of Education

SECTION THREE

The Content of a Christian Philosophy of Education

*Chapter outlines are included at the beginning of each chapter.

FOREWORD

A fresh interest in Christian education from the grass roots of parental concern promises this book a wide reading. It should be in every church library. It should be required reading for every Christian Day School teacher and Board member. Parent study groups and Parent-Teacher Associations should go through it systematically, chapter by chapter. College students with majors in Education and Christian Education should read this and keep it handy for quick reference.

The very basic differences between secular and Christian education are clearly set forth here. The three most vital cleavage points between them are the creation of all things by a sovereign God, the fall of man and his world into sin, and the regeneration of man and his world by the grace of God in Jesus Christ. Thus, the facts of Creation, Sin and Salvation are the basic theological roots of a Christian philosophy of education. In Section I Dr. Byrne shows that these Biblical certainties should be basic to ideas about education.

Section II is a "must" for parents, teachers and students of education. For we must acknowledge and use wherever possible the findings of social sciences under God. Since all truth is God's truth, these verifiable data can aid us in carrying out God's educational mandate.

The hall mark of real Christian Education is the faith-learning process. This is the subject of Section III. The mark of any Christian institution of learning is not whether teachers are Christian, whether the Bible is read or taught, or chapel is held, but whether each subject in the curriculum is presented from the Creator's perspective. This section, therefore, is a teacher's treasure trove.

Each chapter is prefaced by a complete outline of the content and followed by a list of suggested activities. The book is replete with charts and diagrams which illustrate the narrative. An up-to-date bibliography is appended. A four-page glossary of philosophic terminology in education is also included.

The basic Christian philosophy, the excellent practical suggestions for the integration of school subjects with the Christian faith, and its overall usefulness are some of the reasons I have used this book as a classroom text since its first publication in 1961. And this edition is even better.

PROFESSOR CHARLES G. SCHAUFFELE
Gordon-Conwell Theological Seminary
S. Hamilton, Mass. 01982

PREFACE

Much is being said and written these days about the deplorable state of affairs in the field of education. Christian education has not escaped its share of criticism. Some of the most prominent weaknesses in Christian education include the problem of subject integration, where the individual teacher fails to unify his special field of knowledge with the Christian faith, the lack of a clear-cut philosophy to which we can give complete commitment, the compartmentalization of subject matter, and the failure to capitalize on the rich resources of the Christian faith for education.

No claim is made that this work completely solves such problems, but at least an attempt is made to give them serious consideration. The major premise of this work is the belief that the Christian philosophy of life as recorded in the Holy Scriptures embraces a genuine Christian philosophy of education. An attempt, therefore, has been made to provide a bibliocentric approach to the problems of education. At the same time an effort was made to compare and contrast along the way opposing and present-day points of view in the field of education. The primary thrust, however, is positive rather than negative. It is the prayer of the author that all readers will be able as a result of reading this volume to throw a Christian frame of reference around the various considerations of education while at the same time drawing directly from the content of the Christian revelation to arrive at a satisfactory, adequate, and Christian approach to education. No claim to originality is made but it is our hope that the work will prove a stimulation to deeper thinking in the field, leading to the development of a real Bible-integrated view of education.

The main purpose of this work is to provide an introduction to a Christian approach to education for evangelical Christian schools and colleges. At the same time, it is hoped that the book will appeal to laymen in the church and Sunday school as well as to parents who are deeply interested in evaluating the schools to which their children will go.

The general plan of the book calls for three sections. The first one is devoted to a consideration of the foundations of a Christian approach to education. Here a short analysis of the contemporary scene, both cultural and intellectual, is made in order to give the reader orientation for that which follows. This is followed with a chapter on the Christian Theistic World View or Christian Philosophy of life as a whole from which an educational philosophy can be abstracted. The section closes with some suggestions on how a Christian philosophy of education can be constructed.

Section Two is devoted to a consideration of the implications of the Christian World View for a Christian Philosophy of Education. This, of course, concerns the educative process—the process by which the philosophy gets into the classroom situation where aims and objectives, teacher-pupil relationships, the curriculum, methods, and administration are so vitally evident.

Extensive revisions have been made in this section. First, developments in the field of learning theory in recent years have been noted, particularly as they have reference to the cognitive theories of Jean Piaget and the development theories of Lawrence Kohlberg. Also, a section on the changes in teaching methodology has been added. Finally, the growth of the private school movement in this country led to the writing of a completely new segment, with particular attention given to the Christian Day School Movement. It naturally follows that a revised section has been added to the bibliography to reflect some of the more recent books to reach the market.

Section Three continues a discussion of the implications of the Christian philosophy for the great subject matter areas including Biblical Studies, Social Sciences, Natural Sciences, Humanities, and Communicative Skills. Here an attempt is made to show the direct relevance of the Christian faith to these disciplines.

Needless to say, a great many expressions of appreciation are due for which a preface does not provide a sufficiently intimate medium. For the patience and encouragement of members of my family, of colleagues and friends, and of students, such an expression of gratitude as is conveyed by these few words is all too brief.

To Dr. Paul H. Wood, Dr. Nobel V. Sack, Dr. S. A. Witmer, Dr. Rene Frank, and particularly to Dr. Mark Fakkema, appreciation is due for thoughtful and penetrating criticisms. To those who prayed for me I am grateful. To Miss Elaine Neiman for typing most of the manuscript, I offer sincere thanks. For the errors and shortcomings, however, the author assumes full responsibility.

HERBERT W. BYRNE

Section One

The Foundations of a Christian Approach to Education

Forces and pressures arising out of the contemporary cultural situation have demanded revolutionary changes in thought and action. The educational philosopher, as he faces the present-day situation, is called upon to give satisfactory answers to the problems which beset us. Section One, therefore, is devoted to making a survey of what is demanded in the fields of philosophy and education today. This will lay some foundations upon which we may define and build a satisfactory Christian philosophy of education.

The application of regenerated and consecrated reason to the tenets of the Christian faith is sufficient to develop a systematized statement of belief or a world view. From this it is possible to construct a Christian philosophy of education.

THE NATURE AND DEVELOPMENT OF A NEW
APPROACH TO CHRISTIAN EDUCATION

OUTLINE FOR CHAPTER 1

A. THE INTELLECTUAL CONTEXT OF CHRISTIAN EDUCATION
  1. Introduction
  2. Greek Thought
  3. Roman Thought
  4. Christian Thought
  5. Medieval Thought
  6. Modern Thought

B. THE DEMANDS FOR A NEW APPROACH TO CHRISTIAN EDUCATION
  1. From the Critics
  2. From the Culture
  3. From the Field

C. THE DEVELOPMENT OF A NEW APPROACH TO CHRISTIAN EDUCATION
  1. The Nature of Christian Education
  2. The Development of a New Approach

1 | THE NATURE AND DEVELOPMENT OF A NEW APPROACH TO CHRISTIAN EDUCATION

A. THE INTELLECTUAL CONTEXT OF CHRISTIAN EDUCATION

1. Introduction

Freeman Butts, in his *Cultural History of Western Education,* says, "We think the way we do in large part *because* the Greeks thought the way they did. Thus, to understand our own ways of thinking we need to know how the Greeks thought."[1] That this statement is largely true seems evident. Even in so-called Christian circles this condition prevails. In fact we have yet to see a genuine Christian philosophy of education worked out and practiced in our Christian schools and colleges.

It is important for Christian educators to face this issue squarely for a number of reasons. First, Greek intellectualism with its consequent scientific naturalism is definitely the intellectual context within which many Christian educators work. Second, this subject is relevant because Christian education has had the tendency to compromise with this context. As never before we need to develop a distinctively Christian approach to education spelled out in terms of a definite Christian philosophy of education. Third, many of our Christian teachers, while subscribing clearly to orthodox theological positions and enjoying genuine Christian experience, have been so steeped in this context that it is hard for them to break away from its premises in the classroom.

It is our purpose briefly to outline the history of thought on the secular front. By tracing such a development it is hoped that we can come to a much greater appreciation for the intellectual heritage on the Christian front while at the same time opening our eyes somewhat to the task of re-educating ourselves to breaking away from the context of thought provided by Greek intellectualism.

2. Greek Thought

The Greeks were not only interested in noting the existence of reality, but they sought also to *explain it*. Most of them ex-

[1] New York, McGraw-Hill Book Co., Inc., 1955, p. 45.

plained reality on the basis of the action of the gods, but some concluded that natural phenomena are explained by the working of natural forces. They began to depend to a large extent upon reasoning power to provide answers. Analysis of the literary product of this way of thinking has led scholars to identify it as a pattern of thinking known as objective reasoning. This type of thinking, as interpreted by modern thinkers, is paraded as the first recorded effort to develop an intellectual movement which questioned convention, appearance, or anything accepted, and to seek for something better. Socrates is perhaps the best illustration of this. To him, "knowledge is virtue," to *really* know what is good prohibits one from doing evil.

Plato, too, has had tremendous influence on Western thought. Although men have argued over the significance of Plato, in general it is agreed that he leaned toward other-worldly thought. His doctrine of Ideas is the best illustration of this. In this, Plato maintained that only the ideal is real. Actualities are only copies of the perfect ideal. Knowledge is made possible only because actual entities appear to be like or resemble the ideal. Actual life experiences are only reflections of life's true reality, and to Plato life's true reality centers only in the Perfect One, God.

This other-worldliness of Plato, it is claimed, made an appeal to sensitive natures and, therefore, gained easy access to early Christian thought. Then, too, it is thought that his constant striving for moral and social perfection also lent itself both to the Christian spirit and practice.

In contrast to the other-worldliness of Plato was the this-worldliness of the Sophists who flourished in the Fifth Century B.C. They were free-lance teachers and speakers who advocated this new way of thinking called reasoning. They maintained that metaphysical issues were beyond solution, therefore, scholars should concentrate on human nature and human relations. They became famous for their statement: "Man is the measure of all things." They were concerned with the sense world and used reason as a tool to achieve success in that world.

Aristotle has been posed as one who compromised between Plato and the advocates of this-worldliness. His metaphysics is summed up in his views on form and matter. Matter is by nature purposeless. Form is mind or spirit at work transforming matter into something that has life and purpose, it is creative, active, and purposive. His "form" is close to Plato's "ideas" but not quite the same. In fact, he arrives through the famous doctrine of *theoria,* the undisturbed meditation on God, at God who is unmoved Mover, the Final Cause.

Aristotle was not a materialist because he believed in the purposiveness of life here on earth. Life in his view is striving toward some end. This is why his views have been attractive to some Christian thinkers.

In addition to formal philosophy as represented by the outstanding Greek philosophers, the Greeks have helped to pattern Western life through what has become known as classical culture. This is represented by architecture, sculpture, literature, and the arts. Brinton, in his book, *Ideas and Men*, has pointed out certain characteristics of Greek culture which have been handed down to affect our age (Chapter 2).

1. This life and this world, not the world beyond death, is prominent.
2. The satisfaction of natural human desires and needs is the primary motivation for living.
3. "Nothing in excess" established the principle of discipline and control in life process, the Golden Mean of Aristotle.
4. Intelligent competition provided good motivation for one to do his best at anything worth doing.[2]

Brinton goes on to point out (p. 65) that the classic culture was aristocratic because its ideal was beyond the average man to achieve. He also points out that the Greek was earthbound, tied to sensual experience, without hope of immortality, with no belief in a God morally interested in his fate, and although he had some sense of right and wrong, he had no feelings equivalent to what is meant by a sense of sin. Being earthbound he could not gain strength and consolation by most of the means we associate with religion. Patriotism was the only inspiration the Greek had and this did not last long. The outbreak of civil war, the increase of selfishness and individualism, and the inevitable class struggles for power were sufficient to humble Greece. No pagan gods, Apollonian virtues, Golden Means or intellectualism were sufficient to ward off disaster, and Greece fell into division, strife, and ultimate defeat at the hands of the Romans.

Before moving on into the Roman period we must pause to note the part played by Hellenistic Greeks who lived in the three centuries B.C. up until Roman domination. This is the age of the scientists including Archimedes, Euclid, Aristarchus, and Erastosthenes, who did their best work in mathematics, astronomy, and physics. Progress was considerable. In fact, many modern concepts are traceable to Hellenistic sources. This period also featured the artistic and literary achievements of such men as Plutarch, the moralist and biographer; the historian, Polybius; the poet, Theocritus; and the meditative emperor, Marcus Aurelius. It was dur-

[2]Brinton, Crane, *Ideas and Men* (Englewood Cliffs, N. J., Prentice Hall, 1950).

ing this period that the *koine* Greek, the language of St. Paul, was developed. Science, however, declined to await its rise again in another day. It faded before Christianity bloomed in the First Century A.D. so no one could rightly say that Christianity suppressed the cause of science.

3. Roman Thought

Roughly at the beginning of the Christian era the Roman Empire came into being. For about four centuries Western society was a simple political unity. Rome became the great transmitter of Greek culture. This we know partially through the great writings of Vergil, Cicero, Tacitus, Catullus, Seneca, Horace, and others. However, Rome was noted for her practical emphasis and utilitarianism, her emphasis on law and order, her talents for organization, her institutions, her citizenship. Many believe that Rome's greatest contribution was a democratic concept of law. In the final analysis, however, Rome merely perpetuated Greek culture in a social context of democracy.

In evaluating this ancient period the evangelical is encouraged to note the general idealistic frame of mind of the great Greek thinkers, for some of them insisted that nature and man have meaning only in relation to an eternal, purposive, spiritual sphere. Undoubtedly this is at the heart of Socratic-Platonic-Aristotelian philosophy. However, it is clearly evident that the force of their views was intellectually directed through the power of rational thought. In addition, it is also clear that Democritus advocated a thorough-going materialism in which nature was ultimate. Still further, the Sophists with their theory of relativism, in which all of reality was pictured in a state of constant flux, added their voices to that of Democritus. The overall result is that Western thought has been, and still is, dominated largely by elements of Greek intellectualism and materialism. While the great philosophers deplored this materialistic bent in Greek culture, they were powerless to stop its development through efforts to compromise, and Greek culture thereby came to its inevitable doom. Ancient culture lacked the dynamic to achieve high moral and spiritual standards. Thus, this has been the heritage of Western thought.

4. Christian Thought

Into the void, which Greek confidence both in natural reason and in mysticism had failed to overcome, Christianity moved with personal and social power. However, on the Greek side of thought Christianity is viewed not as a supernatural force with the power of personal divinity, but rather from a naturalistic and historical point of view. Actually this perspective is the view of an "outsider." We shall now move to an interpretation of Christianity as a whole from this point of view and assess its effects on Western thought.

The thinker who tries to assess Christianity from a position that he calls "outside" actually has to deny the existence of the supernatural to do this. This is inevitable because, as Brinton put it, "The core of Christian faith, the belief in the existence of the supernatural, the divine, is forever proof not merely against naturalistic and historical attacks, *but involves rejection of naturalistic and historical explanation.*"[3] While such critics admit that Jesus actually existed and became the dominant and motivating force in Christianity, the Christianity which actually was perpetuated since His day, organized Christianity as they call it, has actually been developed largely from supplementary sources. In doing this, the critics say, Christianity actually has gone *beyond* Jesus.

To begin with, it was the Apostle Paul who organized and institutionalized Christianity and developed it from Jewish sectarianism to Christian universalism. Beyond this the success of Christianity is explained on the basis of the peculiar effects that the combination of its theology, its ethics, and its government had on the whole. The main group of Christians, the intellectual maintains, was the Roman Catholic Church which fought its way through persecutions and heresies and became strong thereby so that by the Fourth Century it had become the triumphant and established religion of the Western world.

The Greek intellectual who takes a look at Christianity from an "outside" position is not without his reasons for the triumph of Christianity in the Western world. Brinton has listed such reasons as follows:

1. Christianity is a syncretism, a combining of elements drawn from other religions.
2. The other-worldliness of its faith appeals to the common man who needs an escape from his problems.
3. It also appeals to upper classes and intellectuals who were dissatisfied with life on the one hand and attracted to its new theology on the other.
4. Christianity appeals also to the practical man who wants action and power.
5. Christianity insisted that the elements it had borrowed from other religions were Christian monopolies, not mere copies of other religions.[4]

[3]*Ibid.*, p. 135.
[4]*Ibid.*, pp. 157-62.

Thus, from the naturalistic and historical point of view, Christianity is merely a development of concurrently favorable factors which mutually interacted upon one another.

In assessing the outcomes of Christianity as a way of life, the intellectual is frank to say that organized Christianity is vastly different from that originally pictured in the New Testament. In this he admits there is a difference between professed Christians and real Christians. On the other hand, as a way of life he maintains that there has been and still is a wide variety of ways of life that bear the label of Christianity. Orthodox believers, however, are marked by definite loyalty to the principles of theism. Organized Christianity has been perpetuated also with certain unique elements. They include an other-worldly attitude, a general distrust of the flesh, unselfishness, love for fellowmen, a general distrust of rationalistic thinking, loyalty to Christian theism, and a democratic spirit.

Finally, the intellectual fully recognizes the impact which the controversies within the ranks of Christendom as well as the attacks from outsiders has had on Western thought. In general, this is the intellectual theory regarding Christianity which has been handed down to the present day.

5. Medieval Thought

Moving into the Middle Ages we face a period of intellectual history stretching from about 500 to roughly 1500 A.D. Some scholars speak of the period from 500 A.D. to Charlemagne as "the Dark Ages," a period following the break-up of the Roman Empire relatively barren of intellectual progress. Some scholars speak of the Middle Ages as a period without material wealth and scientific technology but one of moral, social, and spiritual progress. Others, among the positivists, radicals, and anti-Christians, claim this period was barbarous, full of superstition and ignorance. Here, of course, one sees the clash between the church and opposing interests.

Without a doubt this period is one which was largely dominated by the Roman Catholic church. What formal thought existed was sponsored largely and preserved by this church. In fact, men trained in the church almost had a monopoly on intellectual life. The church was lecture platform, press, publisher, library, school, and college.

Outside the church, learning was restricted largely to the upper classes of chivalry fame, who occasionally reached a high level of scholarship. These together with the rise of the universities represented intellectual efforts not sponsored by the church. The universities perpetuated the quadrivium, and trivium on the higher levels of education. However, it is primarily to the church that we owe the preservation of Greek and Latin literature. Gradually, the full fabric of civilization was restored so that in the twelfth, thirteenth, and fourteenth centuries a fully developed and restored culture appeared once more with the church holding the dominating hand.

In medieval thought, theology was indeed the "Queen of the Sciences." Two men and their views dominated the scene — Augustine and Thomas Aquinas. The former, however, has had greater influence.

Augustine clearly held to other-worldly ideas. These ideas are prominent in all his writings. His great work, the *City of God*, put the Christian point of view in the form of a philosophy of history in which Christianity was shown as a process in time.

From Augustine in the early period we trace the course of thought to its climax in the late years of this period to the formal position known as Scholasticism. Scholasticism was at best a compromise system of thought. Scholastics appealed to reason in an effort to support the doctrines of Christianity. In this Thomas Aquinas led the way and sought to bring to his support both the authority of the church and the views of Aristotle.

In social life the medieval attitude toward man in society took on at least three aspects — first, the notion of a stratified society in which each man plays the part God sent him to play; second, the concept of a just price and an economic order not dependent on the play of supply and demand; third, the concept of a natural law to be understood by natural reason, and regulating as well as explaining human relations on earth. Behind all of these ideas was the idea of this world as unchanging. Here again one can see the emphasis placed on natural law which is a demonstration of God's law. This concept of natural law was passed on to later generations. On the one hand, it led to a rather stable society. But on the other hand, it has also motivated rebellion against authority. Later on, in the modern period, we shall see further effects of the concept of natural law.

We may conclude from the short consideration of the philosophical and social concepts of the medieval period given thus far that Greek intellectualism largely prevailed during this period in spite of the general and nominal dominance of theistic concepts in man's thinking sponsored primarily by the Roman Church. It is easy, therefore, to see how such thought was handed down to our modern period. One other aspect of medieval life — the scientific — must also be examined because the roots of the scientific spirit and practice clearly were laid in this period also. We know now that the medieval period provided modern man with many foundations for his present approach, not only to social, economic, and religious matters, but also to science. From the Twelfth Century on social conditions developed which were conducive to the prosperity of science. Intellectually, the study of logic, mathematics, and the liberal arts underlay the habits of mind which led to the development later on of the scientific spirit, the scientific method and practice. Scholasticism laid great emphasis on deductive thinking. This gave rise to the antithesis in the development and use of inductive principles but we now know that deductive principles are also useful in scientific thinking, method and practice. It was not really Biblical fundamentalism that delayed the development of science. Instead, it was a literal adherence to the works of Greek thinkers like Aristotle and Roman thinkers like Pliny and Galen. Add to this the superstitious spirit of the people, an uncritical reverence for classical authority, over-emphasis on other-worldliness, neglect of studying the commonplace for a preference of the miraculous — these and similar reasons explain why science was late in its development. In spite of these, science made strides through the patient labors of mathematicians, laborious translations of Arab works on science and mathematics, widespread increase in inventions of work tools and the discovery of printing. The beginning of the rise of the middle class also made its contributions with new ideas and demands on society. A revolution against church authority by Christian reformers, on the one hand, and popular advocates of carnal living were sufficient to motivate greater freedom of thought. In making a critical evaluation of the Middle Ages, one is forced to certain generalizations. First, it is quite evident that it was a period dominated by the commonsense acceptance of the supernatural. Most intellectuals accepted theistic presuppositions, believing that God directed life for man's good. It was a period strangely mixed with both the supernatural and the natural, a culture of credulity and superstition, a culture of mysticism yet one of violence, a culture of extremes and contradictions, but on the whole a culture consumed with the search for God. Overall it was a culture shot through with an attitude favorable toward the Christian view of life. Men in general felt that much of their lives were in the hands of God who worked in society.

It is quite evident to evangelicals that loyalty to Christian theism in the Middle Ages was largely intellectual. Christianity in its original setting was dynamic; its power rested on revelation and regeneration as the basis of this dynamic. It did not depend on ideas or a theory of knowledge, but on a Person, the Lord Jesus Christ.

While Christianity finds itself formally on the side of Greek idealism as it was opposed to naturalism, it had to oppose the classic emphasis on rational competence. An evaluation of medieval thought shows clearly that competence in the intellectual approach to life was quite dominant during that period. It also shows just as clearly that Greek life was geared to the carnal and natural. Both of these approaches are self-evidently opposed to the Biblical outlook on thought and life.

The organized church of the Middle Ages without doubt compromised with intellectualism and naturalism as a way of life. True Christianity cannot afford to move away from its adherence to inner life as a unique phenomenon from above. Many of the best minds during the medieval period, though ranged on the side of Christianity, weakened their position by merely recasting pagan principles of thought and life in theistic terms. In addition, the moral failure of Roman Catholicism is well known.

Whereas the ancient period with its philosophical idealism and the medieval period with its nominal Biblical theism both affirmed the existence of the supernatural, the transition to the modern period, which was gradual, was a change-over to the denial of the supernatural. In this, Scholasticism played a large part.

Thomas Aquinas developed the scholastic approach by means of a synthesis of science, philosophy, and theology. He thus weakened the hold on Christian revelation and inner dynamic. Luther and Calvin later on tried to swing thought back to the true Christian position but as a whole they failed. The combination of Greek intellectualism, scholasticism, and science was sufficient to gain the ascendancy. This opened the door to the development of new modes of thought opposed to Christian theism and to the ultimate allegiance to nature that we find today.

6. *Modern Thought*

From the Medieval period the trail of intellectual history leads us into the Modern Period. This period traditionally has covered the time gap from the Renaissance to the present day. Historians seem to be able to identify at least two major segments of time within the modern period. The first segment embraces the Renaissance and Reformation up to the Eighteenth Century. The second period begins with the so-called Enlightenment of that century and stretches to the present.

The period of the Renaissance and Reformation was one marked by revolt and reform movements. These movements were protests against scholasticism and Roman Catholicism. On the one hand, represented by the Protestant reformers, efforts were made to effect a return to Jesus, New Testament Christianity, and Christian Theism as interpreted from this perspective. On the other hand, represented by the humanists and rationalists, efforts were launched to revolt, not only from scholasticism and the Roman Church, but also completely away from Christian theism. The force of those latter movements was sufficiently strong to lay the groundwork for the complete shift to naturalism during the Eighteenth Century.

In assessing the movements of the Fifteenth to the Eighteenth Centuries it is important to recognize that there was an intellectual battle between those who advocated ancient thought structures as the proper basis for developing modern culture and the advocates of the claim that modern thought structures were adequate. Three intellectual constituents took part in this conflict: Protestantism, humanism, and rationalism.

Humanism advocated an outright return to classical culture. It questioned immediate custom and scholastic philosophy. It was an active rebellion of artists and scholars. They rebelled against clerical authority and maintained that men *make* their own standards and truth and do not merely discover it. They tended to be aristocratic, however, and failed to touch the masses but left a legacy of self-sufficiency and an appeal to the practical rather than theological which contributed directly to the stream of thought leading to naturalism.

Rationalism discarded Romanism almost completely. In fact, the rationalist banished the supernatural completely and placed man within the framework of nature. Standards of right and wrong were not accepted from any authority but were discovered in the "nature" of things, in the mathematical reality of the universe. The achievements of natural science lent themselves to the support of this view.

Protestantism resulted from a revolt against the Roman Church. It advocated a return to Christian Theism as advanced by Jesus and the early church. By breaking up into many groups and sects Protestantism demanded religious toleration. This made it easy for some to become religiously skeptical, insisting that one view was as good as another. Geared also to nationalism, those who opposed Protestantism claimed Protestantism was prejudiced and narrow. Both of these facts contributed to a situation which made it easy for relativism to arise among its advocates outside religious circles. The Reformers were rather pure in their insistence upon a return to classical Christianity but their case was weakened educationally when we observe that above the elementary school level they compromised with classical learning.

The Eighteenth Century marks the transition from a culture dominated by theism to one dominated by naturalism. In this century attempts were made to substitute a new cosmology for the one advanced by Christianity. For this reason this period is called the Enlightenment. A new optimism gripped the thinkers of this period. Many firmly believed that mankind could attain a state of perfection on this earth outside and independent of Christian doctrine.

Where Greek idealism and Christianity had failed, this age turned to the work of Newton and Locke for the presuppositions thought to be sufficient to bring man perfect bliss. Newton's laws of science laid out the pattern and Locke's ideas about reason provided new thought structures. Nature and reason would unite to supplant theology and Christianity as the hope of men. Once nature is understood man could regulate his plans and actions accordingly. Reason would destroy superstition, revelation, and faith. This view was championed by Voltaire, Pope, Montesquieu, the English deists, Rousseau, Hume, Jefferson, Paine, and Adam Smith.

Other ideas advanced during this period included a rejection of the doctrine of original sin, a belief in progress brought about solely by reason, antagonism for organized Christianity, particularly an aversion for the clergy. The authority of reason was substituted for the authority of God. Man is born good but made bad by society and environment. Hope for recovery lies in the use of reason. Once we get in tune with Nature and use our reasoning powers properly man cannot fail, for Reason will rid us of superstition, revelation, fear, and faith. This new thought structure was developed into a new faith characterized by four outstanding elements:

1. The essential goodness of man
2. The inevitability of progress
3. The ultimate reality of nature
4. The absolute uniformity of nature

Although there were mild reactions to these views, particularly on the part of the romanticists following in the train of Rousseau, there were no essential changes in these views as they were passed along to the Nineteenth Century.

The inevitable result of this new philosophy is best illustrated in the French Revolution, but the Nineteenth Century, in spite of this, saw a perpetuation of the basic ideas of the Enlightenment. The rapid growth of science and technology, while in themselves harmless, actually contributed to this perpetuation. Darwin's theories of evolution seemed to provide further evidence of man's progress upward. In fact, his theories not only provided apparent explanation of progress but actually made progress seem inevitable. Nationalism and the rise of great states seemed to accentuate this progress also. Thus, it appears that the Nineteenth Century merely became an extension of the basic ideas of the Enlightenment, and these ideas were fundamentally naturalistic.

Christian forces often rallied in protest to the inroads of naturalism. This was true in the Seventeenth Century, illustrated by the Methodist and Pietistic movements and again in the Nineteenth Century revivals. In the main the primary results of these movements were to be seen among English speaking peoples. Although the revival of traditional Christianity was not completely widespread, it did leave its impact on the English people. The outcome of this impact has been called the Victorian Compromise. Moderation in politics, nationalism and economics, together with an emphasis on freedom and conventional Christianity marked this movement. While great material progress took place, the intellectual heritage remained, by and large, that of the Enlightenment.

In spite of the passage of over 150 years, the ravages of the French Revolution, and the World Wars of the Twentieth Century, man continues to hold on to the optimistic spirit of the Enlightenment to this very day. The central postulate of the Twentieth Century mind is still the ultimacy of nature.

This is to continue to say that man is essentially an animal and that moral distinctions are only subjective and relative. It is a denial of the reality of the supernatural. From the Biblical standpoint it is a denial particularly of a special divine revelation. Thus, the naturalistic emphasis prevails around the world.

This century has witnessed a mild reaction against naturalism in the forms of idealism and personalism but these movements have not been strong enough to win. Instead, we have witnessed the rise of new alternatives to Christianity in the form of Fascism, Nazism, and Communism all based on the presuppositions of naturalism. Although great tragedies of the past half-century have shaken man's confidence in his basic optimism, we still face a death struggle with naturalism as represented in Communism. Today, the issue is clear. It is Christianity arrayed against naturalism.

The challenge comes to Christians today — we must not think like the Greeks, but like Jesus Christ. May God help us to spell this out in the field of Christian education!

B. The Demands for a New Approach to Christian Education

1. *From the Critics*

Modern education is under fire and has been now for the past several years. Many people are demanding a new approach to education. The question arises as to how the advocates of Christian education stand in the light of the present searching criticism.

Evidence of dissatisfaction is coming from a number of sources. Chief among these is parents. They are markedly dissatisfied with the caliber of instruction their children are receiving these days. Even in Christian schools parents are tired of following old patterns.

Many free lance writers have also attacked education in general. Among these can be found newspaper editors and reporters, authors of magazine articles and books. Even the educational philosophers are responding to the pressures of the hour. Space prohibits the mention of a goodly number of recent publications which reveal marked criticism of our present system and a direct frontal attack on the great American educational philosopher, John Dewey. Educators themselves are not averse to sharp evaluation of their work.

Of particular note, however, is the fact that Christian educators who have been operating upon the premises of the old Hebrew-Greek-Roman approach to education are now beginning to question the very bases of this approach. They are beginning to see that to make a synthesis of thought from such sources is inadequate to face the problems and needs of the present. Among these there is an inner circle who believe that the presuppositions for an educational system which is truly Christian must be found in the Bible as the Word of God. They do not hesitate to make the claim that education cannot truly be Christian unless it is so founded.

2. *From the Culture*

In addition to the above factors the very nature of the cultural situation in which we now live demands a new approach to education. A needy world demands and must have a satisfying philosophy of life and an adequate philosophy of education. We live in the midst of constant change and crisis and this age stands in need of the kind of education which provides a stable place to stand. We need the kind of educational philosophy which can stem the tide of searching criticism while at the same time giving certainty in the midst of confusion. The writer believes that the time has come for evangelical Christians to develop a truly Bibliocentric approach to education. To this end this work is dedicated, with the hope that it will stimulate new thought in the field.

3. *From the Field*

The educational philosophies of naturalism, pragmatism, and idealism dominate the present scene. Modern children of these views are materialism, scientism, secularism, and relativism. Against these, Christian theism is arrayed.

Perhaps it is more proper to say that scientific naturalism prevails today. Reality is conceived in terms of material atomic constitution. Here nature is complete totality of being. Man is an evolutionary result of nature and thus is essentially a part of nature. The function of education in this view is virtually nothing more than to afford man an adjustment to his environment and to make that environment the best possible. The end of education is found either in the individual or the group. No place is found for the supernatural, therefore, knowledge is confined to natural phenomena. The inevitable method of this position is the scientific method.

Educational humanism is closely related to naturalism. Reason is at the heart of this view and the method becomes one of developing it. The accomplishments of the past provide the curriculum for education. Valuable as the good experiences and accomplishments of the past have been, this view is also earthbound. History reveals the failure of this type of philosophy to meet human needs. It, too, leaves out the supernatural.

The second alternative to Christian philosophy is idealism. Its emphasis on absolutes, the reality of the spiritual, its emphasis on moral laws, its belief in freedom and the existence of God, are commendable. But its denial of the reality of evil, its finite God, its hazy conception of God, and its elevation of abstract concepts to the ultimate level above God all serve to weaken its position from the Christian theistic standpoint.

The challenge of this situation demands from Christian educators a new approach to education. In such an approach educators must do more than negatively point out the failures of other systems. They must demonstrate positively and qualitatively that the bibliocentric approach is adequate for our day. Before turning our attention to how this will be done, let us review briefly in out-

line form two representative philosophies of education which hold
the field at present — naturalism and humanism. In doing this we
shall see some of the demands which come from the field itself.
The heart of *naturalism* is the emphasis placed on nature as ultimate reality. It is to be expected, therefore, that nature and the
natural sciences would be at the center of any definition of education propounded by this view. Education takes the form of sociality and vocational training here. Man is a by-product of nature
and God stands on the periphery of its hierarchy of educational
values. The diagram below illustrates this position with its implications for the educational curriculum.

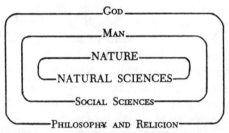

The philosophies of realism and pragmatism are closely related to this position. Realism defines education as the conditioning of the nervous system by physical means so that men can
live in harmony with the laws of nature. The pragmatist defines
education as a process of the reconstruction of experience with
primary emphasis on biological and social factors rather than
physical factors. Here the purpose of education is to help the
pupil live in a changing industrial community and to become more
efficient in scientific techniques which lead to the solution of
present-day problems.

Closely allied to the position of naturalism is that of *humanism*. Human values are central in this view. Perhaps the view is
best represented in the works of Robert Hutchins. Emphasis is
placed on the classics with intellectual development as a direct
corollary. Humanists believe that the combination of the acquisition of one's cultural heritage and modern scientific genius results
in the right kind of leadership. To them education virtually becomes the acquisition of knowledge and mental discipline. Here,
too, it is seen that God is found on the circumference of education.
Implications are seen in the chart on page 32.

It is at once apparent that the above philosophies place either
man or nature at the center of education. The purpose in either
case is sociality or an efficient individual prepared for society. To
the Christian these views are fragmentary.

It is to be noted that in some circles there appears to be a

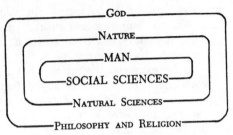

mild reaction to these views. While still holding to many of the tenets of scientific naturalism, nevertheless some are beginning to see that to restrict the goals and concepts of education to sociality is to fall short of the dynamic which is required to produce the kind of pupils who can cope with present-day problems and contribute toward cultural progress. Instead, emphasis is being given by some on the *direction* in which growth should take place. This gives prominence to purposes and objectives in spite of the fact that such evaluation is measured by the degree of desirable behavior competencies attained.

To the Christian it seems unfortunate that the adjustment function has been limited to social reactions. It has been assumed too long that material things bring the greatest satisfactions. Jesus said, "Man shall not live by bread alone." It is an inescapable fact that man's view of the universe affects his social thought and behavior. At the same time it is amazing to see that, almost by common consent, this vital aspect of man's complete adjustment to his environment has been neglected by the school. As a result, spiritual forces in the universe go unrecognized. The inevitable outcome is that man thus misses the forces which give purposiveness, meaning, and timeless quality to life. To the Christian it becomes imperative that the school make possible the integration of personality around some great cosmic principle which will elevate man to a destiny beyond that of materialism.

C. THE DEVELOPMENT OF A NEW APPROACH TO EDUCATION

1. *The Nature of Christian Education*

The development of a new approach to education depends directly on a clear conception of what we are dealing with. Christian education is a distinctive kind of education which demands distinctive treatment.

The Christian believes that education must be centered in Christ to have meaning. Without this the character goal cannot be reached. This means that education involves more than a teacher and a learner.

First, education for the Christian is an outgrowth of God's revelation. It is the process by which man comes to a knowledge of God's interpretation as He has made it known in creation and revelation. No narrow intellectualism is implied here. The ramifications and full implications involved in the creation and revelation preclude any possibility of this. To say this, however, is not to imply that the human mind is passive. It does mean that our minds are receptive to God's interpretations, but from that point on man becomes creatively productive with those facts.

Second, education is an outgrowth of the Christian world view. The Christian believes that God has revealed Himself through a process of revelation both natural and written. This revelation is inherently subject to logical development and analysis. Furthermore, it is the only source of truth. Therefore, it is possible to set up working principles and patterns by which life processes can be directed. This is called a world view. Since this view is all-inclusive, education must of necessity be a part of it. The process of education, then, leads to an interpretation of this view. The function of education is to lead the pupil to a knowledge of God's will and to the doing of His will. Because we are persuaded of the truth of our position, we want our children to be trained in it, and this demands Christian education.

Third, to the Christian, education is a well-balanced function. Social pressure as well as philosophical concepts influence education. The complexity of modern life forces one to think of the interests of both society and the individual. The Christian believes that salvation should eventuate in service.

Fourth, education for the Christian is conceived in terms of comprehensiveness. It is to include both the individual and society. By this is meant the total individual and all in society. It is comprehensive both as to its setting and to its application. With regard to its *setting*, comprehensiveness includes the development of the whole man—physically, mentally, morally, spiritually, socially, and culturally. With regard to its *application*, education is concerned with both instruction and training. Instruction is primarily mental in character. Training refers to the use of knowledge. Christian education, therefore, means the kind of instruction and training which leads one to a knowledge of the Scriptures and of Jesus Christ as Saviour and Lord and to the living of a holy life. The agencies through which this kind of education is realized include the Christian church, the Christian home, and the Christian school, including Sunday schools, day schools, special schools, and parochial schools.

The Christian Theistic World View embraces a definition of Christian education. The heart of this view is the Triune God.

It is to be expected, therefore, that philosophy, theology, and ethics will be at the center of any Christian theistic definition. Education takes the form of evangelism, instruction, and training. Man is a product of the creative power of God and the regeneration of the Holy Spirit. God is at the center, not at the periphery of this view. Instead, nature is at the periphery. The diagram below reveals this position with its implications for the educational curriculum.

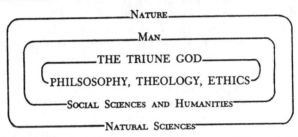

The implications of this view are many. Although God is at the center, the point at which man meets Him is through the Mediator between God and man — the God-man, Christ Jesus. Man is not suppressed in this view. He is dealt with as an end, not as a means. The curriculum is rather the means to an end. It is the whole-man-in-his-environment which is the point of focus in theocentric education. Furthermore, the development of this person is the process involved. First, the man is saved, then growth begins. The goal is the "perfect man in Christ."

Because man has an environment, Christian education is concerned with it also. This constitutes the cultural heritage and should be made available to man. The social sciences and humanities are closest to man in many ways but that does not necessarily mean a hierarchy of subject matter. All truth reveals God and makes a contribution to the educational development of the pupil. The natural sciences also have their part to play.

2. The Development of a New Approach

From what has been said above we have noted that Christian educational concepts are derived directly from sources provided by Christian theology, the Bible and Christian philosophy. Actually, from these studies a Christian philosophy can be abstracted which can serve education in several ways: (1) by providing a world view which gives unity, (2) a philosophy of life which gives meaning, (3) emphasis on true values and objectives which give purpose and direction, and (4) systematization of content by showing relations and inter-relations in the totality of truth which provides a workable pattern for the curriculum.

From the above discussion we discover a working principle for the development of our new approach to education. God stands at the center of the Christian world view. He has revealed Himself to mankind. This revelation provides the basis upon which the Christian philosophy of life can be built. Such a philosophy is comprehensive enough to include all aspects of life, one of which is education, which in turn provides guide lines for the whole educational process embracing content, methods, administration, principles, and relations. The implications of this working principle can be seen in the chart below.

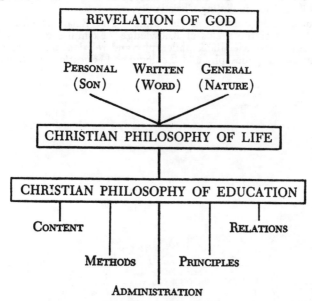

In the chapter which follows each of the various facets which go into the development of our world view will be briefly considered. From this discussion it will be possible to make a summary of the world view in outline form. In succeeding chapters we can see some of the implications for the development of a new approach to Christian education.

Suggested Class Projects and Activities

1. Write a paper or have a discussion on the social, cultural and educational characteristics of the present day.
2. Make a comparative chart on contemporary philosophies to show the following about each philosophy:
    (1) Definition
    (2) Early leaders
    (3) Modern proponents
    (4) Main tenets

3. Create a comparative chart on the main tenets of modern philosophies to show major points on:
   (1) Metaphysics
   (2) Epistemology
   (3) Logic
   (4) Axiology

4. Create a comparative chart showing how the Christian philosophy compares with other philosophies.

5. Do research on how men have defined education.

6. List, define and describe the methods by which philosophers obtain their information.

7. Make a list of the major assumptions of the most important philosophies, including Christianity.

8. Pursue a discussion on the topic, "The Relations and Interrelations of the Fields of Knowledge." Examples might include religion and education, philosophy and religion, philosophy and education, philosophy and theology, and education and theology.

THE CHRISTIAN THEISTIC WORLD VIEW

OUTLINE FOR CHAPTER 2

A. DEVELOPMENT

   1. Foundations
   2. Sources of Content
   3. Organization of Content

B. THE CHRISTIAN THEISTIC WORLD VIEW

   1. Philosophical Approach
   2. Theological Approach
      a. The Centrality of God
      b. The Creation
      c. Revelation
      d. Redemption
   3. Summary Statement

C. GENERAL IMPLICATIONS FOR CHRISTIAN EDUCATION

   1. The Nature of Education
   2. The Purpose and Objective of Education
   3. The Curriculum of Education

2 | THE CHRISTIAN THEISTIC WORLD VIEW

A. Development

1. Foundations

The foundation of the Christian Theistic World View is in God who is the Source of all life and truth. The Christian believes that God has created the universe and revealed Himself thereby. In addition, God has chosen to "speak" to men and we have a record of this in the form of the Holy Scriptures. The foundations of the Christian world view, therefore, are securely laid in a Personal God who has chosen to reveal Himself to mankind.

The history of Western philosophy reveals that four primary types of philosophical assumptions, upon which world views are built, have been formulated. *Naturalism* works on the assumption that truth is obtained only by the inductive method or the scientific method of the physical sciences. The basic weakness of this method to the Christian is that it denies the reality of the spiritual and supernatural. *Rationalism* assumes that a world view can be formulated through the use of pure reason. Such a position is no longer popular nor considered tenable, for pure reason is only a fragment of experience. Then, too, it is built upon arbitrary assumptions. *Idealism* claims that reality is mental in character and can be demonstrated by coherence. Coherence is arrived at through the use of the empirical method. Probability is as far as one can go with this method.

No less than others the Christian begins with an assumption. He has a conviction that the supernatural world is just as real as the natural world. God does exist there and has chosen to bridge the gap between the two worlds by a process of *Self-Revelation.* Such revelation is transcendent; it comes from God Himself. The Christian World View is built upon the assumption that reality is supernatural as well as natural, divine as well as human, that there is revealed knowledge as well as natural knowledge. This is the point of disagreement with all other views. No claim is made that written Revelation covers the whole gamut of truth. However, it does provide a means whereby all truth is measured.

2. Sources of Content

It has been pointed out that revelation from God is the source of our philosophy. It is to be expected, therefore, that God and His revelation can be relied upon as a source of philosophical content. It remains for us, however, to organize and systematize this content into the orderly arrangement of an educational philosophy in the Christian framework. This demands the particular combination of the contributions of Biblical Studies, Christian Theology and Christian Philosophy.

Examination reveals that the revelation of God — personal, written, and general (in nature) — can be analyzed into a number of facets. The first and primary source is *Biblical*. Herein is contained the Word of God in written form. The Bible contains the "idea" of education and shows how God makes provision for it, the historical development of the Hebrew-Christian heritage, the record of the life and teachings of Jesus Christ, the Master Teacher, and the records of the early church. In the Bible we find the primary principles laid down for the establishment and perpetuation of a system of Christian education. Furthermore, in Jesus Christ we find the basis upon which to build both the philosophy and practice of Christian education.

The second facet to be analyzed is *theological*. In theology is contained the organized system of Biblical and Christian truth. Here the very heart of the Christian faith comes to expression in the great doctrines of the Bible and the church. Because God stands at the center of the Christian philosophy, theology becomes all the more important for education because it gives a systematized approach to the great doctrine of God. Thereby we can come to a fuller understanding of Him, of His purposes and plans for men and the universe. Herein is also set forth the great redemptive plan of salvation which also stands at the heart of the Christian World View.

The third facet is *psychological*. Psychology provides a study of consciousness and conduct. At the heart of this study stands the importance of human personality. Because psychology turns the searchlight on the pupil and the best methods of understanding and dealing with him, there are direct implications for education involved.

The fourth facet is *sociological*. Sociology is a study of man in his social relations. Here emphasis is placed on man himself as he stands in relationship to other men. Here, too, emphasis is laid on the great institutional framework in which man works. The school is one of the great institutions of men. The environment in which man expresses himself and lives is also of great importance in education.

The fifth facet is *scientific*. In our modern day no Christian can afford to overlook the implications of science in the development of life and life relations. Any examination of nature, which is the product of God's creative power and design, is of importance to the Christian. The substance and content of the creation reveal God and has direct implications for education.

The sixth facet is *philosophical*. Great cosmic problems present themselves to man to be solved. Not only is it within the province of philosophy to develop a systematized world view, but an examination of the basic causes and reasons behind the universe leads to a solution of many of man's intellectual and spiritual difficulties. No system of education is complete without recognizing and dealing with certain great issues of life, such as origin, death, and destiny.

3. *Organization of Content*

The overall result of this examination, analysis and systematization is to bring together the truth-content of God's revelation combined with the speculations of Christian scholarship into an organized system of synthesized truth that we call a world view. Leaning heavily upon God's revelation we are thus able to formulate the philosophy known as the World View of Christian Theism. Out of this there are direct implications for a Philosophy of Christian Education with regard to purposes and objectives, the nature and place of the teacher, the nature and place of the pupil, the nature and function of the teaching-learning process, the nature and structure of the curriculum content, and the processes of administration and relationships.

B. THE CHRISTIAN THEISTIC WORLD VIEW

1. *Philosophical Approach*

The Christian Theistic World View is an attempt to develop a philosophy of life from which a Christian philosophy of education can be abstracted. Like all other philosophies, this view begins with the reality of self-consciousness. Without this, no meaning is possible. Two things are quite apparent to the self: (1) the self is continuous, it is the same from experience to experience, and (2) there is an awareness of that which is not self but apart from self. If the first fact were not true, meanings and understanding could not be carried over with the passing of time nor would self be able to profit by past experience. A self which is continuous is demanded in order to perpetuate an intelligent existence. The awareness of that outside of self and not a part of self makes objectivity possible.

When self, with the power of consciousness and knowledge, begins to compare himself with the world outside of self, he finds then that there is a great deal held in common. He discovers that the two were made for each other. This brings to the forefront the problem of epistemology which is basic in every philosophy. The self, with the power to interpret, discovers that he lives in a world which has the possibility of being interpreted. The problem of epistemology in the Christian framework will be dealt with at greater length later on.

Granted that man has the power to know and that he lives in a "knowable" world, this makes it possible for a world-view to be set up and to become a part of experience. Thus, the Christian world view, like all others, begins in *experience*. It is to be noted, therefore, that much experience is initiated by and with the self. The Scriptures have clearly stated the matter: "Keep thy heart with all diligence; for out of it are the issues of life" (Proverbs 4:23). It is the heart which deals with the most profound issues of life. It is at this point that experience plays such a vital part to the Christian. The kind of heart a person has determines the kind of world view he exercises. If the heart is not Christian, it is certain that the world view will be unchristian. Of necessity, therefore, the only place that a Christian philosophy can start is with a *Christian consciousness*. Such a consciousness must come through the distinctive Christian experience called *regeneration*. Regeneration comes through the Revelation of God in Christ, and the transformation which comes thereby when received. Therefore, the heart experience of the Christian is bound up in the Word of God both living and written.

Philosophy is a life issue and of necessity must come from the heart by a definite choice of the person. A philosophical choice is a *religious choice*, for religion is the only point from which man can *gain* an overview of the universe. Only by transcending the present cosmic diversity can one fully achieve his philosophy. It is not possible for science to do this because science must begin from a point within the cosmos and of necessity, therefore, is a part of it. Only the heart of man can transcend cosmic diversity. This is true because man is basically a religious being.

The problem of sin enters at this point. Sin has created an antithesis of viewpoints as well as a spiritual difference in hearts.

This fact explains the *presence* of non-Christian philosophy as well as the *nature* of those philosophies. The starting point of all non-Christian philosophy is also the heart — the unchristian heart. It is a *religious* heart but not a Christian heart. A heart can be religious but apostate. It is apostate because it chooses against Christ. The professed philosophy which chooses its starting point solely in science is fragmentary and essentially unphilosophical. It chooses to start with *one* aspect of reality, deifies it, but expects to see the truth. This is an apostate act, for science and human reason belong to a *part* of the cosmos and are therefore antagonistic to true religion. Such a view is known as *immanence philosophy*. It is opposed to God and His Revelation. Where the Christian philosophy leads *to* Christ, the immanence philosophy leads *away* from Him. The first exalts Christ; the latter deifies man. The latter exalts the ideal of personality and of science while the former elevates the true God.

The Christian philosophy begins with a Christian heart, we have noted. A Christian heart is dependent upon Christian experience. Such experience comes by means of the inner working of the Spirit of God in the heart of man. It is, therefore, a supernatural experience but a vital reality to every true Christian. Furthermore, the content of this Christian experience is not fragmentary, appealing only to the emotions, or to the mind, but the decision which culminates in Christian experience involves the exercising of the *total* personality — mind, feelings, and will. This is at the very heart of the Christian Theistic World View.

Closely related to Christian experience is *revelation*. The Christian firmly believes in a Personal Creator who has revealed Himself in three main ways: (1) as Creator in nature — *General Self-Revelation*, (2) in truth through the Bible — *Special Self-Revelation*, and (3) in Jesus Christ His Son — the Living Word, *Personal Self-Revelation*. Through these avenues God has been able to reach the heart of man with a supernatural and authoritative message. In the light of this message all life and all of life is evaluated. On this basis has Christian experience been certified and a Christian world view made possible.

The Christian, then, starts his world view with an assumption. All systems of philosophy are built on assumptions. This was pointed out earlier. Essentially the *assumption* that the Christian makes amounts to a *conviction*, and that is, there is a supernatural world created by God who has revealed Himself to man through nature and spoken to man through the Bible and His Son.

From what standpoint shall the Christian assert his confidence in his assumption — faith or reason? Young presents what is considered the true Christian position.[1] He says both are necessary. Actually *"reason* can never be divorced from *faith."* Man must have faith in his reason; reason should evaluate and substantiate his faith. Where reason excludes faith, man tends toward rationalism. Rationalism rejects revelation and posits the sources of truth in human reason. It is not reason itself but the arbitrary displacement of revelation that counts in this view. Where faith excludes reason, there is tendency toward fanaticism.

Ever since Immanuel Kant tried to divorce faith and reason the forces of naturalism, materialism, and idealism have followed in his train. The ultimate result was to discredit faith. These views picture faith as legendary superstition. They hold that faith conflicts with science and, consequently, that reason is the only sound basis for knowledge. Even among some Christians there is a tendency to doubt the reality of the truth involved *in* faith. To them, faith is a blind trust, a leap in the dark. To the true Christian, however, faith and reason are not incompatible but complementary. The fact that there seems to be disparity between the two is another evidence of sin's destructive and divisive work. The Christian position in the New Testament represents the two as compatible and complementary. Although primary emphasis is given to faith, the use of reason is never excluded. In fact, the New Testament record shows that the believer was expected to use his God-given rational faculty whenever it became necessary (I Peter 3:15; I John 4:1; I Thessalonians 5:21; etc.). Furthermore, there are many instances where the New Testament writers presented evidences of the faith which proved to be direct intellectual appeals.

To the unbeliever there is apparent disparity between faith and reason. The reason for this is the presence and possession of the carnal mind by unredeemed men. Such a mind, according to Romans 8, is enmity against God and set in materialism. It would naturally follow that such a mind would question the validity of faith. The only way by which this problem can be resolved is through conversion. Man must be converted mentally as well as morally. Hereby does man come to know and experience the mind of Christ. Then there will be no conflict between faith and reason. Only then can the believer exercise true faith which is trusting the validity of any pronouncement made by God. Where reason arrives at truth personally, faith is trusting revealed truth.

2. *Theological Approach*

Christian theology provides truth which augments the philosopher's efforts to formulate his world view.

[1] Warren C. Young, *A Christian Approach to Philosophy* (Wheaton, Ill., Van Kampen Press, 1954), pp. 54-55.

a. The Centrality of God

The Christian Theistic World View, formally stated, starts with God. The existence of God is the key truth of this view. His existence provides the foundation upon which to build this philosophy. Since philosophy is the search for unity and Ultimate Being, the reality and existence of God provides both unity and being. All things are related understandingly to God and are derived from God. Christian theology insists that such unity can be found only in the Christian God.

The Christian God is not "a" god or "another" god, but *The God.* To know Him is considered by the Christian to be the essence of knowledge and wisdom. The Scriptures reveal God as a Unity who expresses Himself in Trinity. Man comes to know Him through the process of God's Self-revelation. This, God has chosen to do through the use of three instrumentalities of revelation: (1) the written Word, (2) the Son, and (3) the creation. All things are revelatory of God who is central. The implications of this can be seen in chart form below.

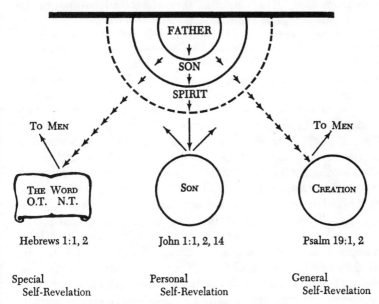

| FATHER |
| SON |
| SPIRIT |

| To Men | | To Men |

| THE WORD O.T. N.T. | SON | CREATION |

| Hebrews 1:1, 2 | John 1:1, 2, 14 | Psalm 19:1, 2 |

| Special Self-Revelation | Personal Self-Revelation | General Self-Revelation |

While it is the heart truth of the Christian philosophy that God is central, the point of contact that God has with man is through His Son Jesus Christ. The Son is the Mediator between God and man. He is the God-man. The Incarnation made this possible. By saying that the Christian philosophy is Christ-centered, we have not changed the God-centered concept. The Triune

God is not only Trinity but also Divine Unity. The Father and the Son are One.

Through Christ God chose to contact man and this was made necessary for two primary reasons: (1) man needed a personal revelation of God, and (2) the presence of sin, which blinds man to God, became a problem to overcome before man could come to know God in the closeness of personal relation and fellowship. Christ is the means whereby the blindness can be removed and the regeneration of the soul made possible (John 6:68, 69; 8:12). In this regeneration the sin-perverted mind of man was also renewed. Here is the point where Christian education is made possible only through regeneration.

b. The Creation

Not only does the Christian philosophy assert the existence of the Triune God, but it also explains the presence and purpose of reality on the basis that *God* brought reality into being (Genesis 1:1). The primary implication of this fact is to make all creation *dependent* on God. The Christian then rejects all pantheistic or partially pantheistic and evolutionary views of creation.

The method which God used to create the universe was by the Word of His power. The universe is present as a result of the Divine Fiat. Here the Christian position stands in opposition to the views of evolution, deism, and idealism. The master assumption of idealism is that all thought is the same, whether divine or human. Immanuel Kant, said to be the father of modern philosophy, adopted this master assumption and principle of idealism. To Kant, thought is creative and the logical corollary to this is a rejection of a temporal creation. To him, creation by an independent God would not be acceptable because such a creation would destroy man's creative thought. This is all the more pertinent for education today because *pragmatism,* largely sponsored by John Dewey, has likewise adopted this master principle. Since God and man are subject to eternal laws of thought, they say, both are temporal and not eternal. Temporal things are all on the move; they are in a state of flux. There is no absolute place of authority. To the Christian this position is untenable. To say that law is above authority becomes meaningless and lawless. There is no place to stand. There is nothing to relate anything else to. Reason becomes impossible. Essentially, this destroys the basis for education.

With regard to the *substance* of creation the true Christian position is one of *contingent dualism.* Since creation is dependent on God, then His level of existence is higher. Analysis of God's revelation reveals that the nature of creation is twofold: (1) rational and (2) non-rational. The position is pictured below.

The *purpose* of creation is revelation. Non-rational creation is that part of creation without the power of exercising the qualities of personality primary of which are intelligence and reason, including all levels of creation below that of man. The real purpose of non-rational creation is to reveal the attributes of God. Rational creation reveals God on the *conscious* level. It has the power of consciousness and awareness because it has been created by a rational and personal God who has these powers — intelligence and reason.

Man stands at the apex of the rational creation as far as this world is concerned. He was created in the image and likeness of God. The manner by which man reveals God is through the proper exercising of His image and likeness. The purpose of man is to glorify God. Man is to express through his character and conduct the character and conduct of God. The attributes of God are to be seen in the world by man through men who voluntarily manifest them.

Free moral agency was granted by God to men in order that they could best exemplify God. Inherent in this provision was the possibility of rebellion against God. The fact of sin in the world can be directly attributed to the further fact that man misused his free moral agency. Holiness could only be achieved by a free, conscious, and voluntary choice on the part of man. Through the exercise of free moral agency man thus revealed God, but it is to be carefully noted that man's participation in sin does *not* reveal God. Sin does not reveal the character of a Holy God. Sin, however, did provide God with an *occasion* to reveal Himself in a new way. This is not to imply that God was forced to so reveal Himself, but simply that He used the opportunity made available to Him through the misuse of man's free moral agency. The fall of man into sin provided God with an opportunity to manifest His displeasure with it, and to manifest His love, mercy, and power in overcoming it. Thus, *indirectly*, the creation included redemption. We conclude, therefore, that the fall of man into sin is subservient to God but not directly revelatory of Him.

c. Revelation

The third facet of the Christian Theistic World View is revelation. God not only is, and not only created, but He has revealed Himself to man. In fact, creation itself is a truth of revelation. Although there are other evidences which point to the *fact* of God, it remained for the *written* revelation to show the *kind* of God who created. Furthermore, the revelation of God provides both authority and substance in building the philosophy of the Christian Theistic World View.

Looking at it from God's standpoint, the existence and creation of God stand foremost, but looking at the matter from man's viewpoint, a knowledge of God comes to man. The Christian philosophy begins with a positive, supernatural, and authoritative revelation.

Revelation is a gift of God. It is the Word of God both Living and Written. No claim is made that all areas of truth are covered and fully dealt with in the Bible but it *is* claimed that all truth is measured by the Written Word.

In carrying out the purpose of revelation which is to reveal Himself, God has used three avenues of enlightenment: (1) General Self-Revelation in nature, (2) Personal Self-Revelation in the Son of God, and (3) Special Self-Revelation in the Bible. These levels of revelation provide not only enlightenment but also standards of measurement by which truth and error can be determined.

The *content* of revelation is fivefold, all coming out of the creation of God in His acts and the Person of God in His Son. These several agencies are: (1) God's Word – the Bible, (2) the material world, (3) the rational world, (4) the Living Word – His Son, and (5) redemption. The implications of this content can be seen in the chart form on page 49.

The highest level of God's Self-Revelation was in His Personal Self-Revelation through His Son, the Lord Jesus Christ. The method by which this was accomplished is called the *Incarnation*. God came in the form of man. The nature of this revelation was twofold: (1) a revelation of the character and conduct of God, and (2) a revelation of God through redemption.

God's Special Self-Revelation came to us also through the Bible. God's Word is holy, not only because it was written through holy men inspired by the Holy Spirit, but also because it reveals

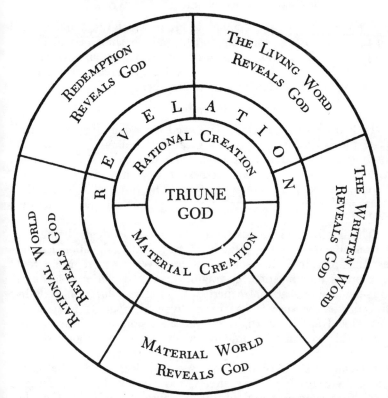

a Holy God and His plan of redemption. We approach this Book with confidence and dependence.

God's General Self-Revelation to man is through nature. It can be seen in two ways: (1) through nonrational or material creation, and (2) through rational creation. The material world reveals the attributes of God but sin has blinded man to this enlightenment. The Bible has been used of God through the Holy Spirit to inform men of these facts. One implication of God's creation and revelation for the curriculum is that essentially there are no such things as secular school subjects.

The rational world reveals God in two ways: (1) through creatures with the power of personality, thought, intelligence, and reason, and (2) through concepts and situations which demand the exercise of rational powers. Man, of course, stands at the apex, as we have seen, of the rational revelation of God. The nonmaterial world in some respects demands the exercise of rational powers to comprehend it. This can be seen through (1) abstract realities which transcend time and space, such as mathematics, language, music, etc., (2) communal life in which the individuality of man is lost in love and common life relationships of which the family is an illustration, (3) conscience which is an inward reminder of the will of God, and (4) Divine Providence which consists of the works of God in and among men.

d. Redemption

Redemption reveals God. The need for redemption lies in the fact of the fall of man, originally created in holiness, into sin and consequent rebellion against God. The results of sin's entrance was to corrupt the image and likeness of God in man and cut man off from the life and presence of God. The result of this was the extension of sin's presence and power to affect all men in all the world.

The implications of this for education are evident. Being cut off from life itself is the tragedy of tragedies. Education has no meaning apart from the context of life. Where there is no real life, there is no education. A fragmentary life-experience leads to a fragmentary educational experience. Modern education finds itself confused because it has been divorced from its integrating core — God Himself. Furthermore, because sin affected the nature of man, this has raised problems for education. The pupil stands as the focus of the educative process. In order to reach the pupil the problem of sin must be recognized and dealt with. The mind of man, as a result of sin's effects, has become blinded, carnal, materialistic, sensual, and doubtful. Because of this, man's thought life is outside that of God's thought life and His will (I Corinthians 2:12-16).

What can man do about it? He finds himself with a nature which impedes his progress toward truth and happiness and in an environment which has also felt the impact of sin, not to speak of being the chief target in the great conflict between God and Satan. The answer does not lie with man, but rather with God. Sin not only affected man, but it also affected God's relationship to man. The effect of sin on God was twofold: (1) in general He was wounded, offended, and wronged by it; His purpose for man was temporarily blocked; for the time being He was dethroned from His own creation; (2) in particular, God was presented with a problem. On the one hand His justice and holiness demanded punishment and banishment of both sin and the sinner. As Judge it was necessary for God to pronounce judgment and the curse upon all sin and its consequences. On the other hand, His love and mercy compelled Him to become a Redeemer. God would solve this problem through the Mediation of His Son who would be both Judge and Redeemer. War was declared with Satan and the field was prepared to meet the need for redemption.

The *nature* of redemption demands a full restoration of *all* that had been lost through sin as far as it was in the power of Divinity to accomplish. To this task God gave Himself, a task which was certainly in accord with both the Divine nature and revelation.

The *purpose* of that redemption was twofold: (1) restoration – to restore all that was lost in the fall of man, and (2) revelation – to reveal the nature and purpose of God.

In approaching this problem from the standpoint of *method,* God was faced with the responsibility of a threefold provision: (1) a solution which was philosophically conceived, (2) a solution which was to be practically realized, and (3) a solution which was to be administratively controlled. The total plan of God by which He solved the problem of sin is called the *atonement.*

Philosophically conceived the solution demanded a plan which would satisfy God, satisfy the demands of His justice and love, and quell all rebellion against God, while at the same time lifting man back into the likeness and favor of God, not to speak of protecting God's reputation before the universe. The author does not presume to probe the depths of God's thoughts with regard

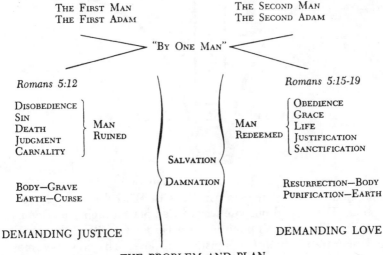

THE FIRST MAN
THE FIRST ADAM

THE SECOND MAN
THE SECOND ADAM

"BY ONE MAN"

Romans 5:12

DISOBEDIENCE
SIN
DEATH   } MAN
JUDGMENT   RUINED
CARNALITY

BODY—GRAVE
EARTH—CURSE

DEMANDING JUSTICE

Romans 5:15-19

OBEDIENCE
GRACE
LIFE   } MAN
JUSTIFICATION   REDEEMED
SANCTIFICATION

SALVATION

DAMNATION

RESURRECTION—BODY
PURIFICATION—EARTH

DEMANDING LOVE

THE PROBLEM AND PLAN

to His plan of redemption but an attempt is made to visualize the problem with its philosophical solution on the preceding page.

God was able to carry out His plan and solve the problem of sin through the mediation of His own Son. This mediation provided a way through which a perfect reconciliation could be brought about within God's Being by a synthesis of His holiness and love which would satisfy the demands of justice and love. A study of God's Word shows that this mediation took place through the Son on five levels of experience for Him: (1) Incarnation, (2) Crucifixion, (3) Resurrection, (4) Ascension and Exaltation, and (5) the Second Coming. The first four of these levels makes possible the realization of the first phase of the plan of redemption — atonement. The fifth level completes the plan through restoration of all creation. The implications of this plan of action are seen in the chart form below. God meets and solves the problem of sin through the cross.

THE CHASM BRIDGED

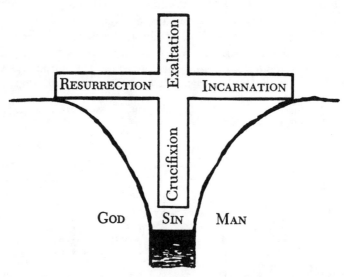

The *purpose* of the incarnation was twofold: (1) revelation of who God is and what man can be with His help, and (2) redemption. The second purpose was carried out through *crucifixion*. Here the problem of sin's punishment was solved while at the same time demonstrating both God's justice and love. The cross became not only a place where God and man meet but the end of the old life and the beginning of the new.

The *resurrection* sealed the victory of the cross and made it available unto men. At the same time the solution of the problem of death and the grave was made known. It provides a sure pledge to man for his own resurrection and victory.

Through His *ascension* and *exaltation* at the right hand of the Father, Jesus presented the work of Calvary and the evidence of the atonement to God and to the universe. There He was crowned King of kings and Lord of lords. From there He would be our Advocate and Intercessor. From there He would keep the promise of sending His Spirit into the world and into the hearts of men to provide a direct relationship with God and the means whereby His life and atonement would be made effective. From there he would be the Administrator of the rest of the plan of redemption yet to be realized. The coming of the Spirit was sufficient to unify the church and form Christ within the believer.

Through the *Second Coming* the plan of redemption will be brought to completion with the redemption of the earth and the setting of the stage for eternal blessedness.

Two phases of the plan of redemption are complete. The plan has been philosophically conceived and practically realized. These two phases care for the *positive* side of the question. The *negative* side remains to be dealt with. Here is where the *administrative control* of God was manifested. How can one account for the presence of evil? Did God plan for it or did He allow it? *Dualism* accounts for sin's presence by trying to show that good and evil are eternal opposites. But there is no basic unity in this view. *Naturalism* tries to account for it through evolution, virtually saying that there is no such thing as evil. This is blindness to reality. Instead, the Scriptures teach that evil exists by divine permission but not by divine design. Moral evil came into existence as a result of moral choice. God was not surprised by this fact and He has also been able to keep control over this fact through divine administration. We may conclude, therefore, that sin and evil in themselves do not reveal God. Rather they are subject to God. God is revealed, however, in the way that He deals with the problem of evil.

Administrative control in solving the problem of evil and in bringing man to the point where he can receive the full benefit of the atonement is all accomplished through the dynamic work of the Holy Spirit. He is God present in the world. When Jesus ascended to the Father following His resurrection, He promised that He would send the Holy Spirit who would be the Divine Agent to carry out all of the provisions of the atonement (John 15:26, 27). This was fulfilled on the Day of Pentecost (Acts 2).

In carrying out His administrative responsibilities the Holy Spirit became the power of God in and among men and the Great Teacher of all time. In His work He would take the things of Christ and make them a reality unto all believers and to the world. In fact Jesus spoke of this relationship as the vine and the branches (John 15). In John 16 Jesus shows how the Spirit will accomplish all of His glorious purposes. The outcome is full sufficiency for all believers (Acts 1:8).

The *results* of redemption were manifold. The problem of sin was solved. Man was restored morally to the image of God. Death and the grave were overcome. New life for soul and body was made possible. Deliverance of the earth from the curse, the complete victory of Christ over evil, and the final incarceration of Satan will be achieved when the Son of God returns soon to complete the final phase of redemption.

At the present time, however, there is one aspect of redemption which is more evident than the others and by which we see a revelation of God, more clearly perhaps, than in any of the other ways. That aspect is *Christian experience.* The life "in Christ" reveals the nature of God personally to those who through Christian experience have that nature imparted to them and to the world by faithful witnessing of God's children. The purpose of this experience is definitely *not* personal enjoyment. It is readily admitted that joy and peace are concomitants of Christian experience but they are not ends in themselves. Men are not only saved *from* something, which should give joy, but they are saved *to* something, which would give greater joy. Instead, the purpose is revelation. We should reveal God.

The process through which man is able to manifest God to the world we call Christian experience. This, in turn, becomes the possession of the believer in two ways: (1) the believer in Christ (through regeneration), and (2) Christ in the believer (through the baptism of the Holy Spirit). The first is provisional and the second is conditional. This kind of life reveals Christ.

3. *Summary Statement*

A study of the considerations in the foregoing statements has now led to the possibility of making a summary statement in outline form of the Christian Theistic World View. Such a statement will make it practical for possible classroom use and further study. The writer is deeply indebted to his colleagues on the faculty of Fort Wayne Bible College for this splendid statement which follows:

SUMMARY STATEMENT OF THE CHRISTIAN THEISTIC WORLD VIEW

God

We believe that God is an eternal personal Being of absolute knowledge, power, and goodness. He is ultimate Reality, the source and ground of all reality and truth.

God and the Cosmos

Christ, the Son of God, is Creator, Designer, and Preserver of all things. In Him the entire universe, macrocosm and microcosm, has its origin, its energy and control, and its final destiny. This relation between God and the world, organic and inorganic, is expressed in such statements of Scripture as Colossians 1:16, 17 and Romans 11:36.

God and Man

Man came into being by a direct, immediate act of the Creator. Unique among all creatures, he bears the image of God in that he has personality and the power of moral choice. He was created for a dual purpose: Godward, he is to *glorify* God and enjoy fellowship with Him; earthward, he is to subdue and hold dominion over the earth and its living creatures (Genesis 1:28).

Man's original state, at creation, has been changed by the intervention of sin. Through deliberate choice of the wrong, man has become estranged from God, the divine image has been marred, and man is now morally corrupted and in need of redemption.

This redemption is provided by God, in the life, death and resurrection of Jesus Christ. By faith in Him as Saviour, and obedience to the Holy Spirit, man may now be transformed unto godlikeness and restored to fellowship with God.

Redemption includes the eternal destiny of Man. By receiving Christ as Saviour, man is fitted for everlasting fellowship with God. Those who reject Christ are destined to everlasting separation from God.

Redemption also assures that the earth, which now suffers the effects of man's sin, shall be restored to its pristine perfection.

God and Truth

Truth, like the created universe, is centered in Christ (Colossians 2:3). It is therefore a unity, integrated by Jesus Christ, and all its parts are meaningfully related to each other and to Him.

If truth originates in God, then He must communicate it to man. He does this by revelation. General revelation is the communication of truth through nature and providence. Special revelation includes the body of truth contained in the Bible, and the disclosure of God and truth in the Person of Jesus Christ. General revelation is in full harmony with special revelation, and finds its true interpretation in it.

Man is endowed by the Creator with the power to apprehend truth. His senses lead to empirical truth; his reason gives him a grasp of the more abstract forms of truth; and faith, which is a positive response to God's revelation, not only enables him by the Holy Spirit to understand the superrational, but also gives him an insight into the meaning of truth at all levels, so that he can "see things steadily and see them whole."

God and Values

As ultimate reality, God sets the standard by which value judgments are to be made. The highest good is realized in the exercise of His will, and on the part of man, in conformity to that will.

C. General Implications for Christian Education

1. The Nature of Education

One direct implication of the Christian Theistic World View is to give us insight into the nature of education. Where God is central, the Creator of the universe, and has made Himself known through Revelation, it follows naturally that education must become a re-interpretation of God's revelation. Education is seeing things as God sees them. It is thinking God's thoughts after Him. Christian education centers in Christ who is the Personal Self-Revelation of God. All other avenues of knowledge also stem from God and are interpreted in the light of Christ's nature and works.

2. The Purpose and Objective of Education

The purpose of education is to show God revealed. The immediate objective of education is to qualify man to reveal God. This is comprehensive because it involves man in his total being — physically, mentally, socially, morally, and spiritually — in his total environment. It includes both information and training. The ultimate objective for education is the Kingdom of God to come.

3. The Curriculum of Education

With God central in the universe and the Source of all truth through creation, it becomes clear that truth proceeds from God. God has chosen to reveal His truth in three ways: (1) through Personal Self-Revelation in the Son of God, (2) through special written Self-Revelation in the Bible as the Word of God, and (3) through General Self-Revelation in nature and the universe. Direct implications for curriculum content are evident. All curricula content is related to God. The Revelation of God becomes the heart of the educational curriculum.

Suggested Class Activities for Chapter II

1. Discuss how the Christian formulates his world view.
2. From what source does the Christian get his information in developing his world view?
3. What part does philosophy have in developing a world view?
4. What part does theology play in developing a world view?
5. What part does the Bible play in the development of a world view?
6. What is the significance of the nature of God in the development of a Christian philosophy of education?

7. Why is the creation considered foundational in the Christian view of the curriculum?
8. Look up Scripture references which point out God's purposes in creation.
9. Create a comparative chart to show how the major theologies compare on defining:

Suggested theologies:

(1) God   (1) Evangelical
(2) Revelation   (2) Roman Catholic
(3) Man   (3) Neo-orthodox
(4) Redemption   (4) Humanism

10. In outline form show the effects of sin in the following ways:
    (1) Upon Adam and Eve
    (2) On the human race
    (3) On the social order
    (4) On the material world
    (5) On God

THE CONSTRUCTION OF A CHRISTIAN
PHILOSOPHY OF EDUCATION

OUTLINE FOR CHAPTER 3

A. PATTERN AND PROCESS

   1. Recent Attempts
   2. A Bibliocentric Theory of the Curriculum

B. PRINCIPLES

   1. Approach
   2. The Concept of Wholism

C. PROCEDURES

   1. Integration
   2. Integrative Means
   3. Biblical Studies
   4. Course Arrangement, Nature and Organization
   5. Interpretation

3 | THE CONSTRUCTION OF A CHRISTIAN PHILOSOPHY OF EDUCATION

A. PATTERN AND PROCESS

1. Recent Attempts

More and more, Christian educators are beginning to realize that to be truly Christian, the curriculum must be Bible-integrated in theory and practice. By this is meant that the Bible is to provide more than theoretical guidance and generalization. Rather, it is to be a vital part of the content and integrated with all subject matter. In fact, the Bible is the integrating factor around which all other subject matter is correlated and arranged. It provides the criteria by which all other subject matter is judged.

On the elementary level an attempt to construct a bibliocentric curriculum was made by the Educational Committee of the National Union of Christian Schools in their recent publication, *Course of Study for Christian Schools*.[1] Dr. Mark Fakkema is a strong advocate of this approach as well. Perhaps he, as no other modern evangelical, has contributed most largely to the general philosophy of Christian education on the undergraduate level. His views are recorded in a pioneer work entitled *Christian Philosophy: Its Educational Implications*.[2] Laying the foundations for a philosophy of Christian education in the Christian philosophy of life, Dr. Fakkema shows the implications of this philosophy in two realms of application: (1) moral discipline and (2) teaching. On the college level, the faculty of Wheaton College in a late bulletin produced the outlines of a theistic approach to the college curriculum. Although this attempt is not specifically named a bibliocentric theory, yet by virtue of its strong theistic basis and the placing of theology at the center of subject matter, this theory can be classified in a bibliocentric context.[3]

Bible colleges have designed their curricula around a Bible core curriculum. In too many cases, however, this is as far as

[1] National Union of Christian Schools, *Course of Study for Christian Schools*, rev. ed. (Grand Rapids, Mich., Wm. B. Eerdmans Pub. Co., 1953).
[2] Chicago, National Association of Christian Schools, (1952).
[3] Earl E. Cairns, *A Blueprint for Christian Higher Education*, Faculty Bulletin of Wheaton College, June, 1953, Vol. 16, No. 3.

they have gone. Other departments too often are operated on the premises of the old Greco-Roman pattern of education. A bibliocentric curriculum is not achieved simply because a Bible department is present. It is not the amount of Bible taught which counts. Instead, the principles of bibliocentric education must permeate the curriculum at all levels and in the classroom of every course. The Bible is the divine catalyst that holds the truth together and gives it significance. We must say, however, that Bible colleges are making some real efforts to develop a truly bibliocentric philosophy of education.

On the seminary level, the former Biblical Seminary in New York has been operating for some time on the principle of a bibliocentric curriculum. The philosophy of this curriculum is published annually in the seminary catalog. The basic premise of this point of view is the centrality of the Bible in all courses of study. Here it is asserted that the Bible illumines all other studies and that the primary task of theological education is to bring the student "to know and experience the theological truth of the Bible." At the Biblical Seminary, they make this theory of Bible study operative in the curriculum in three ways: (1) by the *kind* of Bible study, a methodical, firsthand, and unbiased study of the Scriptures themselves; (2) by the relative *amount* of English Bible required in the total studies, roughly one-third of the hours for graduation, and (3) by the *inter-relatedness* of the courses in Bible with the other subjects. Such correlation saves time, unifies and integrates the whole curriculum.[4]

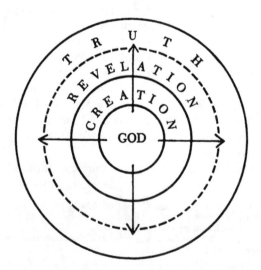

[4]Catalog, 1959-60, The Biblical Seminary of New York, pp. 29-31.

2. A Bibliocentric Theory of the Curriculum

A God-centered pattern of education demands that the Christian educator spell out clearly the processes involved in the total structure of the curriculum. This means that he must base all procedures on a definite theory of knowledge which yields specific curriculum principles and practices.

All avenues of knowledge stem from God and are interpreted in the light of His nature and works. The pattern revealed is somewhat like that pictured in the chart on page 62 above. God Himself is Truth. His works through creation disclose truth. Then, He has provided Special Revelation in His Son and the Bible. Thus, the clues are evident for the development of a Bibliocentric theory of knowledge.

Knowledge is defined as an acquaintance with, an understanding of, and a clear perception of truth. Objectively, it consists of the body of facts accumulated by mankind.

The Biblical view of knowledge presupposes a source of all knowledge, for knowledge is dependent upon truth and truth in turn is dependent upon God. The Bible pictures God as the source of all life and truth. "In the beginning *God* created the heavens and the earth" (Genesis 1:1). "He is a God of truth." It follows naturally, therefore, that any truth which comes to man must be an expression of the nature of God.

Truth is ascribed to the Trinity — the Triune God is a God of truth. God the Father is the source of truth, God the Son is the manifestation of truth, and God the Spirit is the interpreter of truth. In outline form the Biblical theory is as follows:

The Trinity(God) and Truth
> The Father is light and truth — Psalm 36:9; I John 1:15
> The Son is a revelation of truth — John 1:14, 17; John 14:6
> (Truth is a Person)
> The Spirit interprets truth — John 15:26; 16:13

General Revelation
> Through creation — Genesis 1:1; Psalm 19:1, 2; Romans 1:20
> Through conscience of man — Romans 2:14-16

Special Revelation
> In the Scriptures — Hebrews 1:1, 2; Psalm 119:105, 130
> In the Son — Colossians 2:3, 9; John 14:9; 8:12

Man and Truth
> There is earthly wisdom — I Corinthians 1 and 2; James 3:15

There is spiritual wisdom — I Corinthians 1:30; 2:10-16; James 3:13, 17

Wisdom, revelation and knowledge are gifts from God — Ephesians 1:17-19

Knowledge of Christ is most precious knowledge to man — Philippians 3:8; Colossians 2:2, 3

Man is to experience and walk in His truth — II John 3, 4; Psalm 51:6; John 8:32

School and Truth

There is propositional truth — academic content and program

There is personal truth — through regeneration by the Spirit of God and Jesus Christ, the Truth

Direct implications are evident at this point for the total structure of education. A theocentric philosophy of education is made possible by this view. There are several ways this philosophy can serve education: (1) by providing a philosophy of life which gives meaning, (2) a world view which gives unity, (3) emphasis on true values and objectives which provide both purpose and direction, and (4) systematization of content by showing the relations and inter-relations in the totality of truth which provides a workable pattern for the curriculum.

Other implications are evident. First, the fact of God's existence obligates the Christian to be active in the assertion of His existence and centrality. Neutrality is not possible because of man's sin and his need of redemption. These same facts rule out other points of view. The pupil-centered theory is man-centered; but man cannot save himself, for he is utterly dependent on God. The best interest of the student cannot be served outside of the love, mercy, and provision of God. The social perspective also places man at the center. This view is also limited by the comparative helplessness of man. The God-centered view, therefore, is the only adequate basis upon which to build, for it is based on the reality of the divine-human relationship. Furthermore, this perspective discloses the pattern and principles which are basic to the educative process.

The God-centered pattern of truth has direct implications for the purposes and objectives of Christian education. Where God is central, the Creator of the universe, and has made Himself known through Self-Revelation, it follows naturally that education must become a re-interpretation of God's revelation. Education is seeing things as God sees them. It is thinking God's thoughts after Him.

The first purpose of education is to show God revealed. The next follows: to bring students into conformity to the revealed will of God, thus enabling them to reveal the nature of God through their redeemed personalities. This is comprehensive because it involves man in his total being in his total environment. It includes both information and training.

If God is central in the universe and the Source of all truth, there are direct implications for curriculum content as well. All subject matter is related to God. The revelation of God becomes the heart of the subject matter curriculum. The diagram below shows the relationships involved:

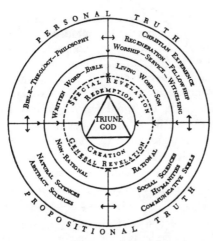

CHRISTIAN THEORY OF KNOWLEDGE

In the diagram above it becomes evident that God has chosen to reveal truth through the two phases of His activity: creation and redemption. The truths of redemption have been transmitted through God's Special-Revelations in the written Word — the Bible, and the Living Word — His Son. In creation, God's general revelation is evident through both the rational and nonrational creations. It is to be expected therefore that all curriculum content will be related to these phases of revelation and that subject matter areas will be abstractions from them. Thus, subjects incorporate records of God's nature and works as man is able to develop them into organized form.

The inner circles of the diagram suggest the objective pattern and source of all truth centering in God. The outer circle takes us to man — his experience of truth and his organization of knowledge into a curricular pattern. Here emerges the broad pattern of Christian education — Bible, theology, ethics; Christian experience in worship and service; the social sciences and the humanities; and the natural and abstract sciences.

This pattern yields the bipolar curriculum theory — God and man — giving direction to education under the control of Christ as indicated in the diagram below:

This concept of education under the mastery of Christ is the heart of Christian education. It includes the "setting" for learning, the framework for teaching, and what may be called the structure of Christian education. The history of education indicates that the education of every age has had an inner structure, a coherent power to hold it together. For the Greeks it was citizenship or loyalty to the state; for the Hebrews it was knowledge of the law and obedience; in the Middle Ages it was knowledge and discipline. For the Christian, it is the power and life of Christ sublimating and integrating all of life and expressed in the virtues of faith, love, and obedience. This gives spiritual and moral depth to education and saves it from sterile rationalism and intellectualism.

Dr. James D. Murch commented on this principle by saying:

> When we give Christ His proper authority in curriculum there will be no loss of emphasis upon the Scriptures, for He insisted that "they are they that testify of me"; the church will not be relegated to a place of minor importance, for it is "the body of Christ" purchased by His own precious blood; the pupil will not be neglected, for Christ came to give men life and give it "more abundantly." When the pupil accepts the control of Christ, his attitudes, habits, conduct, relationships, and ideals will be immeasurably enriched.[5]

The Christian curriculum begins properly with the Bible, the Word of God. This is true when conceiving of the curriculum broadly as comprehending all planned educative experiences or more narrowly as the factual materials for subject matter.

The Bible itself becomes the central subject in the subject matter curriculum. Since it contains the record of God's truth as inspired by the Holy Spirit and reveals God's Person, His Son, and His dealings with man, it is also the basis by which all other channels of knowledge are evaluated and used. It thereby becomes the integrating and correlating factor in the subject matter curriculum. Through the Bible the inter-relatedness of all other subjects and truths is made possible and clear. This means that all other subjects and truths have their first point of reference in the Word of God, draw their materials from the Bible wherever possible, and return to the Bible with their accumulation of facts for interpretation and practical application.

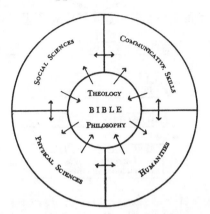

We may conclude therefore that the function of the Bible in the subject matter curriculum is twofold. First, it provides content of its own. Second, it provides a service function to the other subjects. The principles of Biblical truth should be applied to and in all other subjects. Claims to truth from other areas should be tested and evaluated by the philosophical and theological truths of the Word of God. The chart above sets forth this central relation.

B. PRINCIPLES

1. *Approach*

The Christian educator approaches the task of curriculum construction in the light of the demands placed upon him by the requirements implicit in his Christian philosophy of life and theory of knowledge. We noted in the previous chapter that this philosophy is based on the presuppositions of revelation recorded in the Bible.

Having the conviction that God has revealed Himself to mankind, the Christian educator begins both his concepts and practices in education with God, believing as he does that Christian education is actually a re-interpretation of God's revelation. This principle demands that the Christian educator deal with the implications called for by a theocentric or God-centered approach to truth. The chart on page 68 shows the relationships involved.

[5]James D. Murch, *Christian Education and the Local Church* (Cincinnati, Standard Pub. Co., 1943), p. 151.

The Bibliocentric Pattern of Curriculum Construction

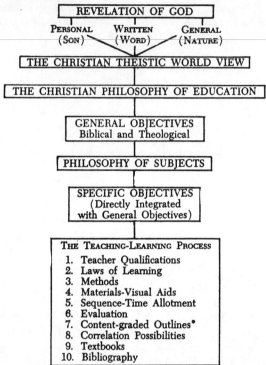

REVELATION OF GOD

PERSONAL   WRITTEN   GENERAL
(SON)   (WORD)   (NATURE)

THE CHRISTIAN THEISTIC WORLD VIEW

THE CHRISTIAN PHILOSOPHY OF EDUCATION

GENERAL OBJECTIVES
Biblical and Theological

PHILOSOPHY OF SUBJECTS

SPECIFIC OBJECTIVES
(Directly Integrated
with General Objectives)

The Teaching-Learning Process
1. Teacher Qualifications
2. Laws of Learning
3. Methods
4. Materials-Visual Aids
5. Sequence-Time Allotment
6. Evaluation
7. Content-graded Outlines*
8. Correlation Possibilities
9. Textbooks
10. Bibliography

*Follow the pattern of bibliocentric interpretation of subject matter.

The chart above shows that the Christian Theistic World View based on Revelation yields the Christian Philosophy of Education. From this philosophy general objectives are abstracted and they serve as guide lines for theory and practice. By integrating and correlating the philosophy of the various school studies with these general objectives the teacher is able to formulate specific objectives for use in the development of the truth represented in the subject to the pupil. The specific objectives are directly integrated and connected with the general objectives in such a way that the implications for the teaching-learning process are consistent and clear.

In the chapters which follow, the teaching-learning process will be dealt with in detail with attention being given specifically to each of its facets. At this point, however, it is necessary for one to see in what way the Christian educator approaches that process. This demands a clear understanding of the fundamental concepts of curriculum construction and specifically how the Christian philosophy of life can reach the classroom situation.

2. The Concept of Wholism

Every curriculum is constructed from some kind of perspective. In some instances this perspective demands an organizational approach to courses of study. In this approach, courses may be organized on the basis of the relation of one course to another. In this view each course forms a part of the whole but is considered autonomous in itself. Relationships are established on the basis of similarities or contrasts in course content. Such courses are arbitrarily put together in curriculum organization. This is made possible by the feeling that truth is somehow inherently coherent.

In other instances the whole of the curriculum is formed by an eclectic approach to organization. This demands that courses be arranged through a process of sampling from each major field of study. It is felt that each part sampled will provide a comprehension of the essential whole. Christian educators must reject these approaches.

Believing as he does that God is the Source of life and truth and through creation has brought the universe into existence, the Christian educator can and must take a wholistic approach to curriculum construction. In this view he maintains that reality can be conceived as a whole because God made it that way. The whole is prior and superior to any of its parts and to the sum of its parts. The whole is greater than the sum of its parts. The various parts of the whole can be understood, not only in their relationship to one another, but primarily within an understanding of the whole. The parts are derived from the whole and therefore are not autonomous. The secret of this wholism, as stated previously, is the Christian world view.

C. Procedures

1. Integration

The actual construction of a bibliocentric curriculum involves working by the principles laid out above and close adherence to the pattern and process demanded thereby.

This whole process involves the problem of integration. It is a problem with which education has been concerned for a long time. At the present time higher education in this country is rather widely involved in the problems implied in curriculum integration. In fact the curricula of higher institutions are under widespread attack because of a basic lack of an ordering principle. The committee which drafted the Harvard Report expressed the view that American education lacks a unifying purpose and idea.

Integration means to make whole, to unify, to bring parts together. It is the means whereby unity is achieved. An undesirable opposite of integration is separatedness and is often expressed through such criticisms as "discrete" or "splintering." Separatedness implies the positive characteristic of connectedness and relatedness provided in the concept of integration. Wholeness and design are further characteristics of this concept.

The history of education reveals that every great culture sought a unifying core or concept for a directive force to its educational system. For the Greeks and Romans the good citizen was undoubtedly such a force. Outside of the church this concept very largely dominated educational circles until Thomas Aquinas attempted his great synthesis. Integration for him consisted largely in harmonizing classical learning with Christianity. In this the Seven Liberal Arts had a major place.

Moving into the modern period, which traditionally has been rooted in the Renaissance, reason was advocated as a basis for integration. It was felt that reason in one individual would be in harmony with reason in all other individuals. The liberation of reason would lead to the realization of a perfect humanity and to a system of harmonious relations between individuals and society. This conviction was deepened when scientists began to popularize a belief in the intelligible order and system throughout nature. Nature, too, is rational because it reveals a coherent pattern which is in tune with reason. A synthesis of science and reason was sufficient to gain many adherents to the notion that scientific naturalism provides the unifying core and concepts.

Today educators have come to see the marked insufficiencies of these past efforts to achieve integration, particularly the use of reason. It is quite evident that reason has lost control over the vast cultural forces which seek to bring almost complete disintegration. There seems to be an almost frantic effort to find a new basis for integration at the present. All of this provides the Christian educator with a real opportunity to demonstrate the sufficiency of a bibliocentric approach to this problem.

There are two general ways by which integration in the curriculum can be accomplished. The term universe provides the clue. The etymology of the word reveals that it means all things combined into one. A collection or aggregate may be shown to be one by disclosing either a pattern which the elements jointly exhibit or a common quality which they individually possess. In the former case, the elements may be quite unlike one another but they fit together into a design, or an organic whole, or system or structure. In the latter case, the elements may have no significant relations of dependence or interdependence and thus cannot be said to constitute a whole, but they are in some important respects like one another and thus are all instances of one kind of thing. The sciences have been classified according to the first type of integration. An example of the second type is found in situations where concepts demand some kind of relationships. An illustration of this type of course integration is found in courses such as Philosophy of Science, Philosophy of Art, Philosophy of Religion, etc.

The Christian approach to integration involves the principles inherent in a wholistic view of life and truth. Life itself is full of constant reminders that man needs a sense of balance and perspective. The principles of centrality and coherence are used constantly in Christian circles. In theology, we speak of a God-centered, Christ-centered and Spirit-filled life. These terms are used to describe a well-balanced and integrated personality.

Other clues are evident when the problem is viewed from the standpoint of psychology. Perception and understanding require a wholistic approach in order for the student to "make sense" out of the unintelligible. In other words, the mind seeks a sense of balance. Psychologically considered, a well-balanced personality bears fruit in self-control. The experimental evidences provided by the advocates of Gestalt Psychology reveal clearly how much the human mind seeks integration.

In Christian experience, we speak of the "heart." In Christian philosophy the coherence theory of knowledge is prominent in epistemological considerations. The Christian doctrine of the creation directly implies a wholism. Therefore, in the curriculum as a whole, a focus is needed, something which will provide unity, orderly arrangement, intelligent relationships, and systematic organization. The Christian believes that the Bible provides him with the basis for integration, particularly in the subject matter curriculum. This is seen on two levels: the level of principle, providing us with a universe of thought centered in God; and second, the level of practice, which is the level of the teaching process, whereby interpretation and application are made possible in the Christian frame of reference.

2. Integrative Means

Integrative means provide instrumental power by which unity and coherence are realized. The Harvard Report on education reported four possible means by which integration could be attained: Religion; Western Culture; Change: Contemporary Problems; and Pragmatism and Natural Science. The conclusion was that these means were either impracticable, too narrow, or intrinsically deficient. Thus, Conant points out that "the search continues and must continue for some over-all logic, some strong, not easily broken frame within which both college and school may fulfill their at once diversifying and uniting tasks. This logic must be wide enough to embrace the actual richness and variegation of modern life — a richness partly, if not wholly, reflected in the complexity of our present educational system. It must also be strong enough to give goal and direction to this system — something much less clear at present."[6] The Christian educator believes that he has God-given integrative means based on the presuppositions of Christian theism. These means are provided to him through what is called synoptic studies which are studies aware of their own distinctiveness but also functionally providing a perspective for seeing things in connected wholes. They include the disciplines of Bible, Christian Theology, and Christian Philosophy, hereafter referred to as Biblical Studies.

Before moving on to the specifics of applying the principles above we must pause to note at least three levels where such principles are practiced. From the discussion thus far it is evident that there is a philosophical and theological level based on the presuppositions of the Christian faith. There is a second level called the level of autonomous disciplines based on the creativity of God. This level will be dealt with in succeeding chapters. There is the third level of interpretation when the Christian faith acts as the key to interpretation and integration and in the judgment of subject matter disciplines. We shall move to a consideration of those studies which comprise the integrative core and then show how these studies affect curriculum construction at the various levels mentioned above.

3. Biblical Studies

The concept of integration as applied to the subject matter curriculum provides a basis for understanding the relatedness of courses, of areas of knowledge and subject matter, and of the curriculum as a whole. It can also be applied to personality, to the structural operation of the total school program including the administration, and to the relation of student life and instruction. All of these factors will be dealt with in time but at this point attention is focused on the heart of school life — the subject matter curriculum, where the teaching-learning process takes place.

It is the claim of the Christian educator that Biblical Studies represented by Bible, Christian Theology and Christian Philosophy, provide the synoptic basis and wholistic approach by which inte-

[6]General Education in a Free Society (Cambridge, Mass., Harvard University Press, 1945), p. 40.

gration and interpretation of the total subject matter curriculum are made possible most adequately. The chart below pictures the relationships involved in this view.

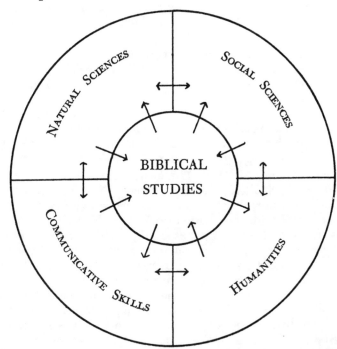

The chart shows the direct implications of revelation for the Christian educator and his approach to the organization of truth into curriculum form. To him revelation is conceived in two forms: special and general. Biblical Studies constitute the written and organized approach to the contributions of Special Revelation. All other studies constitute the approach to General Revelation. No set pattern is evident for the organization of truth into courses in the area of General Revelation, but nature and culture are evident sources of truth in this area.

Biblical Studies include those disciplines which regard the whole of knowledge and reality as one of their specific tasks. In this task they perform a *synoptic* function, that is, seeing things together, seeing things as a whole, and seeing things connected together as a whole. Their very nature demands this kind of treatment; their methods are inclusive and their content or substance provides a synoptic basis for integration and interpretation.

Of central importance in this area of truth is the discipline of *Bible.* This discipline stands alone in its own right as a subject, but it also operates synoptically by providing a service function to all other disciplines in the subject matter curriculum, and even to school administration as a whole. In a later chapter this matter will be explored more fully but the following list reveals the strategic place that Bible has in the curriculum.

1. It provides the historical record of God's revelation.
2. It provides much content for study.
3. It tests and measures all truth by its principles.
4. It releases the thought-structures by which thinking can be guided.
5. It provides great principles which form the substance of Christian Theology and Christian Philosophy.
6. It provides the bases whereby integration and correlation are made possible in the curriculum as a whole.

Next to Bible, *Christian Theology* is a strategic part of the area of Biblical Studies. Christian Theology is concerned with the whole of reality as reality is particularly related to its source — God. It is concerned with the relation of God to the reality which He has created and vice versa and especially with the purpose of man within reality. It looks to *revelation* for its source of knowledge and thereby adds a dimension to thought not present in other disciplines. This discipline focuses particularly on the relation of our faith to the church, but its contributions are sufficiently important to education as a whole to merit a peculiar place in the area of Biblical Studies. Some of these contributions are revealed as follows:

1. Theology provides a frame of reference for all knowledge, all truth, and all being. It shows that all truth, sacred and secular, is one in God.
2. The various spheres of life are coordinated according to the dictates of Christian faith expressed in Christian Theology. In this it guides Christian Philosophy.
3. It specializes in a description and explanation of the nature of God — the Source of all reality.
4. In revealing the nature of God, it discloses the clues by which truth can be properly interpreted.
5. It provides structures of thought, such as creation, immanence, and transcendence by which truth can be interpreted.
6. In relation to history, it furnishes the categories of purpose, providence, incarnation, redemption, and destiny.
7. It provides an integrating center for knowledge, expressed through great principles and focused in the Person of God.
8. It discloses God's will for men, thereby giving both a sense of purpose and destiny.

Christian Philosophy constitutes the third discipline in the area of Biblical Studies. In general the function of philosophy is to achieve synoptic integration by relating things systematically. Philosophy is all-inclusive, for it deals with total meanings, questions of purpose and value, and consults data from all experience. In all of this it seeks the organization of all knowledge and experience into a coherent explanation of reality or a world view. It is also more narrowly concerned with ontological and epistemological problems particularly as they relate to each other separate discipline in the curriculum. This it accomplishes through an examination of the basic presuppositions, methods and basic concepts of those disciplines. The contributions of Christian Philosophy may be summarized as follows:

1. It coordinates the various spheres of life as a whole.
2. It relates knowledge systematically.
3. It examines the presuppositions, methods and basic concepts of each discipline and group of disciplines.
4. It strives for coherence, the formulation of a world view.
5. Its method is to consult data from total experience.

In the chart above arrows are extended both vertically and laterally. Biblical Studies not only contribute the clues by which all truth can be organized coherently, but they also provide the bases for correlation by which relationships are made evident. A God-centered view of education demands that He not only be recognized as the Source and Ground of truth and reality, but that He has also provided for the existence of relationships between the various facets of truth. Thus, the truths contained in the wide area of General Revelation have a direct relation to truths in the area of Biblical Studies and to one another. Since truth is a unity, the "parts" of truth contribute to an understanding of the whole. Biblical Studies provide the clues by which this is recognized.

From this discussion it is quite evident that the nature of truth makes it possible for courses of study to draw upon one another and contribute to one another so that the total pattern of truth can be made evident to the student. While each separate discipline has a "thrust" of truth of its own, making it distinctive from all others, there is remarkable overlap in their relationships. These close relationships make it possible, therefore, to lay out a pattern of course arrangements by which certain preconceived goals may be achieved.

4. *Course Arrangement, Nature and Organization*

The relations and inter-relations of truth in the subject matter curriculum make it possible for the Christian educator, particularly in higher education, to arrange and organize course patterns according to pre-conceived ends. Ordinarily such plans are made in terms of either course content or student personality. On the philosophical level the educator is concerned with principles for handling truth-content but in making arrangements for organizing courses of study he should be guided by the needs of the student. Here a school must think in terms of the outcomes planned. In other words, the question arises: what kind of person are we trying to develop through the courses of study offered by the institution? The answer to this question requires a curriculum which is designed to do at least two things: (1) to provide courses which will develop the Christian personality of the student as such, and (2) to offer courses which will assist the student in preparation for serving God in his chosen life task.

The philosophy of the curriculum with regard to the development of both Christian personality and skills is illustrated in the pattern below:

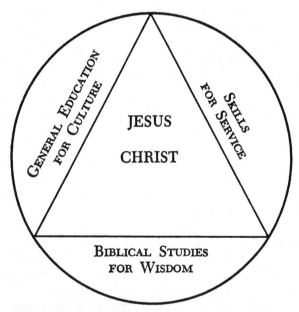

A God-centered pattern of education finds its expression through the life and teachings of Jesus Christ. "In Him was life and the life was the light of men." All Christian education, therefore, must be Christ-centered and Christ-controlled. Christian personality is developed through a unique combination of Christian experience, based upon regeneration of character, and Christian knowledge, both of which lead to Christian service. This approach saves the educator from being narrowly intellectual to the exclusion of the dynamic life principle. Instead, it calls for skillful integration of life and truth and to realize the ends desired. In this pattern the life and truth of Jesus Christ permeate the principles and practice at all levels of Christian education.

On the other hand, this pattern is not narrowly theological because it makes definite provision for intellectual growth and development as well as for an awareness of the outside world of reality, recognizing that the Christian cannot be a true witness or servant without such an awareness. Service cannot be truly rendered without a knowledge and experience of the world of men in which the Christian message is needed and applied. Wisdom, culture, and ability are all needed to enable the student to live his life, carry out God's purposes, and render a service to God and Man.

Biblical Studies for Wisdom has been largely covered in a previous section of this chapter. There the synoptic benefits of these studies provide self-evident advantages to the student sufficient for the discussion at this point. Wisdom here is pictured as more than intellectual apprehension. It is rather an experience of God who is both life and truth. This gives life both balance and a dynamic.

To some the concept, *General Education for Culture*, might imply a liberal arts education. As used here, however, the liberal arts concept as held traditionally throughout the long history of education is not what is implied. The writer is well aware of the nebulous meaning of the term "general education" but the term as used is in line with the current movement in higher education in general today. Despite the vagueness of the term there are some general agreements as to what this kind of education should include. High among these agreements is a growing awareness that each student should have an intelligent insight into many areas of knowledge and into the inter-relatedness of those areas. There is also general agreement on some of the personality attributes which each college graduate should possess. It embraces what might be called a common, necessary type of education. It involves skills in the use of language, a knowledge of the social structure, the development of the skills of correct thinking, an appreciation for the accomplishments of men in the arts and sciences, and an understanding of the highest values of life.

Traditionally, liberal arts education has its roots in Graeco-Roman culture. As developed by them this denoted the Seven Liberal Arts, commonly known as the Trivium and Quadrivium, comprised of grammar, rhetoric, logic, music, arithmetic, geometry, and astronomy. Christian scholars were prone to add language, literature and philosophy to this list. Today, the concept of General Education has broadened the list still more to include the social and natural sciences in some circles. In addition it is conceived in terms of general personal characteristics.

General education for culture represents an area of truth which the Christian educator feels obligated to investigate and master. The Christian faith demands that the Christian lay claim upon all of life. This he does through education which is the process by which man involves himself in God's interpretation as He makes this known in revelation. While Biblical Studies specialize in the area of Special Revelation, General Education is largely a product of God's General Revelation. At the basis of this area lies a temporal creation. God has called all things into being. Principles of truth, goodness and beauty are of His making and expressive of His nature. Therefore, the believer's commitment to Christ not only gives him a faith by which to live but also a world outlook comprehensive enough to embrace all the spheres of life.

Christian educators, therefore, must not withdraw, reject or compromise with the cultural structure with which they are related. Instead, they must be interested in effecting cultural regeneration. This means that critical participation is demanded. It implies that actually the Christian is a participant in two worlds: one of the here and now and the one to come. The Christian lives in a social context that he must be interested in, that he must understand, and witness to and use to the development of his personal skills for the extension of the Kingdom of God.

While recognizing that general education will contribute to the development of intellectual skills and to the broadening of one's horizons and knowledge, evangelical Christian educators must constantly strive to remember the importance of immersing this kind of education in the larger context of the Christian Spirit and practice. The spiritual realities in the school program will create a Christian environment conducive to the development of Christian attitudes, habits, and character sufficient to keep a good balance in one's intellectual pursuits.

While general education has traditionally been designed to develop the student's intellectual life, the concept at present should lead Christian educators to strive for outcomes such as those suggested below:

Proposed Outcomes in a Program of General Education

1. To help each student to see that the Christian world view is comprehensive enough to include areas of truth embraced by the general culture.
2. To acquaint the student with the world around him through a general study of selected natural sciences, social sciences and humanities.
3. To develop for the regulation of one's personal and civic life a code of behavior based on ethical principles consistent with democratic ideals and the Christian faith.
4. To prepare the student for intelligent and satisfactory living as an individual, in the home and in society.
5. To develop ability to understand and express ideas clearly and effectively.
6. To cultivate an appreciation of moral, aesthetic and spiritual values.
7. To provide a sound basis for critical thinking and valid judgment.
8. To help the student toward physical as well as mental well-being.
9. To help each student attain a satisfactory emotional and social adjustment.
10. To assist each student in the choice of a vocation.

To summarize, general education is education that is non-vocational. Its content is comprised generally of the liberal arts and sciences, commonly divided into the humanities, the social sciences and the natural sciences, although not strictly limited to these. These are the subjects which, to the Christian, comprehend one's relations to God, to one's self, to others and to nature.

General education does not aim at vocational competence but rather at developing the student's capacity for responsible living under God in a human society and a natural environment. It cultivates the feelings, enlarges and exercises the imagination, disciplines the mind, trains the judgment, provides historical perspective, and sheds light on the nature of every reality.

While it is recognized that subject matter content will play an important part in the realization of the above objectives, Christian educators must be sensitive to the part played also by the total school program. Still another factor involved here is that which is termed "structure" in the program. Deliberate attempts need to be made to "build structure" into the lives of the students. This, as we have already noted, will be provided by the general example of the staff and the general atmosphere of the school characterized by Christian love, faith, and obedience. The sincere demonstration and manifestation of these virtues will have a "total" effect on students by which they assimilate a great deal of general education. Therefore, general education in addition to developing certain personality traits will also inculcate certain Christian virtues in students.

Skills for service involves the areas of the curriculum which supply the "major" fields for academic study. The students are involved in some type of specialization which will enable them to devote themselves to a chosen vocation in the service of God. There is no limit theoretically to the developments in this curriculum area but each school will need to plan carefully the total scope of its offerings in the light of the resources available and the general objectives previously decided upon.

5. Interpretation

In addition to supplying the clues to integration, Biblical Studies also supply clues for the proper interpretation of truth.

Secular educators approach subject matter content in a secular frame of reference. By doing so they resort to what is called "natural interpretation," to abstract meanings from study-content. This kind of interpretation stems primarily from human reasoning and cannot possibly be the approach of the Christian educator. Natural interpretation places man at the center and leads ultimately to rationalism and humanism, for in this view man is the ultimate authority. The implications of this kind of interpretation were clearly pointed out by Dr. Mark Fakkema who said:

> Secular education is a child of natural interpretation. Secular instruction is a blunt denial of the centrality of our God. It is the "image" disowning his "Original." It is worse than that. Secular instruction marks a rebellion against the Most High in the field of education. Not only has the Creator been banished from His creation but God has been dethroned and man has been enthroned.[7]

The approach by the Christian educator to interpretation is known as *supernatural interpretation*. Here the educator thinks God's thoughts after Him. Essentially, man's interpretation is a re-interpretation of God's revelation. The Bible is the guide for the process and becomes central in the thinking of the Christian educator. Interpretation here thus becomes God-centered and Biblical. The Holy Spirit is present to assist man in the process and in spite of sin's effect on man He carries on His work to

[7]Mark Fakkema, *Christian Philosophy: Its Educational Implications* (Chicago, National Association of Christian Schools, 1952), p. 85-T.

ultimate success. The duty of the Christian educator, therefore, is to get in complete harmony with the person and work of the Holy Spirit.

Operating upon the basis that there are both cultural and spiritual products in the curriculum, the Christian educator can proceed in his interpretation of specific subject matter in a twofold way: (1) He will try to discover the factual knowledge provided for him by the subject under consideration and how it is organized for study; (2) He will apply the principles of supernatural interpretation to these facts in order to discover first the attributes of God, and second, to reveal the implications of these attributes both personally and socially. This reveals the *spiritual* knowledge within the facts. This process may be stated in another way. The subjects in the curriculum are revelatory of God. This is objective revelation. The process, however, is not complete until objective truth becomes subjective truth for the learner. The learner, then, must receive the God-revealing truth of the subjects and unveil this truth in his daily life, character and conduct.

A *pattern of interpretation* emerges from the foregoing consideration which provides the basis for classroom procedure in this development of subject matter. The truth to be revealed would include:

1. Cultural and factual knowledge to be used in practical situations in the whole of life.
2. Direct parallels between Biblical Content and factual content whereby close relationships are revealed.
3. The attributes of God, incommunicable and communicable.
4. The consequent analogical character which man is expected to manifest as a child and image of God.
5. Application of revealed truths to society as a whole.
6. Clues for the building of the kingdom of Christ among men through the Church.

This kind of interpretation is made possible through the clues provided by the application of the synoptic principles of Biblical Studies. A particular area of the curriculum is interpreted in the "light" of the whole. For example, a philosophy of Social Sciences depends directly on the Christian view of man, society, and history. Thus, a very practical procedure for classroom use in the handling of subject matter is indicated. The process of thinking will follow somewhat the following pattern:

Facts ———⟶ Principles ———⟶ The Christian Point of View

Thus, both facts and principles derived from the facts are interpreted by and made significant through the Christian point of view as it is related to them. Both facts and principles in the Biblical

Studies area enable the teacher to evaluate facts and principles outside of the Biblical Studies area.

SUGGESTED CLASS ACTIVITIES FOR CHAPTER III

1. Show the relations of Christian philosophy in general to education.
2. Discuss the implications of the chart entitled "The Bibliocentric Pattern of Curriculum Construction." Do you agree with its general pattern?
3. Point out practical examples where the concept of "wholism" has a place in Christian thought and practice.
4. What is meant by a "wholistic" approach to Christian education?
5. Draw a chart or sketch to show the centrality of God in Christian thought and education.
6. Can you think of other attempts to formulate a Bibliocentric approach to education?
7. Formulate your own theory of knowledge from the Christian standpoint.
8. How is knowledge defined? Wisdom? What is the difference between the two?
9. Discuss the implications of the fact that God has revealed Himself to the field of education.
10. What are the practical advantages of a Christian philosophy for education?
11. What do Biblical Studies have to contribute to all other subjects?
12. What can other subjects contribute to Biblical Studies?

Section Two

THE IMPLICATIONS FOR A CHRISTIAN PHILOSOPHY OF EDUCATION

Having discussed the *foundations* of a Christian philosophy of education in Section I, we can now move to direct consideration of the *implications* of these matters for a Christian philosophy of education. This, of course, concerns the educative process — the process by which the philosophy gets into the classroom situation. Of primary concern in these considerations will be aims and objectives, teacher-pupil relationships, the curriculum, methods, and the school system.

THE EDUCATIVE PROCESS – ITS NATURE, AIMS AND OBJECTIVES

OUTLINE FOR CHAPTER 4

A. THE NATURE OF THE EDUCATIVE PROCESS

    1. Definition
    2. The Nature of the Educative Process
    3. The Content of the Educative Process

B. THE NATURE AND FUNCTION OF AIMS AND OBJECTIVES

    1. Definition of Terms
    2. The Source of Aims
    3. The Function of Aims and Goals

C. AIMS AND OBJECTIVES HISTORICALLY AND PHILOSOPHICALLY CONCEIVED

    1. Early Views
    2. Humanism
    3. Idealism
    4. Realism
    5. Naturalism
    6. Pragmatism
    7. Statements by Individuals
    8. Modern Developments
    9. Survey and Evaluation

D. THE GOALS OF SECULAR EDUCATION

    1. The Elementary School
    2. The High School
    3. Higher Education
    4. Confusion in Secular Ranks

E. GENERAL OR ULTIMATE OBJECTIVES AND FUNCTIONS OF CHRISTIAN EDUCATION

    1. The Basis of the Purpose of Christian Education
    2. The Purpose of Christian Education
    3. The Individual Objective in Christian Education
    4. The Integration of Personality and Christian Maturity
    5. The Social Aim of Christian Education
    6. The Social Objective of Christian Education and the Church
    7. The Prophetic Aim in Christian Education
    8. The Functions of Christian Education

F. THE PLACE OF OBJECTIVES IN THE EDUCATIVE PROCESS

    1. The Use of Objectives in Christian Education
    2. General Objectives for Christian Education

4 | THE EDUCATIVE PROCESS —
ITS NATURE, AIMS AND OBJECTIVES

A. THE NATURE OF THE EDUCATIVE PROCESS

1. *Definition*

The educative process is that which focuses attention on instruction. It is concerned with what takes place in the classroom situation. It involves both teaching and learning, and is, consequently, also called the teaching-learning process. It embraces a teacher with something to teach and a student who is a learner. It is the process by which the Christian Philosophy of Education gets into the classroom situation.

2. *The Nature of the Educative Process*

The teaching-learning process is actually *one* process. Where there is no teaching, there is no learning. Teaching is always connected with learning. In fact, teaching and learning are essentially part of the same process. Both aspects of this process are complex and possess several facets. Teaching involves attitudes, aims, materials, methods, preparation, and presentation. Learning includes motives, attitudes, desires, perceptions, comprehension, and other factors. Actually, very little is known about learning *per se* but the more light we receive on it, the better our teaching becomes.

The teaching-learning process is also a *manifold process*. The task of the Christian teacher is to be aware of the nature of this many-sided task and to develop skill in the manipulation of its several facets. In this whole process the teacher works with the Spirit of God in integrating these varied factors to focus them on the learner in an attempt to realize the great goals of Christian teaching. Thus, the task of the Christian teacher is to work with God in bringing the pupil to Godlikeness and kinship. "We are laborers together with God" (I Corinthians 3:9). We are "workers together with Him" (II Corinthians 6:1). This is the essence of Christian education.

3. *The Content of the Educative Process*

We have seen that the Christian Philosophy of Life has direct implications for a Christian Philosophy of Education. This in turn is revelatory of the educative process which involves content and methods. From the standpoint of content the Christian Philosophy of Education begins with purposes and objectives. These are instrumental in the hands of the teacher who meets the pupil in a teaching situation and contacts him with the necessary methods of accomplishing the objectives. Thus we have a pattern set up by which we can operate in the educative process. It appears as follows:

1. Purposes and objectives provide guide lines for initiating and culminating the educative process.
2. The teacher stands before the student as the oracle of God with the truth of God.
3. The focus of the educative process is the pupil.
4. The structure of Christian education provides the atmosphere in which the whole process takes place. This structure is provided by Christian love, faith, and obedience.
5. The curriculum provides the truth-content by which the revelation of God is organized and presented to the student. Herein we find justification for course content with every subject assuming importance by the extent to which it is revelatory of God. The pattern by which this is accomplished is fourfold: (1) evangelism, (2) information, (3) worship and (4) fellowship.
6. The methods provide the mediums of communication through which the curriculum content reaches its destination. Such methods should be spiritual, varied, graded, unified, integrated, comprehensive, flexible, personal, social, and Biblical. They should be integrated with the principles of learning and teaching.

An attempt is made to picture in the chart form which follows the various factors which comprise the teaching-learning process.

From the chart on page 89 one can see the magnitude, diversity, and density of the teaching-learning process. Our purpose in that which follows is to consider each of the several facets of this process.

B. The Nature and Function of Aims and Objectives

1. Definition of Terms

The word *aim* means to point so as to hit something, to direct efforts, intent or purpose. The first two concepts here are given preference. They place emphasis on initiation and function. The term *objective* is used in two primary ways: (1) to define something real, or actual, independent of the mind, and (2) to point

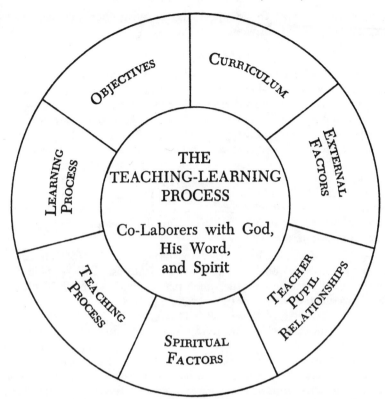

out "goals." The latter definition is most common and will be used in this discussion. A third term related here is *function*. It is defined as the normal or characteristic action of anything. It also describes a special duty or performance required of a person or thing in the course of work or activity.

In education these terms are vitally connected. An aim may be thought of as that with which the educator starts. The objective is the goal, the place of arrival, the ultimate resting place. Function is the process involved in bringing aims and objectives together. It is illustrated something like the following:

Aims ⟶ ⟶ Function ⟶ ⟶ Objectives

Another way of approaching this matter is the practice in vogue among some educators of thinking of purposes in terms of immediate and ultimate or general aims. Immediate aims concern the present while ultimate or general aims concern the future. We feel, however, that the method above is superior because it is clearer. It avoids confusion.

2. *The Source of Aims*

The popular conception in secular education posits the source of aims in what is called "survival values." Thus conceived, aims are considered abstractions from the salutary experiences of society in propagating itself. Thus, statements of objectives become virtually a social policy and a program of social action. When society changes there must be corresponding adjustments in objectives. This social concept is the predominating one at present in American education. Of course, the social policy accepted here is the democratic ideal. The main concepts in this ideal include the principles of (1) the general welfare, (2) civil liberty, (3) the consent of the governed, (4) the appeal to reason, and (5) the pursuit of happiness.

Other educators have tried to derive the aims of education from an historical analysis of social institutions. Others have derived theirs from a scientific analysis of current life. Still others have predicated aims on the psychological study of the original nature of man. All of these methods are able to derive *present day* values, perhaps. Both science and history are limited to fact-finding now. A sense of moral obligation is missing. Only an educational philosophy can supply the lack. The *Christian*, therefore, relies on the philosophy of the Christian world view based on the revelation of God to give him a sense of values and future security from which the aims of education can be abstracted. Here, of necessity, Christian theology and philosophy will be the primary sources of Christian aims and objectives. The nature of man is also a vital factor in this matter. The needs of the human heart and life also rank high in educational values.

3. *The Function of Aims and Goals*

Generally speaking, aims and goals provide direction for the whole educational process. More specifically, there are values for the teacher and pupil. Aims and goals give the teacher the inspiration of a worth-while endeavor. He is constantly motivated by a sense of destiny and purposefulness. Furthermore, aims and goals serve as guide lines in the selection of materials and methods by which the pupil is moved toward the objectives set up. Ultimately, aims and purposes provide a method of evaluation. They are points of reference in the evaluation process.

Aims and goals motivate pupil responses. When pupils are clear on why things are being done and where they are going, the chances for cooperation and effective learning are greatly enhanced. When objectives begin to meet pupil needs, there is greater interest, concentration, and effort. These factors motivate learning.

All of these reasons for the importance of aims and goals are clearly recognized by secular educators. The *Christian* educator concurs in what these statements imply. He would add, however, one other important function of aims and goals. They provide the means whereby integration and correlation of the Christian curriculum is made possible. Representing as they do a summary of the main points of the Christian world view, aims and goals become practical guides in providing unity and integration for a God-centered and bibliocentric philosophy of education and curriculum construction.

C. Aims and Objectives Historically and Philosophically Conceived

1. *Early Views*

The primary purpose of education for the Greeks was preparation for citizenship. Individual development through liberal education was considered by many the best process for achieving this goal. Socrates (469-399 b.c.) stated that the aim of education was to dispel error and to discover truth. Aristotle (384-322 b.c.) believed that the true aim of education was the attainment of happiness through perfect virtue.

The Romans adopted the Greek citizenship ideal. They added, however, certain practical virtues along with stress on the values of participation in government. During this time the Christian church accepted and employed the liberal arts curriculum stripped of its pagan elements.

During the Middle Ages, emphasis was placed on content. Submissiveness and obedience were primary qualities of character.

During the Renaissance Period, secular education virtually returned to the Greek and Roman ideal of preparation for good citizenship. The original and dominating aim during this period was humanistic instruction, self-culture, and individual development.

During the Reformation, education was dominated to a great extent by religious aims. The aim of preparing youth to become Christians and church members was strongly emphasized by men like Luther, Calvin, and Comenius. On the other hand there was a broadening purpose at work which laid emphasis also on the importance of citizenship and life. In America the schools of this period were dominated by the religious aims of denominations.

However, in order to see how the progress of ideas through the years affected educational thought along this line, we shall now turn to a more detailed consideration of some of the main philosophies with their statements of purpose.

2. Humanism

It remained for the rise of humanism in the Fifteenth to Seventeenth Centuries to stress a return to the Greco-Roman ideal of liberal education. The essence of this view is that education should consist of the thorough mastery of a limited body of subject matter which in itself contained the power to call forth, train, and develop the highest gifts of body and mind which ennoble man. This knowledge was comprised of the writings of the important Greek and Latin authors. To them, the best individual and citizen was the "learned man." The classics formed the curriculum and served as a model for every school to emulate.

Two views of educational objectives arose from humanistic roots. One is knowledge as the aim of education. The purpose of education is to organize all knowledge. The second view was mental discipline. The purpose of education, especially the classics, was to discipline the mind, to develop the knowledge-getting faculties of the mind, such as memory and reasoning. A sound mind in a sound body was emphasized along with moral character. Later on, at the insistence of Locke, mathematics was allowed entrance into the fellowship of the classics. The humanists felt that it was not so much the content of the classics which proved helpful, rather it was what they could do for the learner that was important. Thus the advocates of mental discipline placed emphasis on the *method* of acquiring knowledge rather than content. Although today these views are rejected by the majority of secular educators, a neohumanist point of view stressed by a small minority places importance on the current belief that a list of "great books" forms a sufficient basis for education.

3. Idealism

This philosophy is represented most clearly by Herman H. Horne. For him, the ultimate objective of education is the adjustment of the human being to God. The result of this is an integrated individual who lives in an integrated society and grows in the image of the integrated universe.[1] The specific goals include the guidance of the pupil in seeking truth and avoiding error, in feeling beauty and transcending ugliness, as well as achieving good

[1]Herman H. Horne, "An Idealistic Philosophy of Education," in the *41st Yearbook of the National Society for the Study of Education*, p. 186.

and conquering evil. Thus, the individual should seek culture, knowledge, and development. For society, the educational ideal must aim at efficiency, character, and citizenship.

4. Realism

Realism became the foe of humanism. With the rise of the vernacular languages in Europe, Latin was displaced as the language of the scholars. Francis Bacon advocated the scientific method for teaching. The "sense realists" began to emphasize the place of objective truths, methods, and materials. Comenius advocated audio-visual methods, universal education, and the principles of maturation, gradation, and kindlier discipline. Later on, *practical* subjects were placed in the curriculum. All of these developments served to suppress the influences of humanism. Thus, the aristocratic aim for education arose. The production of the Cavalier, the man of letters and action, became the aims of education. Closely allied to this today is the position of Bertrand Russell who pictured the aims of education for the individual as personality characterized by vitality, courage, sensitiveness, and intelligence.[2]

5. Naturalism

Naturalism struck still another hard blow at humanism. Rousseau placed the needs of the pupil at the center of education. "Everything is good as it comes from the hands of the Author of Nature." Naturalism thus opposes the doctrine of original sin. Man is born good, not bad. Since nature is unchangeable, he says, education must conform to nature. Pestalozzi insisted that the natural instincts of the child should provide the motivation for learning. This is known as the "doctrine of interest." He believed also that cooperation and sympathy should provide the means of discipline. Froebel emphasized the importance of the *whole* child. To him, education was more than *preparation* for life; it *is* life. He submitted the idea of "self-activity" as the basis for developing the inherent powers of children. Thus, one can see the direct influences of realism and naturalism on the educators of that day. The development of physiology, genetics, psychology, and evolutionary theory, all scientific influences, laid the basis for the present-day dominating philosophy of pragmatism.

One of the best modern developments of the naturalistic position is that represented by Stella Van Petten Henderson in the

[2]Bertrand Russell, *Education and the Good Life* (New York, Boni and Liveright, 1926), pp. 60 ff.

work, *Introduction to Philosophy of Education*.[3] A summary of this view is as follows:

1. Man, a product of evolutionary forces, is biologically the most highly developed of the animals.
2. Man cannot be understood apart from the natural world out of which he has come, but he is different from other living creatures.
3. Life consists of constant interaction between man and his environment. Man seeks to satisfy his desires and sets goals according to his ability to set purposes to guide his activity.
4. Learning results through the modification of constant changes in the life situation.
5. Since man is fundamentally social, he is dependent upon society for his development. Education, of necessity, includes individual growth in a social setting.
6. The purpose of education is not only to preserve the social heritage but to progress constantly toward the highest possible standard of human excellence.
7. A teleological interpretation of the meaning of life, that life has purpose, cannot be proved.
8. Since man's ultimate destiny cannot be known, the most important question is: what does it mean to be *human?*
9. Man's *human* characteristics include the consciousness of himself as a person, the use of symbols to express thought, and through the use of symbols the ability to reason, create, and express moral distinctions.
10. The highest development of man's *human* characteristics, which is self-realization, is the true purpose of education.
11. Self-realization can be achieved only in a social situation. Since man's ultimate destiny cannot be known, cooperative self-realization, the ideal man, seems to be the chief end of man.
12. Since human excellence is so dependent on society, the purpose of the school is to help create a perfect society in which self-realization may be most likely achieved.
13. The "good life" leads to the satisfaction of the biological, social, and spiritual needs of man on the highest ethical and moral levels.
14. The school curriculum should be made on the basis of *human* needs.

6. Pragmatism

John Dewey developed the philosophy of *pragmatism*. Essentially, it is an outgrowth of naturalism. Actually, his views on education were not original. What he did was to combine the ideas of his predecessors on education with his ideas on democracy and

[3]Stella V. P. Henderson, *Introduction to Philosophy of Education* (New York, McGraw-Hill Book Co., Inc., 1947), Chapters 2, 3 and 4.

pragmatism into a philosophy of education. Those ideas included the following:

(1) The emphasis of Vives on vernacular languages
(2) Rousseau's views on child development
(3) Froebel's views on the whole child and self-activity
(4) Comenius' views on universal education
(5) Francis Bacon's views on scientific method
(6) Pestalozzi's views on natural instincts of the child as the basis for motivation
(7) Mulcaster's views on kindlier discipline
(8) Priestley's, Leibnitz's, Franklin's, and Mann's views on practical, useful subject matter

Of course, the above list does not exhaust the sources of Dewey's views. He did, however, merge them with his views on democracy and pragmatism and apply them to the American school situation. *Pragmatism* is the doctrine that the ultimate test of whether or not a thing is good depends upon whether or not it works.

Two primary views on the aims of education have been spawned by pragmatism: (1) the social concept and (2) the creative concept. In the latter view, the purpose of education is to make it possible for the individual to develop harmoniously through free spontaneous expression in solving problems which arise in life situations. This view is also known as the child-centered view and has been advocated by Rousseau, Pestalozzi, Froebel, and Dewey. The character development type of education is also embraced by this view.

In the *social concept*, the aims of education are determined by life situations and the problems which arise out of them. The primary emphasis, therefore, is given to the development of the most efficient individual — the whole man in a better society. Man is to be fitted to find his place in the social structure. Social efficiency in *all* social relations is the goal. This is education for all. This view has been advocated by Rousseau, Froebel, Pestalozzi, Spencer, Bobbitt, and John Dewey. It dominates the philosophy of present-day education. Self-realization becomes the ultimate aim and goal of education.

An illustration of this position is submitted by Mort and Vincent in their *Introduction to American Education.*[4] The "scope and sequence" chart developed in the Core Curriculum for Virginia Public Schools reveals how the objectives of society, so conceived,

[4]New York, McGraw-Hill Book Co., Inc., 1954, p. 28 ff.

became the objectives of education. In the left hand column of our chart the major functions of society are listed as follows:

MAJOR FUNCTION OF SOCIAL LIFE	GRADE I HOME AND SCHOOL LIFE (Center of Interest) ASPECTS SELECTED FOR EMPHASIS
Protection and conservation of life, property, and natural resources	How do we protect and maintain life and health in our home and school?
Production of goods and services, and distribution of the returns of production	How do the things we make and grow help us?
Consumption of goods and services	How does our family provide itself with food, clothing, and shelter?
Communication and transportation of goods and services	How do members of our family travel from place to place?
Recreation	How can we have an enjoyable time at home and school?
Expression of Aesthetic impulses	What can we do to make our home and school more beautiful and pleasant?
Expression of religious impulses	
Education	
Extension of freedom	
Integration of the individual	
Exploration	

In the right hand column each grade represents a selected center of interest. They are listed as:

Grade   I — Home and School Life

Grade   II — Community Life

Grade   III — Adaptation of Life to Environmental Forces of Nature

Grade   IV — Adaptation of Life to Advancing Physical Frontiers

Grade   V — Effects of Invention and Discoveries Upon Our Living

Grade   VI — Effects of Machine Production Upon Our Living

Grade   VII — Social Provision for Cooperative Living

Grade VIII — Adaptation of Our Living Through Nature, Social, and Mechanical Inventions, and Discoveries

Grade   IX — Agrarianism and Industrialism, and Their Effects Upon Our Living

A Comparative Study on Philosophical Formulations of Educational Aims and Objectives

Philosophy	Ultimate Aims	Immediate Aims
Humanism	Man's eternal happiness with God achieved through the culture of the classics.	Self-realization through liberal education.
Realism	Man's eternal happiness with God achieved through actual living in a real world.	Social culture and adjustment through classical liberal education but in accord with the laws of nature.
Formal Discipline	Development of the whole man — Locke.	Virtue, wisdom, breeding, learning. Mental and character development through exercise.
Rationalism	Intellectual freedom from all repression and tradition.	All things both divine and human should be tested by reason.
Naturalism	Preparation for life and adaptation to environment, both subjective and objective.	All knowledge comes through science and should be tested by the scientific method.
Development-alism	The psychological development of the child through the laws of learning. Advocated by Hall, Pestalozzi, Froebel, and Herbert.	To guide and control child development through nature study. To harmoniously develop all the child's powers. To stimulate the child's creative self-expression and self-activity.
Scientific Determinism	To bring man and society into conformity to laws of science. To develop a science of education. To solve educational problems through the scientific method.	To prepare future scientists. To prepare an enlightened society, trained to live by the scientific method.
Social Traditional-ism	To prepare the individual for life in conformity to accepted social standards preserved in the social heritage.	To prepare the individual for social adjustment and efficiency.
Social Experi-mentalism (Pragmatism)	Preparation of the individual for social reconstruction according to the philosophy and pragmatism of John Dewey.	Training of the individual for intelligent group cooperation and social planning.
Idealism	Adjustment of the individual to God. Thereby integration of personality is achieved for man and society.	Guidance in seeking truth, beauty, and goodness, culture, knowledge, character, efficiency, and citizenship.
Christianity	Redemption is the ultimate goal Personal—Christlikeness and fellowship with God. Social—The Kingdom of God through the Church resulting in the following attributes: (1) Perfect brotherly love (2) Sacrificial service (3) Good citizenship (4) Christian culture. Physical — earth restored to its pristine perfection.	Generally—to reveal God. Personally—to qualify man to reveal God through restoration and sanctification; to excite and direct the self-activities of the pupil so that he will volitionally strive for the best possible integration of personality on the human level, but directed toward Christlikeness in all areas of life. Socially—the highest development of every individual pursuant to social serviceability. Prophetically—the Second Coming of Jesus Christ and the hope of the life to come.

24. Self-realization: Dewey, Tufts
25. Satisfying wants: Thorndike, Gates
26. Insight: Gentile

8. Modern Developments

The distinguishing aim of the Enlightenment period, which paralleled the separation of church and State, was preparation for citizenship. This was intermingled with the religious and humanistic emphasis. During the Nineteenth Century, there was a marked change in educational aims and purposes. Butts has noted a six-fold conception of the purpose of education as expressed in the various levels of the American educational system: (1) character and moral development, (2) mental discipline, (3) literacy and information, (4) vocational, (5) civic and social, and (6) individual development.[6] During this period the ideas and aims of Pestalozzi, Froebel, and Herbart greatly affected elementary education. At the close of the century, G. Stanley Hall and John Dewey laid the groundwork for revolutionary changes in the American educational process. Dewey helped to re-shape and re-state the aims of education. Both the individual and society must be stressed. The purpose of education is self-realization. The Educational Policies Commission of the National Education Association has become famous for its classic statement regarding the purposes of education: (1) self-realization, (2) good human relationships, (3) economic efficiency, and (4) civic responsibility. These, however, reflect the Dewey school of thought. Previous to this the Commission on Reorganization of Secondary Education, also a branch of the N.E.A., in 1918 had become noted for its Seven Cardinal Principles of Education: (1) Health, (2) command of fundamental processes, (3) worthy home membership, (4) vocation, (5) citizenship, (6) worthy use of leisure time, and (7) ethical character. All of these purposes more or less reflect the Dewey school of thought. Emphasis is secular, social, and, in general, a preparation for citizenship.

9. Survey and Evaluation

What is the *Christian* reaction to these views? It must be admitted that humanism has affected some Christian schools. This is revealed by the prevalence of the knowledge aim as the directing force in the curriculum. In certain *Christian Day Schools*, some think that knowledge of the facts of subject matter is the end of education. In many *Sunday schools*, the success of the teacher is largely measured by the memory of texts and stories. Apparently,

[6]R. Freeman Butts, *A Cultural History of Education* (New York, McGraw-Hill Book Co., Inc., 1947), pp. 498-501.

5. Sound social character which includes a knowledge and practice of spiritual values, desirable attitudes, and home and civic responsibility[7]

2. *The High School*

The Seven Cardinal Principles of Education have served as high school goals for many years. Others have formulated objectives, including the Committee of Ten (1892-1893), the Committee on College Entrance Requirements, the Ten Socio-Economic Goals of 1934, and the goals formulated by the American Youth Commission in 1937. Again, Lueck, who believes that the high school should continue the process of educating pupils for enriched living in a free society, is representative of the modern view. He lists the following goals for the high school:

1. Health
2. Social cohesion
3. Vocational adaptability
4. Problem solving
5. Home living
6. Cultural development
7. Sound social character to include desirable attitudes, social skills, and spiritual values[8]

3. *Higher Education*

The functions of schools on this level are twofold: (1) to provide a broad, cultural education at higher levels, and (2) vocational education at the professional level. President Isaiah Bowman of John Hopkins University has listed the functions of higher education as follows:

1. *An understanding* of the realities of experience toward which we have an evolving attitude: knowledge is not a standardized body of fact and doctrine, but an incomplete revelation of the world that is constantly enlarged by new investigation.
2. *Experience* in critical methods of work: the use of sources, the value of logical processes, the need for analysis, each of which has varying significance according to the nature of the field of investigation.
3. A knowledge of the *history of science and learning:* how men made progress in learning to observe and to think and how that progress came to benefit mankind.
4. An appreciation and some *technical study* of the *environment;* man's geographical surroundings, man working under measurable conditions, man and nature in interaction. The closely associated study of alternative choices, opportunities, limitations, and compulsions of the environment and not the study of civilization in a vacuum, as if man did it all himself without regard to terrain.

[7]William R. Lueck, *An Introduction to Teaching* (New York, Henry Holt and Co., 1953), Chapter 2.
[8]*Ibid.*

5. An *experimental knowledge* of the way the modern world works: the applications of humanitarian concepts, the growth of codes, and the origin and present-day operation of social machinery.
6. The acquisition of an *outlook or a philosophy* that embraces all men understandingly in their different environments, occupations, and cultures.[9]

In recent years there has been a reaction against extension, specialization, and segmentation of the college curriculum, as well as the questioning of the value of the elective system. Instead, there seems to be general movement, particularly in the lower division, to provide a continuation of the general education begun in high school. Thus, in some circles in higher education the whole curriculum structure is being re-thought, with the emphasis placed on general education supplied by the liberal arts. Such is the case at Washington University under the leadership of Dr. Huston Smith, where a special committee on the Aims of Liberal Education recently produced a brochure on the philosophy of higher education entitled *The Purposes of Higher Education.*[10] It must be pointed out candidly that it was clearly recognized by Dr. Smith that this work was not motivated and directed by a clear and single philosophy. Instead, it was produced as an eclectic philosophy by the contributions of a variety of personnel. In spite of this handicap, it was felt that the project had worthy fruitage and the conclusions of the study resulted in the formulation of a set of objectives for higher education. They are as follows:

I. Knowledge
   A. About man's physical and biological nature and en-environment
   B. About man's social nature, environment, and history
   C. About man's cultural history and situation
   D. About the processes that make for personal and group fulfillment

II. Abilities
   A. To use one's own language
   B. To think critically
   C. To make value judgments
   D. To participate effectively in social situations
   E. To handle a foreign language

[9]Isaiah Bowman, *The Graduate School in American Democracy* (Washington, D. C., U. S. Government Printing Office), p. 9.
[10]Huston Smith, *The Purposes of Higher Education* (New York, Harper and Bros., 1955), Part II.

complish this, the purpose of Christian education must be the purpose of Jesus. "The Son of Man is come to seek and to save that which was lost" (Luke 19:10). This is the initial purpose. Wrapped up in the general purpose, however, is an ultimate objective — the perfect man in Christ. "That the man of God may be perfect, throughly furnished unto all good works" (II Timothy 3:17). Thus, from the moment the initial purpose is realized, there must be constant and steady development for every true Christian toward the ultimate objective. This ideal holds up the highest possible standard in every area of life. In fact, Christians are admonished to "study to show thyself approved unto God, a workman that needeth not to be ashamed, rightly dividing the word of truth" (II Timothy 2:15).

To the Christian teacher, the constant purpose of education is education for daily life. Dr. C. B. Eavey, with this in view, defined the purpose of the Christian teacher as one which assists "each individual pupil to live as he was created to live, in order that he may become what His Creator destined him to be."[14]

In the carrying out of the true purpose of Christian education, the early Christian church recognized that four functions were inherently essential, recorded for us in Acts 2:41, 42, as follows: evangelism (vs. 41), education (vs. 42), edification, (vs. 42), and fellowship (vs. 42). Rooted in the deepest tradition and practice of the Christian church is education. The highest possible standard of growth and development has been sustained in the Christian school. Christianity and education have always worked in close harmony. In fact, it is dangerous to disassociate the one from the other.

Originally no distinction was made between a "secular" school and a "Christian" school. Early church fathers quickly adopted so-called secular subjects for the curriculum, stripped of pagan effects, of course. The Christian church at large has championed the cause of education. The history of education is replete with instances where the church initiated one educational system after another. Much democratic emphasis and insistence upon education for the masses can be attributed to the Christian church.

Today, two general types of Christian schools are apparent. One kind follows the "secular" pattern and provides what many call a general education. This is seen on the primary and secondary levels in grade and high schools and on the college level. These schools provide instruction and guidance in the command of fundamental processes and preparation for so-called secular

[14]C. B. Eavey, *The Art of Effective Teaching* (Grand Rapids, Mich., Zondervan Publishing House, 1953), p. 14.

pursuits. Even, here, however, evangelism and Christian character should be emphasized. Many such schools are sponsored by churches and others by private enterprises.

The second general type of Christian school provides a more special kind of education culminating in full-time and professional preparation for life-service. This is generally within the ranks of the church. Bible schools, colleges, and theological seminaries on the level of higher education represent this group. Graduates are generally channeled into some phase of the Christian ministry.

Although the curriculum emphasis is a little different in various Christian schools, the purpose remains the same. Perhaps modern Christian schools have fallen into the original pattern of the early catechumenal and catechetical schools, but on a much higher academic level.

Included in this latter group of schools is the Sunday school. Here the setting is directly in the ranks of the church membership with the use of church building facilities. Emphasis is placed entirely on the spiritual and on character and conduct. This school provides marvelous assistance to the school in the home and in the community. In all such schools, however, the purpose remains the same, for backed by a specific philosophy of life, these schools will always maintain a special philosophy of education.

By way of summary, education for the Christian places stress on the quality of life. Teaching does not consist so much of books, lessons, and classes as something happening to the learner. Purpose gives importance to life rather than subject matter. In this sense, Christian education is different from religious education. It is not a general religious viewpoint toward which we strive, but rather a specific Christian viewpoint and life.

3. The Individual Objective in Christian Education

We noted previously that the aim or purpose of Christian education is to produce Christian character. Pupils must be Christlike pupils. Thus, the character of Christ is the goal for the individual. Jesus said, "Be ye therefore perfect, even as your Father which is in heaven is perfect" (Matthew 5:48). The secret of Christlike personality is to be found also in His words: "Abide in me, and I in you" (John 15:4).

The analysis of the character of Jesus is revealed in the Scriptures. "He that hath seen me hath seen the Father" (John 14:9). Jesus was like God. His Godliness was expressed in all areas of His life and conduct. "Jesus increased in wisdom and stature, and in favor with God and man" (Luke 2:52). Here we see the intellectual, physical, social, and spiritual aspects of His character from

that the intellectual organization of the self necessarily carries along with it the moral organization of the self.[15]

To become integrated a personality must become a unity, an integer, and the educational process should be one by which a person becomes a unit. In the words of Paul, "that the man of God may be perfect, throughly furnished unto all good works" (II Timothy 3:17), we see the picture of an integrated personality.

An analysis of the human personality reveals that there are various manifestations of the ego or the self. Man is more than intellect; he is also feelings and will; he is spirit, soul, and body. The purpose of education is to integrate the powers of the personality so that they work as a whole. Knowledge should not be divorced from the feelings or the will. Here, again, it is to be noted that education is education for life and living. At this point is where much modern education has failed. Failure to observe the needs of the moral and spiritual aspects of man's nature, and to provide educational assistance in these realms, has resulted in a fragmentary type of education and a stunted personality. Thus the moral and spiritual development must be integrated with the other aspects of the self. As this integration progresses in the individual, there results to a greater degree in him the powers of self-mastery, self-control, and self-determination. All of this, however, must, to be effective, be guided by the Christian philosophy of life. To be complete the integration of personality includes not only education for life, but also for death. Since attitudes toward death affect life, they also affect education.

The purpose of the integration of personality, therefore, is to help man increasingly to be raised to the higher spiritual levels which are supplied by the Christian philosophy of life and the grace of God. The self-realization of the Dewey school of thought, therefore, seems to fall short of an adequate goal. One is tempted to think more of *self-indulgence* than self-realization through self-expression. A faulty psychology and philosophy here are revealed. The Christian viewpoint provides a higher level upon which to integrate the personality.

It can be safely said, therefore, that the purpose of Christian education is the development of human personality but it is development toward a designed end, guided by obedience to the will of God. In this sense, the personality is freed. Sin causes a disintegrated personality but the Christian school must integrate

[15]Edward A. Fitzpatrick, *Philosophy of Education* (Milwaukee, Bruce Publishing Co., 1950), p. 85.

that which sin has disintegrated. This includes, of course, the restoration of the personality to the image of God. From this point on, the life is centered in God and lived in the center of God's will.

5. The Social Aim of Christian Education

Two primary concepts are at the very heart of the Christian religion: (1) man is built in the image of God and should strive toward the perfection he finds in Him, and (2) man is a social creature, he was made for fellowship with his God and fellowman. The social purpose of Christian education, therefore, includes more than individual development; it includes social development and this, in turn, implies the highest possible development of each individual. In this view life is seen in its wholeness — the rounded development of the individual who lives in harmony with his fellows. The nature of this harmony requires a philosophy of life, and this rests upon the Christian theistic world view. This view demands the highest possible degree of social serviceability. The curriculum and learning processes must be developed to this end. The child must be trained to take his place in society and to so live and work that social relationships will conform to the ideal.

6. The Social Objective of Christian Education and the Church

The social goal of Christian education places stress on what Christians can do together for the common welfare. Two agencies are used by God in bringing to realization His social objective: (1) the Church, and (2) the Kingdom.

The Church is composed of the body of Christ, the corporate body of believers. The goal here, therefore, is to form a great Missionary Society in which the goal is to enlist every disciple of Christ in this body and to develop them into efficient apostles. The method to be employed is witnessing and evangelism, expressed in the Great Commission. In order to facilitate this objective, the Church, as the Kingdom of Christ, moves out into society as a spiritual leaven with a spiritual program called the Kingdom of Heaven. The objectives in such a program include the following:

1. Investigation — Find the Man — Luke 19:10 — "Seek"
2. Evangelization — Win the Man — Luke 19:10 — "Save"
3. Identification — Hold the Man — Colossians 2:6, 7—"rooted"
4. Information — Build the Man — II Peter 3:18 — "grow"
5. Sanctification — Fill the Man — Acts 1:8; 15:8, 9 — Purity and power
6. Consecration — Use the Man — Romans 12:1, 2 — Service

The way this process works out in curriculum construction is discussed more fully in the chapter ahead on curriculum.

It is at once apparent that general or ultimate objectives determine the direction of the educative process. The *specific* objectives provide the means by which the subject matter is adjusted to pupil needs and to the teaching-learning process. The determination of these objectives is arrived at through three channels: (1) knowledge of the Christian World View, (2) the needs of the pupils, and (3) application of the subject matter truth to these needs. There are also certain principles which should guide the use of these objectives. (1) They should be integrated and correlated with the general objectives of the Christian World View, pointing toward the ultimate ideal. (2) They must cover as completely as possible all the component elements of the ultimate goal. (3) They must be related to objective and concrete truths as far as possible. (4) They must reflect the needs of the pupil. (5) They must be stated in terms that are meaningful to the teacher and pupil. (6) They should be carefully correlated with the various units and lessons in the subject matter curriculum.

2. General Objectives for Christian Education

We have now arrived at the point where this whole discussion on objectives can be summarized in the form of a statement of general objectives for Christian education. For the Sunday school, such a statement was made under the discussion of the social objectives of Christian education because the Church is classified as a social institution which has a social function. The following objectives can be used in the Sunday school situation but they are more properly designed for other types of Christian education and for classroom guidance. They were developed in faculty seminar sessions at Fort Wayne Bible College in 1956-57. An attempt was made to follow the procedure outlined by the chart preceding in the section on the "use of objectives in Christian education." There is first a statement of the Christian philosophy of life and world view. From this was abstracted the statement on general objectives. From this latter statement, each teacher was expected to formulate specific course objectives to be used in the classroom presentation of the subject matter.

THE CHRISTIAN WORLD VIEW

God

We believe that God is an eternal personal Being of absolute knowledge, power, and goodness. He is ultimate Reality, the source and ground of all reality and truth.

God and the Cosmos

Christ, the Son of God, is Creator, Designer, and Preserver of all things. In Him the entire universe, macrocosm and microcosm, has its origin, its energy and control, and its final destiny. This relation between God and the world, organic and inorganic, is expressed in such statements of Scripture as Colossians 1:16, 17 and Romans 11:36.

God and Man

Man came into being by a direct, immediate act of the Creator. Unique among all creatures, he bears the image of God in that he has personality and the power of moral choice. He was created for a dual purpose: Godward, he is to *glorify* God and enjoy fellowship with Him; earthward, he is to subdue and hold dominion over the earth and its living creatures (Genesis 1:28).

Man's original state, at creation, has been changed by the intervention of sin. Through deliberate choice of the wrong, man has become estranged from God, the divine image has been marred, and man is now morally corrupted and in need of redemption.

This redemption is provided by God, in the life, death and resurrection of Jesus Christ. By faith in Him as Saviour, and obedience to the Holy Spirit, man may now be transformed into Godlikeness and restored to fellowship with God.

Redemption includes the eternal destiny of Man. By receiving Christ as Saviour, man is fitted for everlasting fellowship with God. Those who reject Christ are destined to everlasting separation from God.

Redemption also assures that the earth, which now suffers the effects of man's sin, shall be restored to its pristine perfection.

God and Truth

Truth, like the created universe, is centered in Christ (Colossians 2:3). It is therefore a unity, integrated by Jesus Christ, and all its parts are meaningfully related to each other and to Him.

If truth originates in God, then He must communicate it to man. He does this by revelation. General revelation is the communication of truth through nature and providence. Special revelation includes the body of truth contained in the Bible, and the disclosure of God and truth in the person of Jesus Christ. General revelation is in full harmony with special revelation and finds its true interpretation in it.

Man is endowed by the Creator with the power to apprehend truth. His senses lead to empirical truth; his reason gives him a grasp of the more abstract forms of truth; and faith, which is a positive response to God's revelation, not only enables him by the Holy Spirit to understand the supernatural, but also gives him an insight into the meaning of truth at all levels, so that he can "see things steadily and see them whole."

God and Values

As ultimate reality, God sets the standard by which value judgments are to be made. The highest good is realized in the exercise of His will, and on the part of man, in conformity to that will.

THE EDUCATIVE PROCESS – TEACHER-PUPIL
RELATIONSHIPS

by Charters and Waples.[2] The 25 most desirable traits were ranked in their order of importance for rural, elementary, and secondary school teachers. Those given highest rank were self-control, dependability, adaptability, enthusiasm, good judgment, and honesty. Other traits listed included attractive personal appearance, health, industry, leadership, magnetism, neatness, openmindedness, originality, progressiveness or ambition, promptness, refinement, scholarship, and thrift.

In 1947, Paul Witty compiled a list of traits from approximately 12,000 letters written by school children. Traits most frequently mentioned in order were:

1. Cooperative, democratic attitude
2. Kindliness and consideration for the individual; patience
3. Wide variety of interest
4. General appearance and pleasing manner
5. Fairness and impartiality
6. Sense of humor
7. Good disposition and consistent behavior
8. Interest in pupil problems
9. Flexibility (methods)
10. Use of recognition and praise
11. Unusual proficiency in teaching a particular subject[3]

Today other general traits are considered essential. They include a knowledge of the pupil, placing the pupil before the subject in importance, a broad general education, use of pupil activities, teacher-pupil planning, participation and interest in community affairs, democratic appreciations and practices, and desire for professional improvement.

3. The Function of the Teacher

In secular education, the strong tendency has been to shy away from indoctrination. Instead, the role of the modern teacher is considered to be *functional*. Primary emphasis is not laid on impartation of factual knowledge but rather on guidance. The teacher motivates, inspires, leads, guides pupil activity and growth, and wins pupil cooperation. The purpose of all this is social adjustment and efficiency, leading ultimately to good citizenship.

The public school teacher has two obligations, one to the parents and the other to society. The teacher acts *in loco parentis*. As such he is expected to be true to his trust in teaching the child in behalf of the parents. The teacher has no obligation to build a new society, but by making contributions to the character of the pupil he bears great influence toward this end.

[2] W. W. Charters and Douglas Waples, *The Commonwealth Teacher Training Study* (Chicago, University of Chicago Press, 1929), p. 18.
[3] Paul A. Witty, "The Teacher Who Has Helped Me Most," *Journal of the National Education Association*, XXXVI:386.

B. THE TEACHER IN RELIGIOUS EDUCATION

1. *The Place and Function of the Teacher*

The position of religous education is best represented perhaps by the viewpoints of the National Council of the Churches of Christ in the United States of America. To them, the *place* of the teacher in religious education is based largely on the effects of the personality of the teacher on the pupil. Such influence, they feel, is based on genuine, personal interest, mutual admiration, and the practice of democratic principles.[4]

The *role* of the teacher in this viewpoint is also considered *functional*. The purpose of the teacher here is to create group fellowship in which growth in "Christian" personality is encouraged. The power of influence is to be felt in both individual and group life-situations. This approach is definitely in the John Dewey tradition by which primary emphasis is placed on pupil interest and needs and pupil life-situations. The goal is social adjustment and efficiency. Dangers include the possibility of confusing pupil interests and situations with physical activity situations, the possibility of neglecting the Bible, and using trivial and commonplace life-situations. There are undoubtedly some values to be derived in using pupil interests and gearing the teaching process psychologically to pupil capacities, but to restrict this process to sociality is fragmentary to the Christian educator. On the other hand, the Christian teacher is aware that influence does play a great part in the educational process. Because of this the Christian teacher provides Christian atmosphere and environment, he builds Christian structure into the teaching process which is provided by placing emphasis on Christian love, faith, and obedience. Notice, however, that sociality is not the goal here, but spirituality.

2. *Qualifications of the Teacher*

In religious education, the law of perfect love to God and fellowmen, as expressed by Jesus, is made the basis for teacher qualifications. The basic motivations and qualifications are listed as follows by the National Council of Churches.

1. Devotion and personal loyalty to Jesus Christ and Christian zeal to serve; a feeling of the significance of the teaching opportunity and determination to do one's best.
2. A genuine liking for and belief in pupils of the age in one's group.
3. The ability and gladness to give the time needed.
4. The habit of democracy in daily living.
5. Continual growth as a wholesome personality and as a Christian.
6. Enthusiasm for the task of Christian education.[5]

[4]The National Council of Churches of Christ, *The Curriculum Guide for the Local Church* (Chicago, Division of Christian Education, 1950), pp. 74, 75.
[5]*Ibid.*, p. 76.

III. TEMPERAMENT AND DISPOSITION

1. General good health
2. Good cheer, joy, optimism
3. Sympathy, tenderness, love
4. Patience, perseverance, objectivity
5. Sensitivity, responsiveness, serenity
6. Sense of humor, enthusiasm
7. Self-control, peace, caution
8. Kindliness, courtesy, politeness
9. Poise, attractiveness, purpose
10. Zeal, reverence, exaltation

IV. SOCIAL BEHAVIOR

1. Address, understanding
2. Tact, sympathy
3. Leadership, attractiveness
4. Resourcefulness
5. Punctuality, practicalness, responsibility
6. Reliability, sincerity
7. Truthfulness, honesty
8. Tolerance, respect
9. Altruism, unselfishness
10. Ambition, dependability

V. MORAL LIFE

1. Purity
2. Respect
3. High moral standards
4. Sensitivity
5. Unflinching devotion to the right
6. Fairness
7. Impartiality
8. Loyalty
9. Earnestness
10. Dignity

VI. SPIRITUAL LIFE

1. Absolute surrender to God
2. Vivid sense of the reality and presence of God
3. Recognition of Jesus Christ as the only way to God
4. Wholehearted dependence on the Holy Spirit
5. Keen, deep interest in the salvation and the spiritual life and welfare of others
6. Humble, growing sense of victory over selfishness, worldliness, and sin
7. Intelligent and genuine conviction concerning fundamental truths
8. Willingness to serve and to give without thought of recognition
9. Given to importunate, effective prayer
10. Deep, sincere love of God and of pupils

3. The Function of the Christian Teacher

The nature of the teacher and the teaching process determine the functions of the teacher. The Christian teacher is a *Christian educator*. The terms "Christian" and "educator" provide us with the clues revealing the function of the Christian teacher. As a Christian the function of the teacher is to reveal God. As such, he is a witness both by life and voice. In life, he witnesses through giving a living demonstration of Christlikeness. Through voice, he gives expression to the truth concerning the nature of God revealed in Divine Revelation as seen in nature, in the Bible, and in His Son Jesus Christ.

As an educator, the Christian teacher functions in accordance with the mandate of God to teach and in accord with the educational and pedagogical principles contained in the whole educative process. Dr. Mark Fakkema has some interesting observations to make with regard to the first of these emphases. He pointed out that the teacher has a mandate from God. I Peter 4:10, 11, A.V. says,

> As every man hath received the gift (spiritual talents), even so minister the same one to another, as good stewards (restored images) of the manifold grace of God. If any man speak, let him speak as the oracles of God; if any man minister, let him do it as of the ability which God giveth: that God in all things may be glorified through Jesus Christ, to whom be praise and dominion for ever and ever. Amen.

An analysis of this text, says Dr. Fakkema, reveals four basic elements for Christian teaching: (1) ministering what has been received, (2) speaking as oracles of God, (3) working with an ability which is of God, and (4) God must be glorified through Christ.[7] As ministers, Christian teachers should witness to the manifold grace of God and to the nature of God revealed in the subject matter under consideration. As an *oracle of God*, the Christian teacher is the mouthpiece of God. With Jesus he says, "My teaching is not mine but his that sent me . . . he that speaketh from himself seeketh his own glory" (John 7:16-18). The Christian teacher is an oracle of God. The abilities and talents which he possesses are to be considered God-given and should be used in His service and for His glory. By exalting Jesus Christ we bring honor and glory to God.

The function of the Christian teacher is also seen in relation to God-given pedagogical principles. The teacher not only is obligated to be a witness, but also must *operate* properly as a witness. This brings in the matter of methodology which will be dealt with later on, but it will be sufficient to lay down the pattern of operation at this point to show what the function of the Christian teacher is with reference to this relation to both subject matter and the goal.

Generally speaking, someone has said that the teacher's function is revealed by the nature of the teaching process itself. Since teaching is helping the pupil to learn, the function of the teacher is to help. Since teaching is awakening the pupil, the function of the teacher is that of awakening. Teaching is helping to know, therefore the function of the teacher is imparting knowledge. Teaching is to inspire, therefore the teacher should be an inspirer. Teaching is guiding and correcting, therefore the function of the teacher is guidance and correction, etc. Here, however, we are speaking in broad generalizations. More specifically, the function of the Christian educator is determined by God-given pedagogical principles by which the teacher operates in relation to subject

[7]Mark Fakkema, *Christian Philosophy: Its Educational Implications* (Chicago, National Association of Christian Schools, 1952), p. 105-T.

the Religious Education Association which adopted outright the social philosophy of John Dewey, and the result is a socially constructed religious education. These, too, make the pupil an end of religious education, therefore the place of the child is central in religious education. In fact, the child-centered theories and creative concepts of the teaching process have dominated religious educational circles now for many years. The failure of liberalism, however, is quite evident today, therefore the advocates of religious education are finding themselves hard put to justify their practices.

3. In Christian Education

God, not man, is central in Christian education. God is the end, not the pupil. To be like God is the great goal of Christian education. The result is, therefore, that the pupil becomes the *focus* of the educative process, but not the end. The entire educative process is directed toward the child but becomes a means to an end in bringing the pupil to *Christlikeness*. The Christian philosophy of education is Christ-controlled, pupil-related, Bible-integrated, and socially applied. With God in control through the Spirit of Christ, He must be central. All things stand in relation to God and this includes the pupil. All the influences of Christlikeness are brought to bear on the pupil in this view, making him the focus of the process. Thus, the pupil is a sinner who needs redemption. As a redeemed sinner he needs sanctification and information.

E. FREEDOM, AUTHORITY, AND DISCIPLINE IN SECULAR EDUCATION

1. Freedom and Authority

In secular education, freedom is assumed to be a natural function of individuality, for where there are no individual differences present there is no need for freedom. In spite of this, traditionally education has held to the position that the pupil should give unquestioning obedience to the authority of the teacher. This position gave rise to one position characterized by extreme authoritarianism. At the other extreme is found the viewpoint of progressive educators who follow in the train of Rousseau by asserting that freedom is a natural derivative of nature which recognizes the demands of individual differences. This, of course, is the position of the adherents of the philosophies of naturalism, some forms of realism, and pragmatism. It is recognized, however, that there are varying points of view within the framework of these general philosophies. The practice, held to be necessary in these views, is one of *laissez-faire*. At the very foundation of this position is the belief that child nature is inherently good and free from corruption. The rule is not to impede the workings of natural law in both nature and the child.

There are mediating positions, of course. Some, who reject the inherent goodness of the child, favor a tempered *laissez-faire* policy because they observe the evils of authoritarianism. They feel that authoritarianism leads to teacher tyranny and pupil suppression, both of which are unhealthy for the educative process.

Still others try to synthesize freedom and authority. Freedom, they say, is not license, for license leads to chaos in the educative process. Freedom demands control in order to be true freedom; freedom depends on observance of the law. The teacher represents this law but he is not expected to abuse it. Still others interpret such freedom as freedom from the law as well as freedom under law. Here the purpose is to give liberty to the pupil in the exercise of individual differences of preference which lead to reformation of the social structure.

In all of these views, it is recognized that some measure of control physically is necessary, for the protection of the pupil himself. This is based on the fact that the experiences of the race have taught us that some activities simply cannot be engaged in if the preservation of the individual and society is to be realized.

2. Discipline

It is generally recognized in secular education that law and order are necessary to effective instruction. The primary question is *how* it should be done. One view states that the teacher, by virtue of his position, has the *right* to set up regulations for obedience. Another view finds the secret in *interesting* instruction. Where there is mutual interest, there will be mutual cooperation and unanimity, they say. A third view places the source of discipline in the class itself. Here, discipline is maintained by group pressure, cooperation, mutual helpfulness, and purpose. When all these methods fail, what is to be done? Some advocate pressure from the teacher immediately, others disapprove of any method of punishment, others would use it as a last resort. In the first view punishment is used on the pupil because it is deserved; in the second instance, the welfare of the group is uppermost in mind; in a third view, punishment should be educative, leading to the reconstruction of the individual.

3. Evaluation

The Christian finds it possible to concur with the general view in educational circles that the teacher does have some semblance of authority and is expected to exercise it. He must reject, however, many of the foundations upon which the exercise of this authority is based.

The Christian philosophy is definitely opposed to the views of Rousseau. He virtually denied the need for authority and discipline in the classroom. Although the Christian recognizes that secular educators today do not concur with the extremes of Rousseau's position, yet there are definite evidences that his views have deeply affected secular education. The issue is clearly one of theology. Secular education concurs with Rousseau in his views on the inherent goodness of child nature. The assumption is that where this inherent goodness is not interfered with, the child will, under favorable circumstances, develop favorably. Here, the Christian position sharply opposes that of secular education. To the contrary, the Scriptures teach that child nature is inherently corrupt. This is evident also in experience. The history of education and of the race will confirm this. Some of the Scriptures which bear this out include the following — Psalm 51:5; Proverbs 22:15; Ephesians 2:3; Romans 3:23; Mark 7:21-23. Furthermore, the Bible is also clear on the use of correction and punishment — Proverbs 13:22, 24; 19:18; 23:13, 14; 29:15.

It must be admitted, however, in view of the very unrealistic descriptions of human nature and the social effects of war and the atom bomb, that some educators are beginning to swing back to a more realistic view of authority and discipline, even to the point of advocating some mild form of coercion and punishment. Others see the need of living according to the rules of society. To them, the citizen must learn to live according to these rules and the purpose of the school is to prepare pupils for just this sort of thing. Such a position is certainly realistic because it is recognized that society places certain restrictions and controls upon the individual. It is necessary, therefore, to prepare the pupil for this kind of environment or he will be completely disqualified to face it.

F. FREEDOM, AUTHORITY, AND DISCIPLINE IN CHRISTIAN EDUCATION

1. *The Source of Authority*

Secular educators posit the source of authority either in the State or the parents; Catholics posit it in the Church. The true Christian educator, however, believes that the source of all authority lies in God. God, as Creator, Preserver, and Administrator of the universe, gives abundant evidence of His authority in providence over both temporal and spiritual affairs. This is the Scriptural position. "Let every soul be subject unto the higher authorities, for there is no authority but of God. The authorities that be are ordained of God" (Romans 13:1). This principle has been recognized throughout the course of human history. It is even recognized today in the oath which the President of the United States takes as well as affirmations in court. Thus, to the Christian, ultimate authority rests with God and it is here where the educator, the teacher, and the parent, must trace their authority. In fact, if the secondary authority of those mentioned above is not in accord with God's principles of authority, actually the pupil is not obligated to recognize it.

The Christian teacher must recognize that his authority in the classroom does not inhere in his person, but in God. Every Christian teacher should make this plain. This being so, no Christian teacher can possibly be a dictator. His authority is not authoritarian, but *authoritative*. More specifically, parents have been appointed the primary obligation to maintain authority over the children. Essentially therefore, teachers derive secondary authority from parents through delegated power. The complexities of education are such that parents need assistance. The teacher, therefore, stands in the position of *loco parentis*. Thus, the source of authority for the Christian teacher is in God and through the parents.

2. The Nature of Authority

The nature of authority is derived from the nature of God. His sovereignty, truth, love, mercy, and justice are to be manifested through authority. The teacher, therefore, finds initiation for his authority in God, not in the child, nor the position of the teacher. Through the proper manifestation of authority the teacher gives a manifestation of God to the pupil. Through this manifestation the teacher witnesses and reveals God.

Human authority has been classified as judicial and moral. Judicial authority has been defined as the right to command, to make laws, to enforce obedience. Moral authority, on the other hand, is that kind which is based on opinion and the experience of the race. The Christian believes that the teacher has responsibility for both of these kinds of authority. As a social institution in which the teacher is responsible for the instructional processes, judicial authority becomes necessary in order to preserve law and order and in assuring the success of the educative process. Moral authority becomes a derivative of the teacher's own Christian character and the experience of the church. In both cases, however, this authority centers in God.

3. The Purpose of Authority

Henry Schultze pointed that there must be a theocentric objective to the exercise of authority by the teacher.[8] The purpose of authority is *not* for the benefit of the teacher. Authoritarianism

[8]Henry Schultze, "Authority a Liberating Force in Education," in *Fundamentals in Christian Education* (Grand Rapids, Mich., Wm. B. Eerdmans Publishing Co., 1953), p. 110.

is just as much condemned in Christian circles as anywhere else. The purpose of authority is not for the sake of the pupil. To make man the center of the educative process is an erroneous concept of both education and authority. This view has aroused a great deal of friction because it is fundamentally false. Selfishness is at the heart of it, and selfishness does not work. Instead, *the real purpose of authority for the Christian is to reveal God and manifest God.* God is the source of authority and the means whereby it is directed.

It becomes the responsibility of the teacher to keep this fact before the pupils constantly. This fact will also direct the method by which all authority is exercised. It must be in strict conformity to the will and nature of God.

Authority in the school system has led to the establishment of rules and regulations by which the school is managed and conduct is organized and controlled. This is not only good for the school and for the individual pupil, but it actually serves to prepare pupils for the kind of society which they will face upon graduation.

4. *The Results of Authority*

Schultze has pointed out that the right exercise of authority leads to liberty not bondage.[9] The popular conception of liberty is that it is the privilege of unrestricted thought and action. In reality, says Schultze, this is not possible. Restrictions are self-evident and necessary for human efficiency and preservation. This fact has given rise to the multiplicity of rules and regulations by which life is both liberated and restricted. God restricts, man restricts, and nature restricts. True freedom, therefore, can be found only in conformity to things as they actually are. "Ye shall know the truth and the truth shall make you free" (John 8:32). True freedom is freedom under law and authority. The Christian, consequently, insists upon the sovereignty, truth, love, and justice of God. To be free, man must choose to live in harmony and conformity with these.

5. *The Method of Authority*

From the foregoing discussion it is at once apparent that the method of authority must conform to the nature and will of God. This includes the "spirit" of the method as well as its practice. Louis Berkhof has listed some fundamental requirements by which the Christian teacher should exercise his authority.

1. The teacher should cause the children to understand that he is ruling the school in the name of God.
2. The teacher, in the exercise of his authority, should act in strict conformity with the Word of God.

9*Ibid.,* p. 111 f.

3. School discipline must be motivated by love and not lose sight of the ends of justice.
4. The teacher must rule with equity and justice, and maintain order with a firm hand.
5. So-called pupil government is of dubious value, especially on the elementary level of schooling.[10]

The Christian teacher should be motivated by love in the exercise of his authority. He should feel a definite responsibility for the pupil both academically and spiritually. Love is necessary for the teacher in order that he may have a proper understanding of the pupil and patience with him. Furthermore, the exercise and manifestation of love on the part of the teacher will certainly motivate the pupil both physically and academically as he moves in the environment of the classroom situation. Thus, we are brought again to the question of building structure into the life of the pupil. Such structure is provided by manifestations of love, faith, and obedience. Love for God and manifestation of responsibility toward Him on the part of both teacher and pupil helps to provide a much better atmosphere in which obedience can be both expected and practiced. Here is the secret of the control factor in education.

6. *Discipline*

For the Christian teacher, discipline is not confined to mere control. Discipline in the Christian school has a training aspect to it in addition to controlling the teaching-learning process. In this sense, it is an intrinsic part of the educational process.

As in all other aspects of Christian education, God must be the center of the disciplinary process. Submission and obedience to His will is the very heart of Christian education and experience. There is really no such thing as being a disciple of Christ without submittting to His discipline.

Instead of being negative, Christian discipline is positive, because its exercise makes a contribution to Christian character and conduct. Temperance and self-control should be constantly emphasized in the Christian school as a fruit of the Spirit. A redeemed heart, then, is the first step in school discipline. The motivation for such discipline is the constant effort upon the part of the Christian pupil to please God. Where there is the manifestation of unchristian traits and conduct, it becomes the obligation of the teacher to reveal to the pupil that it is sin which is the cause of his actions. The teacher should encourage the child to react negatively to sin in any form, in spirit or in practice. Thereby the child soon comes to condemn unchristlike attitudes and conduct. He learns to evaluate his own attitudes and conduct in the light

10Louis Berkhof, "The Christian School and Authority" in *Ibid.*, p. 104.

of the criteria provided by the spirit and conduct of Jesus Christ. Thus, the moral powers of the pupil must be trained to respond promptly and accurately to the will of God. Obedience issuing in Christlikeness is the goal of the Christian educative process.

In the classroom situation where occasions arise which call for the exercise of control in order that the teaching-learning process may proceed with law and order, it becomes necessary for the teacher to use secondary measures of discipline. Jaarsma has referred to these as (1) preventive discipline and (2) remedial discipline.[11] In preventive discipline the teacher uses firmness but kindness in suppressing overt activity and in keeping order. Love, firmness, and kindness are combined to maintain a Christian atmosphere even in situations like this. Remedial discipline refers to punishment. Corrective measures become necessary. Here the emphasis should be placed on displeasing God. There is no set procedure involved here, but the teacher should be led by the Holy Spirit in dealing with these situations. Prayer and the use of the Word quite often become effective in dealing with this kind of discipline requirement. Where absolute rebellion is faced, corporal punishment may become necessary as a corrective measure. Even this, however, needs to be done in a Christlike spirit. Such punishment should be administered with the permission of the principal and not during the class hours. Chastisement is the Scriptural word to describe this kind of discipline (Proverbs 19:18; Hebrews 12:5-12). The need for this kind of discipline should become progressively unnecessary the older the child grows. This is particularly true where there is a real Christian experience along with growth in grace. Corporal punishment, however, should not be considered the end of the matter. Where sin has been committed, the pupil should be led to confess it, repent of it, and ask God's forgiveness. Here is where the true correction resides.

We may conclude from this discussion that the primary purpose of discipline is not negative but positive. On the one hand it cleanses from both the heart and life of the pupil those things which are foreign to his nature and well-being, while at the same time, and uppermost, it strengthens the pupil in real freedom through the provision of a sense of security and a basis for satisfactory personal and social relationships (Proverbs 29:15).

G. INTEREST AND MOTIVATION IN EDUCATION

1. *In Secular Education*

Interest is Latin for that which "is between." Commonly considered in education, it is that which establishes the proper relationship between the pupil and the curriculum.

[11]Cornelius Jaarsma, "Discipline in the Christian School" in *Ibid.*, pp. 408-09.

One theory says that interest and motivation can be explained from the standpoint of some kind of tension which is deeper than mere attention. Attention does not always mean that a pupil is interested in what the teacher has to say or is doing.

Others explain interest on an emotional basis. It is an emotional attachment which is self-active and accompanied by a feeling of worth and approval.

Still others say that interest is purposeful. The pupil is motivated because he wants to achieve a goal. Interest thus becomes a means to an end. Still another view is based on the principle of apperception. Here interest in that which is already known is sufficient to motivate an interest in the unknown. The interesting teacher, therefore, is one who can make new things parallel the old.

Where there is lacking a true relationship between child nature and the curriculum, lessons must be made interesting. Making lessons interesting, however, means that some inherent interest is lacking. Some extrinsic motivation, therefore, must be brought into play to gain the desired results. As practiced, these have included such things as examinations, marks, rewards, and punishments.

2. *In Christian Education*

To the Christian teacher, attention is the mental focusing of consciousness on a sight, sound, idea, or emotion; it is concentrated consciousness. The teacher, however, must go beyond mere attention to achieve his goal. Interest is sustained attention. There are three kinds of attention: (1) involuntary, (2) voluntary, and (3) non-voluntary. Involuntary attention is spontaneous or flitting; it turns to any slight distraction. Voluntary attention is accomplished through force of will. But the teacher cannot force attention; it must be of the pupil's own free will. Non-voluntary attention is that kind in which the pupil becomes so absorbed in the study that he is oblivious to what is going on around him. This is the point of most genuine interest which the Christian teacher seeks to reach. The evidence by which the teacher can know his pupils are interested is the *kind* of attention being given by the pupils. Where interest is not present, the teacher by analysis should remove all hindrances in the teaching situation that are evident. These would include all discomforts, unnecessary disturbances, distractions, and lack of good teaching techniques.

Jesus used the principle of apperception. He constantly referred to the commonplace things in which people engaged or which they used. From this point of common knowledge He was able to lead them into the spiritual realm and make spiritual applications. Real interest can often be motivated by the teacher in this way. It must only be used as a means to an end, however.

The principle of self-activity is concerned directly with motivation. The pupil must do his own learning. Teaching is more than the impartation of information. It is also directing activities so that desirable learning will take place. It is necessary, therefore, for the teacher to stimulate thinking. This he can do in several ways. One is by way of apperception as we saw above. The teacher can develop readiness to learn by creating a favorable learning environment. He can inspire the pupils by a good example and appreciative attitudes toward them and the subject. He can ask questions.

As a means of motivation, punishment fails. It may be a corrective device, but certainly not a tool for learning. Loyalty is won, not commanded. We can only put into the pupil's lives that which they put within themselves. The purpose of the Christian teacher is to develop love, not fear.

There are definite dangers in prizes and rewards. Bribery is no better than force. Essentially, it leads to selfishness. Only one person can win a prize, therefore, jealousy may arise. Prizes take pupils' eyes, at least temporarily and partially, off their work. Sometimes dishonest methods are used to win prizes. Where rewards are used, the teacher should be careful to point out that the glory should go to God who made it possible for the pupil to gain his reward. The real basis for receiving a reward, therefore, is the opportunity which it provides for the recipient to honor God who made it possible.

Rivalry is a strong motive, but it should be used so that it does not cultivate wrong attitudes and wrong standards of value. The best type of competition is not with others but with one's self.

Better methods of motivation arise out of making the lessons interesting, knowing the pupils, meeting their needs, assisting them in the teaching-learning process, variety in activities, asking questions, use of audio-visual aids, and good objectives.

H. THE LEARNING PROCESS

1. *In Secular Education*

Several theories have been devised to explain the nature of learning in secular education. Perhaps the earliest of these was that of *faculty psychology*. Two schools of thought known as *assimilation* and *discipline* became primary. The premise of this position was as follows: mind functions as an entity distinct from the rest of the human organism. The mind can assimilate ideas and be disciplined in the use of them. To this view, mind consists of compartments and faculties, such as memory, judgment, reasoning, imagination, purpose, motivation, etc., as functions.

Thus, learning becomes a process of taking in ideas and assimilating them and exercising and forming the mind thereby. The teacher, therefore, transmits ideas and compels the learner thus to be exercised. The form of teaching was logical, deductive, and verbal memory.

The second theory was represented by the school of *association psychology*. To this view, mind consists of the association of ideas, not as an organ which assimilates ideas and exercises itself. Learning results from the connection of ideas according to mental laws. Teaching consists of relating new ideas to old ones, the principle of apperception. Some realists hold this view also.

The third theory became known as *conditioning* or *connectionism*. John B. Watson and his mechanistic psychology were strong advocates of this position. In this theory the nervous system, not ideas, becomes central. The mind is composed of neural connections in the brain and is centralized in the cortex with its multitude of connections. Learning becomes a matter of connecting stimuli and responses and establishing them. Establishment takes place through conditioning the responses. Some realists hold this view.

A fourth theory is modern. It is a theory based on *insight* and was advocated by the *Gestalt* and *Wholistic* schools of psychology. The core term in this view is *wholeness*. Man does not react to isolated stimuli but rather to organized wholes. Learning, therefore, becomes a matter of the organization of responses in relationship. It may come in a flash when the whole is perceived. This is insight. Teaching is the presentation of organized wholes perceptible to the learner. Many idealists accept this view.

Another theory was advanced by John Dewey. Learning was explained in terms of *experiencing*. In this view mind and personality are experience. Human behavior is not individual but social, therefore, experience is the interaction of the organism with its environment and this environment is largely social. Learning, thus, is experiencing. The heart of experience is to face problems and solve them. The scientific method is the medium through which this is done. Teaching, consequently, becomes a matter of guiding the learner's experience to achieve foreseen ends which are valuable. Pupils learn by doing. This is the view of pragmatism.

A contemporary theory is known as *creative expression*. This is an eclectic view which combines the latest findings of both psychology and sociology. Learning is expression which takes place in a social setting. The expression is creative because it originates within. Impressions are not "stamped in" but energize and motivate action. The whole-person-in-action seeks activity. Teaching becomes a matter of guiding the expressions of the whole-person-in-action in security to desirable ends.

In recent years developmental psychologists have focused on learning theory by submitting the thesis that child learning is essentially different from adult learning based on fundamental neurological differences between early life and adult maturity as well as differences in ways of perceiving the world and processing the information received about it. In the light of these differences they advocate a complete redesigning of school programs for young children in which educational events coordinate with the child's readiness to learn. Highly prominent in these theories are the teachings of Jean Piaget and Lawrence Kohlberg.

It is quite apparent that general agreement on learning is lacking among secular educators. Unlike science, learning is very subjective in character and thus hard to define. Current emphasis, therefore, is shifting away from the older stimulus-response positions to the view that stimuli can be processed in many different ways by the human central nervous system. The shift is also away from exclusive preoccupation with conditioning theories of behavior to the study of higher mental processes.

Perhaps Mueller has summarized the current situation rather well when he says that

> Almost all psychologists agree on certain basic, observable facts of learning — for example, the effect that immediate reinforcement has upon motivation, the shape of learning curves. But vigorous disagreement arises when attempts are made to fit a given learning process into a tightly knit theory that can account for all the variables and provide the basis for research designs. In the setting of the classroom, the importance of learning by conditioning, insight, creativity, and understanding are universally agreed upon. But the major question still remains: How are these achieved psychologically? Like the phenomenon of electricity, learning behavior is a great deal easier to measure than to define. We know what learning is by its effects; its true nature remains a mystery.[12]

2. Christianity and Theories of Learning

There are elements of truth in all main theories of learning. The Christian, however, must take issue with many of these representative theories while at the same time extracting elements of truth from them. To the Christian, faculty psychology violates the basic unity of personality. Association psychology destroys the

---

[12]Richard J. Mueller, *Principles of Classroom Learning and Perception* (New York, Praeger Publishers, 1974), p. 58.

spiritual identity of the person. Original sin becomes impossible and redemption unnecessary in this view. Instead, the power of man rests in ideas. The connectionist is a rank materialist. The Christian must reject the basic assumptions of Thorndike and Watson. Gestalt psychology also is considered too mechanistic. Social theories overstress the social aspects of man. The theory of self-expression is stressed in the creative view. In God's sight, self-expression apart from divine grace is the essence of sin. Although an eclectic theory is acceptable in some respects, yet in the final analysis only a scriptural point of view is acceptable to the Christian.

We come now to a definition of learning. Learning has been defined in the Christian sense as

> the process by which the I comes into conscious control of the self in his interacting with the environment. In and through the psycho-somatic the I or person is constantly interacting with the environment. In the dimensions of his personality, changes occur in which the I integrates in the whole-person-in-life. These changes become a permanent ingredient of the total personality as the person commits himself to them.
>
> As a child in the course of the learning process comes to accept life, he is said to mature. This means he is coming to order the dimensions of his personality responsibly. In the child of God the I is coming to order his total self in keeping with God's will. He comes to accept life responsibly as a member of the body of Christ, as a citizen of the kingdom of God.[13]

It is apparent from this definition that the Christian is not truly educated until he experiences God. Learning to the Christian is not narrowly conceived in intellectual terms, change, or adjustment, but it embraces all of these and much more — regeneration by the Spirit of God.

The Christian can go along with most of the findings of scientific psychology on the physiological basis of learning. He will insist, however, that beyond the physical nervous system lies the soul or spirit which is responsible for conscious responses.

Because the Christian point of view is the whole-person-in-life, learning is not confined merely to "mental" processes. Instead, other factors are present. These include purpose, maturation, emotions, motivation, understanding, apperception, and the pupil's attitudes. Certain external factors also affect learning directly, such as class spirit, class size, building and equipment, and others. These factors are descriptive of an integral phase of learning termed "concomitant learning."

Then, too, the Christian insists on the importance of certain spiritual factors in the learning process. These include the capaci-

[13]Cornelius Jaarsma, *Fundamentals in Christian Education* (Grand Rapids, Mich., Wm. B. Eerdmans Pub. Co., 1953), p. 330.

ties of the regenerated heart-life of pupils, the Person and work of the Holy Spirit who is the Spirit of Truth, the power of the Word of God, and the spiritual affinities of the nature of man to respond to the wooings of the Spirit and divine truth. Furthermore, the power of faith provides a way for truth and personality to meet most effectively. The more frequently one dwells upon an object by faith, the more he feels its power.

It may be well at this point to stress a word of caution. It is not true that we can learn only by doing. Many of the things which we wish our children to learn most cannot possibly be taught by doing. Of course, many use the term "doing" to include "thinking" in doing, but it is pragmatically used to indicate physical and manual activity, the engagement in some type of "motion" or experience. But to restrict our Christian education to learning by doing is to make it as static as most dogmatic kinds of instruction. While we hasten to admit that we can learn by doing, we can also learn by the imaginative rehearsal of activities as well as by the actual practice of activities. How can we teach children, for example, the sacredness of the marriage bond, the value of a stable family life, and the importance to themselves and to the world of parenthood by "doing"? These are not extreme illustrations. Frankly, we are challenged with the possible fact that the most important things in education cannot possibly be learned by doing. They must be learned through the imagination or through vicarious experience. This does not imply, however, that such learning must of necessity be dead or dull. Jesus employed at least three approaches to learning: (1) He initiated the learning experience, (2) He allowed His pupils to initiate learning experiences, and (3) He employed interaction, exchange, and discussion. Many teachers feel that the third approach is most fruitful. While in the main we would concur with this feeling, let us not overlook the importance of learning in other ways. After all, learning is an individual experience.

The student expresses himself because God gave him the powers of expression. Therefore, the teacher must present the student in his perceptual field with those truths in life which will lead to conceptualizing in the Christian framework of love, faith, and obedience. In this way, there is far greater possibility that he will love the truth and commit himself to it. Only until truth is accepted in the heart will commitment to it really be given (Romans 10:10).

Learning cannot take place until the facts of information are received and retained by the mind and memory. Such information, however, is quite useless unless the student comprehends and understands the facts retained. Such understanding leads to significance and recognition of relationships. Being able to converse about his understandings leads to self-activity which, in turn, allows the student to form convictions. However, when the student reaches the level of application of knowledge, this is wisdom which is the highest step in the learning process. This is where learning by doing becomes important. When he knows how to use knowledge, the student can commit himself completely to it. His faith in it leads him to commitment. Jesus showed that by practicing the will of God we prove its truth and that faith leads to *living* truth (John 7:17, 37-39). He also pointed out the close relation between truth and life (John 15). James adds a word to impress us that true knowledge will be used in conduct (James 3:13).

Wisdom gives knowledge the insight for action. Christian wisdom is from above and is a gift from God. It is seeing things as God sees them and doing His will. This is the essence and apex of the learning process.

3. New Developments in Learning Theory

Changes now being proposed in education are based on greater knowledge of the new discoveries in educational psychology. In 1964 Benjamin Bloom of the University of Chicago proposed the thesis that at least half of all human intelligence is developed by age four. This was reflected in the book *Stability and Change in Human Characteristics*. This thesis was very largely supported by White and Watts at Harvard and revealed in the book *Major Influences on the Development of Young Children*. This view has gained rather wide acceptance among educators in this country.

Major questions were raised: What must we teach? How are we to educate? What is child learning? Many answers to these questions were supplied by Jean Piaget, the famous European psychologist. For more than fifty years he has been studying the development of intelligence in children. His work had its greatest impact in the new curricula that were the main educational thrust of the sixties. One illustration of this is the "new math." Less well known, perhaps, but equally important, are the implications of his work for the practice of teaching. His main theory in working with children was in the "semiclinical" interview, a relatively nondirective open discussion with a child that deals with a particular issue or problem. He used questions posed by the children themselves as a starting point. He thus discovered their real interests. This has led to what may be called "thematic education," that is, instruction in all subjects by emphasis on the open classroom. Piaget also stressed the importance of starting where the child is in language and conceptual development. This focuses on the importance of keeping verbalisms and abstractions to a minimum

in working with children. In early years children need to con-
cretize their language by relating words to things. They also need
close personal relationships in learning experiences.

One of the emphases in Piaget, however, that some American psychologists differ with is his denial of the ability of the child
to do abstract thinking until he reaches age seven. Because of cultural factors in our society many believe that our children are able
to do abstract thinking long before age seven. Among those advocating the possibility is Jerome Bruner who says that young children are often underestimated in their ability to learn. He advanced the premise that "any subject can be taught effectively in
some intellectually honest way to any child at any state of development," at least among school age children.[14] Significant work
to support this thesis is currently underway at several places in the
United States. Oscar Moore at the University of Pittsburgh found
that three-year-old children can learn to write stories on a coded
key typewriter with the use of pictures. Experiments at the High/
Scope Research Foundation, Ypsilanti, Michigan, show that educators and parents are learning how to give even crib-bound infants an educational head start. Thus, some form of school can and
should be provided for small children.

Dr. Kagan at Harvard, in research on the power of infants to
think, found that babies react much like adults when confronted
with new situations. Burton White, also at Harvard, points out
that year two is very critical for the child. At the Harvard Pre-
School Project, 1965, they discovered that the period between ten
months and eighteen months is the most significant period in the
child's life. They also discovered that three-year-olds have relatively the same cluster of abilities as six-year-olds. The role of the
mother in guiding the child's learning experiences becomes very
significant. The critical factor, therefore, in any child's learning is
the home.

The significance for Christian education and the Christian
home is apparent. The great need is to help prepare parents to be
Christian and to give their young children the right kind of general and Christian instruction at a very early age.

In educational practice this new theory can be seen in current
usages of the open classroom. The basic premise of the open classroom is faith in the child's desire to learn and in his ability to
assume responsibility for choice. This requires more emphasis on
guidance and less on teacher control. Children learn better from
guides and fellow explorers than from authoritarian leaders.
Greater freedom leads to greater interest and more involvement,
and thus to better learning. To educate children who love to learn,

[14]Jerome S. Bruner, *The Process of Education* (Cambridge, MA, Harvard University Press, 1960).

we must recognize that both love and learning flow from the conditions of real life — the possibilities of choice, self-responsibility, and the freedom to relate to the people around us.

The way all of this comes out in the teaching-learning process might be pictured as follows:

For children:[15]

Listening	— get attention, interest, focusing on	*knowledge*
Exploring	— searching and involvement	*understanding*
	—provides options, choices, cooperation	
Discovery	— self-discovery, not telling	*attitudes*
	— sees meaning and value under the leadership of the Holy Spirit	
Appropriating	— implications for own life, behavior	*appreciations*
	— makes learning personal	
Responsibility	— lives the truth, uses it	*action*

For youth and adults:[16]

Familiarization	— giving facts	*information*
	— student rather passive	
Feedback	— testing information	
	— using questions, alternatives	
	— student responds, inquires	*understanding*
Exploration	— search for meaning	*appropriation*
	— discovery through small groups	*appreciations*
	— more pupil participation	*attitudes*
Responsibility	— meanings, applications of truth, usage	*action*
	— pupil fully active	

Let us not forget that in all of these learning processes the work of the Holy Spirit is apparent. He is present to activate the teaching and the learning, providing motivation, enlightenment, and application to the heart and life.

---

[15]See Charles T. Smith, *Ways to Plan and Organize Your Sunday School* (Glendale, Gospel Light, 1971), Ch. 2, for more details.
[16]See David A. Stoop, *Ways to Help Them Learn* (Glendale, Gospel Light, 1971), Ch. 3, for more details.

4. *Influence of Developmental Theory*

In addition to the cognitive aspects of learning it is important to recognize the facet of interpersonal relationships in the learning process. In both secular and Christian education circles the importance of this has been clearly recognized.

Richards surveyed two decades of research in this area in secular education to determine the basic issues involved.[17] In the early 1950's many studies were made comparing so-called "teacher-centered" vs "student-centered" classes. Such studies assumed that greater participation was provided in the latter method and that group emphasis would result in greater learning. Efforts were sought to prove the superiority of the student-centered methods. It was concluded that the assumptions were wrong, that student-centered methods were not necessarily superior particularly in terms of cognitive outcomes. On the other hand some studies did point up group work as providing a supportive climate in which people can work. It is also evident that the schooling method itself, while valid, does not provide all ingredients necessary to produce mature Christians. This does not mean, however, that we should abandon the schooling idea and method. Instead, we need to institute a wide variety of teaching-learning methods and be sure that the life-reality of Biblical truths are revealed to and experienced by pupils in the teaching-learning process.

The developmental theories of Jean Piaget and Lawrence Kohlberg have also greatly influenced moral education. Piaget's position is that cognitively children cannot handle adult concepts; therefore they cannot process Biblical and moral concepts until they reach the maturity level to do so. If this is true, then the absolute truths of God's objective revelation not only do not exist, but are withheld from children because they are outside human experience. Such a position demands that we not be concerned with Biblical communication but rather with environmental conditions which stimulate internal development.

Kohlberg has taken virtually the same position on moral development. Limited by their cognitive development children use data in their physical and social environments, using them at their level of development. Teachers, therefore, should not indoctrinate but help chilren grow from lower moral stages of development to higher ones only as they are ready to do so.

Larry Richards, we believe, has given an effective answer to some of the implications of both Piaget and Kohlberg.[18] He points

---

[17]Lawrence O. Richards, *A Theology of Christian Education* (Grand Rapids, Zondervan, 1975), Ch. 9.
[18]*Ibid.*, Chs. 15, 16.

out several responses to these theories. First, it is not necessary to "fully know" truth perfectly in order to know truth. What adult fully knows the meaning of theological truths like omnipotence or moral truths like forgiveness? These things, therefore, should not be withheld from children because they do not "fully know" meanings.

Second, we should not expect children to respond on an adult level of understanding. Let them respond on *their* level because it is the intent of the heart rather than the head which is more important to God.

Third, if data is so necessary in reconstructing one's perception of reality, as Piaget and Kohlberg insist, then all learners, including children, must have the *proper data* — both theological and moral — to work with. Children need these data *during the process* of their development, not at the end. This gives God and His Word a chance to operate all along in the process.

I. THE TEACHING PROCESS

1. *In Secular Education*

Among secular educators teaching and learning are viewed as one whole. Only theoretically can one separate the two. This does not mean, however, that the various components of teaching and learning cannot be examined separately. In doing this, objectives stand in the forefront of the teaching process. Subject matter becomes a means to an end in meeting the objectives, and the process is concluded by making an evaluation of outcomes.

Although one finds a battle in progress between the traditionalists and progressives today, it has become apparent that the psychological approach in the teaching-learning process is at least the dominating one theoretically. Most of the modern textbooks today advocate following the findings of psychology. This means that child nature determines very largely objectives, subject matter, and outcomes. The teacher approaches his task in terms of child activities instead of formal subject matter. The order of the lesson takes its cue from the present level of child experience. The problems arising in child experience set the structure of the lesson. The method employed will be that of conducting inquiry. Pupils will be given freedom in seeking solutions to their problems and the part the teacher plays is pre-eminently one of guidance.

While in general secular education has not moved away from the more traditional ways of managing the learning process, there have been a few late developments. Instead of following a strictly subject matter oriented process a three-component model is often incorporated into a *systems* approach. This three-component instructional design involves (1) instructional objectives, (2) instructional activities, and (3) performance assessment. Subject matter and learning activities become the general goal rather than the means to achieve clearly stated objectives.

The instructional objectives component is based on behavioristic psychology, a concept which declares that learning results from experiencing a change of behavior that can be described in terms of observable performance. Thus usable objectives must state the intended outcome in terms of terminal behavior, behavior which follows instruction. The writings of Robert F. Mager reflect this performance philosophy. His most popular works include *Preparing Instructional Objectives* (Fearon, 1962), *Analyzing Performance Problems* (Fearon, 1970), and *Goal Analysis* (Fearon, 1972).

Admittedly, there is value in stating objectives in terms of performance, for objectives are clear to the student and measureable for the teacher. Good teaching, however, is not always dependent on behavioristic terms. Certain intangibles and spiritual outcomes to both teaching and learning cannot be captured in this way. Many things are learned spontaneously and in interpersonal relationships in the classroom.

2. *In Christian Education*

Generally speaking, in Christian education the teaching process must follow the pattern of the learning process. The psychological laws most certainly help the teacher in his task. The principle of self-activity demands that the teacher control the activity of the pupil in the right direction and often in that direction. The principle of motivation and interest demands that lessons be made as interesting and attractive as possible. The principle of apperception demands that materials and stimuli be adapted to the experience and mental set of the pupils. The principle of individualization demands that the teacher adapt instruction to individual differences. Finally, the principle of socialization requires that all learning responses be developed in natural social settings and that the environment be conducive to the development of good attitudes.

Another way of looking at the teacher's task generally is to see that his function is one of guidance. In fact, his task is fourfold. First, the teacher must *inspire* the student. He does this through setting up goals which are clearly understood by the student. Where the student is engaged in purposeful activity, he will proceed far more readily with confidence. Second, the teacher *in-*

structs the student. Here materials are provided for the self-activity of the learner. They may be presented as ideas or objects and in many various ways, but the main purpose is to provide information for the student. Such instruction will be varied, graded, and connected to life-situations. Third, the teacher *disciplines* the student. Here teacher-control is exercised to keep the student firmly on the task at hand. This authority, however, is exercised to keep the student operating in the framework of love and kindness. Here is where the divine elements and spiritual factors play a large part in both teaching and learning. Christian teaching must always be "in the Spirit."

Fourth, the teacher *evaluates* student achievement. He will help students judge their own progress and will encourage constant self-evaluation of status and progress.

More specifically, the teaching process must be viewed in three phases: (1) preparation for teaching, (2) presentation in teaching, and (3) evaluation of teaching. In the preparatory phase, the teacher is concerned with study processes. In the presentation phases, methodology is primary. Evaluation, of course, is concerned with measurement. The chart on page 149 shows these relationships.

In the *preparation* phase of the teaching process each teacher is concerned with (1) personal study of the lesson leading to mastery of its content, (2) lesson planning, and (3) the pattern of the learning process. Since the teaching process must follow the pattern of the learning process for greatest success, this factor becomes central in lesson planning. The starting point of the lesson must be a sense of need. Attention and interest are gained only by meeting some need. Interest results in self-activity which is so necessary in learning. The task of the teacher, therefore, is to present truth which meets the need. Such truth must be mastered personally by the teacher and planned carefully for the student. More than that, however, the teacher must show the "way of truth" and then urge the student to accept it. The pattern which emerges looks something like the following:

1. First, get attention and interest — the appeal to *intellect*
2. Second, meet needs — this is the appeal to the *emotions*
3. Third, self-activity and action — the appeal to the *will*
4. Fourth, urgency of acceptance — appeal to the *heart* and *action* which results in character

The implications of this process are quite evident. In preparation the teacher is to follow the pattern in *planning*. The plan will look something like the following:

1. What do I want my students to know? — intellectual appeal

2. What do I want my students to feel? — emotional appeal
3. What do I want my students to do? — appeal to will and action
4. What kind of character am I seeking? — this shows the way of life

It should be carefully observed, however, that in planning the teacher should take particular pains to avoid mere intellectualism and mechanical reproduction on the part of the student. Inductive study will avoid this and lead to considerations of interpretation and application, self-activity and self-application which ultimately result in wisdom.

Clues to the form of the lesson plan are also provided by the learning process. If the study process in lesson planning has been thorough and effective, it will result in somewhat the following form in the lesson plan:

1. Introduction to the lesson — appeal to the intellect — get the attention and hold the interest — make point of contact

2. Development of the lesson — appeal to the emotions by showing how needs are met in pupils' hearts and lives — here the teacher uses objectives, content, methods, and materials

3. Conclusion to the lesson —
show the way of life and how truth can be used — this is the appeal to the will and heart — acceptance in the heart is wisdom —

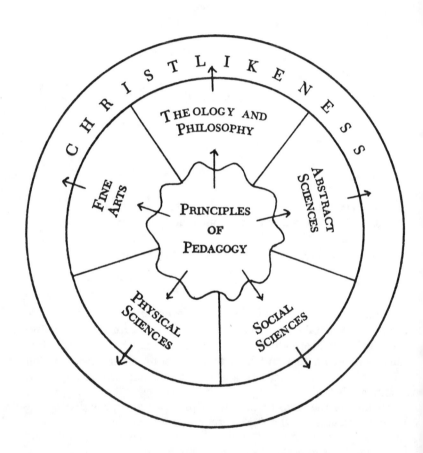

The second phase of the teaching process is lesson *presenta-tion*. The function of the Christian teacher is seen in relation to God-given pedagogical principles. The teacher is not only obli-gated to be a witness, but also must *operate* properly as a witness. This brings in the matter of methodology. God has provided cer-tain pedagogical principles by which the Christian teacher can operate in relation to subject matter and goals involved. The relationship is pictured somewhat as in the chart on the preceding page. Here is revealed the very intimate relationship between prin-ciples of pedagogy which direct the use of subject matter as instrumental in bringing the student to the character-goal of Christ-likeness.

In meeting the student in the classroom situation the effective-ness of the teacher will depend on two things: (1) his contact with God and His truth in the study process, and (2) his contact with the student. In both preparation and presentation the teacher is a co-worker with the Holy Spirit. In the study process the teacher should have an "inner experience" with God so that the lesson is worked deeply into his own heart life. From this point the teacher can move into an "outer experience" of the classroom where he contacts the student. In presentation, the function of the teacher is to begin with the "outer experience" of the student and through the methodology involved lead the pupil to an "inner experience" of the truth as it came from God through the experience of his teacher. The whole process takes the form re-vealed in the following chart:

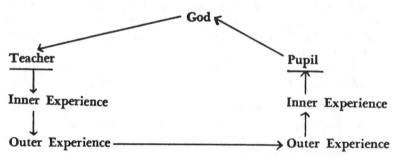

The process may be visualized in another way in chart form below. The teacher, who knows the way and who has had life-experience, should begin with the needs and interests of the pupil, connect these with the Word, and apply them in life-situations for the benefit of the pupil. The process then becomes as follows: from life-situations, as seen and experienced by the teacher, to God's truth and back to the pupil *in* life. Too often the process is parallel and teacher-centered as indicated by the dotted lines in the chart below. Too often teachers teach without any indication of making contact with pupils with the Word in life-situations.[19]

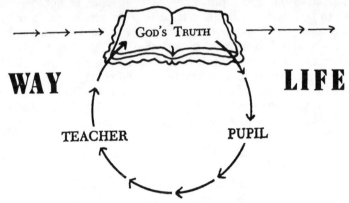

As far as methods themselves are concerned the Christian teacher believes that a combination of methods seems to be the best overall approach. The selection of methods is determined by objectives, the needs and ages of the students, the time and skill at the teacher's command, and other factors. Selection should be made in the light of the teacher's best judgment as to how best he can deal with the subject matter, the pupil, and objectives. Variety and correlation should direct the use of methods.

The Christian educator recognizes the values of tests and measurements but in the final analysis the interests of the student himself are paramount. Teachers, therefore, should supplement test results with personal judgments and will be careful as well to evaluate students beyond the scope of mental accomplishment. Tests can be used as means to an end, as leads, as evidence of trends, but not as final determinants. The Christian teacher should not blind himself to the fact that life itself provides an education.

SUGGESTED CLASS ACTIVITIES AND PROJECTS FOR CHAPTER V

1. Outline your list of the qualifications of a good teacher:
   a. In secular education
   b. In religious education
   c. In Christian education
2. Discuss or write a paper on "The Ministry of Teaching."
3. Compare and/or contrast the place of the pupil:
   a. In secular education
   b. In religious education
   c. In Christian education
4. Discuss the problems of discipline in the classroom.

[19]For a full discussion of this problem the reader is referred to Lois Lebar, *Education That Is Christian* (Westwood, N.J., Fleming H. Revell Co., 1958), chapters 3-6.

5. Discuss how the principle of apperception is useful in motivation.
6. Write a paper on how Jesus Christ practiced the principle of apperception in His teaching.
7. Discuss the dangers of prizes and awards in motivation.
8. Study in greater detail the various theories of learning.
9. Discuss the implications of the various laws of learning for teaching as you see it today.
10. What is your definition of learning?
11. What spiritual and divine elements are present in learning for the Christian?
12. Discuss the limitations of learning by doing.
13. Discuss the relation of teaching and learning from a psychological point of view.
14. What steps are involved in the teaching process?
15. Why is it important to connect subject matter with life situations?

THE EDUCATIVE PROCESS – THE CURRICULUM

OUTLINE FOR CHAPTER 6

A. THEORY AND PRINCIPLES OF THE CURRICULUM

 1. Definition of the Curriculum
 2. Theories of the Nature of the Curriculum
 3. The Scriptural Basis for the Curriculum
 4. Sources of Authority in Curriculum Building
 5. Underlying Principles for Curriculum Building

B. FACTORS WHICH AFFECT CURRICULUM CONSTRUCTION

 1. Educational Aims and Objectives
 2. The Nature of the Pupil
 3. Other Factors
 4. Organization of the Curriculum

C. THE CONTENT OF THE CURRICULUM

 1. Subject Matter — a Definition
 2. Objectives of Curriculum Materials
 3. Criteria for Subject Matter Selection
 4. Procedure for Selection
 5. Areas of Subject Matter Content in Secular Education
 6. Areas of Subject Matter Content in Christian Education
 7. Evaluation
 8. Steps in Course of Study Construction

6 | THE EDUCATIVE PROCESS — THE CURRICULUM

A. Theory and Principles of the Curriculum

1. Definition of the Curriculum

A variety of definitions has been given to the word "curriculum." The word itself is derived from the Latin word meaning "a place of running," "a race course." In other words, the curriculum is a course of study, a line of progress through a series of subjects.

In its broadest meaning, the curriculum is life-inclusive, but this is not too practical for study purposes. It can be thought of instead as that which includes all activities and experiences which are initiated or utilized by the church and school for the accomplishment of the aims of education and Christian education.

A more narrow meaning, yet commonly held, conceives of the curriculum as areas or fields of subject matter organized into learning areas. Its purpose is to perpetuate the cultural heritage and prepare for the present and future. This is the most practical view.

For a long time it was a real issue among educators as to whether the curriculum was inclusive of *all* that goes on under the organized activities of the school, or that it was confined merely to lesson materials. The first view is the one most acceptable today. For day schools, the curriculum then includes classes, chapel services, recreation and physical education, social life, the equipment, the teachers, etc. For the Sunday school, it would include classes, worship, hymns, prayers, lesson materials both Biblical and extra-biblical, the ritual, etc.

What is a Christian curriculum? The meaning of the term, "Christian," will determine the answer. Education is distinctively Christian when the authority of Christ and the realization of His authority in our lives is the justification for all educational activity. All subject-matter will be recognized as a revelation of His truth. All activities will be motivated by His life, will, and Spirit. Whether conceived in broad or narrow terms, a Christian curriculum centers in Christ. It is the medium employed by the school to achieve the ends of Christian education.

The curriculum is given design by the course of study. The

157

basic facts and principles of child development set the stage for this design. This is all guided by the principles of the Word of God. The whole-person-in-life doing the will of God is the object of the Christian curriculum. Therefore, the curriculum may be thought of as guided experience. Properly, the Christian curriculum includes the elements of evangelism, instruction, worship, fellowship, and service.

The outlook of philosophy enters here into the matter of definition. The *realist* would define the curriculum as the repository of subject-matter the nature of which is completely objective. The subjects of major importance, therefore, would be those of the fields of natural and physical sciences. The *idealist* is not as much interested in subject-matter as he is in the student. The curriculum consists of that which is for the best interest and highest development of the pupil. Where the realist emphasizes the objective, the idealist emphasizes the subjective. The *pragmatist* stresses the importance of the social sciences. All subjects, however, should be utilized in problem-solving. Empirical social usefulness is the criterion by which the subject-matter curriculum is evaluated. The realist is interested in subject-matter as such, but the idealist and pragmatist are both interested in what subject matter does for the pupil.

2. Theories of the Nature of the Curriculum

Four major concepts of the organization and purpose of learning areas or subject-matter fields are offered: (1) the information or knowledge concept, (2) the disciplinary concept, (3) the social concept, and (4) the creative concept.

In the *knowledge concept* of the curriculum, factual material is organized for intellectual mastery. The subject matter is graded on a quantitative basis from level to level. One's education is measured in terms of the amount of information he has memorized and retained over the years.

In the *disciplinary concept*, subject matter is used to exercise and develop the learner's mental powers and capacities. Faculty Psychology is at the basis of this view. Here the mind is thought of as possessing certain faculties which are exercised and developed by mastering certain kinds of subject-matter. Here greater emphasis is placed on *how* one learns rather than on *what* is learned.

The *social concept* of the curriculum stresses the needs of the individual as he functions in the social structure. These needs also guide the educator in the selection of curriculum materials. In addition, emphasis is placed on dynamic social changes with the inevitable necessity of adjustment to them as well as the impact of the total environment of a technological, scientific, and democratic culture. Problems to be faced in such a situation include the influence of science and technology, changes in community life, social stratification, changes in family life, changes in occupation and employment, changes in economics, and changes and resulting confusions in the present system of values. The greatest problem, therefore, is: what does the learner need to know to function in modern society? Information, they say, is quite meaningless apart from the social structure.

In the *creative concept*, emphasis is placed largely on the psychological nature of the individual. This approach, therefore, is child-centered or pupil-centered. Man, adherents say, has creative capacity and the development of this power is the primary goal of education. Learning activities are so arranged as to motivate this power. Self-expression, self-appraisal, self-activity, and motivation are the key concepts of this view. The curriculum consists of activities which are adjusted constantly to pupil needs.

What is the Christian's reaction to these concepts? First, in order to evaluate these concepts, the Christian uses the Bible as the basis of such evaluation. Principles of Scripture provide a theological and philosophical basis for sufficient examination. Second, the Scriptures provide guidance by revealing to the educator what he is to teach regarding man and his place in the world. In the third place, education is concerned with the *whole* man. The Christian view pictures man as an integrated personality. In spite of the presence of sin which is disturbing to personality, man has retained the essential framework of an integrated personality. As such, the physical, mental, social, and spiritual elements are interrelated and all interact on man.

Man in his wholeness was created in God's image. As such, he is free and responsive to the world around him. Such freedom allowed him a choice to be like God. Education, as conceived by the Christian, therefore, is a process of man-making, not merely mind-training.

The fact of sin has deeply affected man's nature, and by voluntary disobedience man lost God's presence from his heart and life. In spite of this, however, man still functions on the level of self-will and in accordance with natural inclinations which tend toward evil. Particularly in his mental, moral, and spiritual resources has sin caused distortion and corruption so that man cannot respond as God originally intended. Because he is at once creative and corrupt, man has developed a culture made to serve himself. Any education which overlooks this fact is not complete. Because of this, the Christian believes that redemption plays a large part in educational processes. Christ died to redeem men, and as a result, it has been made possible for man to regain the image of God. Education, therefore, should now be redemptive by calling attention to the fact of sin and God's provision through His Son for deliverance from it.

In spite of man's natural disinclinations for God's truth because of sin, the Holy Spirit accompanies the truth, makes hearts responsive, and transform them. This is the height of the educative process to the Christian. It is felt, therefore, that the school must help the pupil understand, master, and commit himself to the truth which redeems. Furthermore, he should be taught that man's destiny is beyond this world.

In the light of these general observations on the nature and destiny of man, it is possible to evaluate the concepts of the curriculum listed above. With regard to the *knowledge* concept, the Christian readily recognizes that there should be factual material, that grading is necessary, and that there are objective pre-existent truths to be apprehended, mastered, and used. He disagrees, however, that education is measured in terms of intellect. Here the knowledge concept fails to consider the *whole* man. There are other aspects of man's personality besides the mental, and they include the emotional, physical, and spiritual. In the knowledge concept, erudition may be achieved at the expense of the other elements of personality and thus man would be seriously out of balance. Furthermore, it is possible to know *about* God without *knowing* God. It must be recognized, too, that quite often there is little correlation between knowledge and conduct. Knowing the Bible and following Christ are two different things. Jesus said, "Ye know these things; happy are ye if ye do them" (John 13:17). It is possible to have heaven in the head, but hell in the soul.

The Christian can agree with the stress laid by the disciplinary concept on memory and mental development, but he must reject the Faculty Psychology as the basis for it. While it is recognized that there are laws of logic which help to mould the intellect and that there are principles which underlie effective memory, it is also seen that this view has basic weaknesses. First, there is the danger of mental gymnastics with little regard for the subject matter itself. It is possible to perfectly reproduce in a mechanical fashion through memory all of the subject matter, but without the slightest evidence of comprehension and understanding. Mental acuity may be achieved at the expense of desirable emotional and social growth also. Still further, this view is based on a false notion of the learning process. Transfer of training is not based on the power of reasoning or memory, but rather on common elements in the principles, procedures, and skills as well as teaching methods. It does not follow that the criteria for sound thought and of good literature are identical. Thus the "Great Books" core does not necessarily lead to better thinkers. It should also be noted that the Great Books Theory does not necessarily lead to better orientation for the present.

The *social concept* has much to commend it. The Christian recognizes that man is a social being. Cooperation is necessary if worthy goals are to be achieved. Furthermore, social maturation is not considered mechanical. It requires common sense and realism to solve social problems. This, however, is not going far enough for the Christian. Man's deepest needs go beyond the social situation. Society needs a destiny for its justification. Society itself cannot satisfy man's deepest longings, for it neglects intellectual development according to patterns of truth. Furthermore, in the social view there is definite danger that the individual may become a victim of social regimentation and conformity. In view of the value crisis now upon us (and advocates of the social view are quite willing to admit such a crisis), it is apparent that social theory does not and cannot supply the philosophical basis for evaluation. The adequate criteria for evaluation are not to be found in the social situation itself.

The Christian agrees with the *creative concept* in placing stress upon the importance of child and child nature. Furthermore, it is readily admitted that man does have creative ability and capacity. This capacity is inherent in all individuals and is an integral part of the learning process. To suppress originality is to suffocate motivation. There are definite weaknesses, however. First, this view neglects the possibility of developing individuals according to preexistent patterns of thought and action. It tends to de-emphasize the cultural heritage and truth. It tends to reject absolute and divine truth. Instead, emphasis falls on expression with little to express. Furthermore, the norms for judging the quality of expression are lacking. The individual becomes a law unto himself. All systematic learning ceases. The educative process, as a result, becomes aimless, lawless, and capricious.

In summarizing, it can be said that there is truth in all the above theories, but each of them lack certain basic elements. One is a lack of comprehensiveness; some human element is missing. The social and creative concepts deny the existence of pre-existent truth and completely overlook the need for a process of redemption outside of man himself. It can be seen, therefore, upon these bases why an eclectic view is not acceptable to the Christian, for these views are rooted in concepts of man and the world which are contrary to the Scriptures.

These theories are inadequate for other reasons, as well. The natural man, who propounds them, seeks to view the whole of life from a position within life. Because his heart has not been regenerated by the Holy Spirit, he cannot see the transcendent view. Because he believes his views are correct, he accepts life as he sees it and from his own standpoint. Some phases of life he glorifies above others, and, as a result, in education he either glorifies knowledge or personality. A theocentric, Christocentric, or bibliocentric view is impossible for him. To this view we now turn.

3. The Scriptural Basis for the Curriculum

The Christian curriculum begins properly with the Word of God. This is true when conceiving of the curriculum broadly as comprehending all that goes on in the school situation, or more narrowly in terms of factual materials for subject matter. The Word of God as a divine revelation provides both content and principles by which all subject matter content is evaluated and used.

The source of all truth, to the Christian, is God. God, as Creator, speaks to man through His Word, both spoken and written. This is the transcendent point of view. As such, it is outside, over, and above creation. It is the only position from which all things can be viewed coherently. The Christian takes this position not only because it is the result of a new heart regenerated by the Holy Spirit, but also because it is the Christian World View. The Holy Spirit, through the Scriptures, reveals it to us. To the contrary, the natural man is confined to a view *within* creation. Without a new heart, he cannot comprehend the correct point of view, for only the Holy Spirit can give this comprehension. Mere intellectual comprehension and consent does not give one an understanding heart. Instead, the Christian lives by faith in the Word of God. Such faith is not an intellectual leap in the dark where knowledge fails, but it is an act by which the transformed heart accepts life lived out of the Word of God. The result is — we follow the Word of God.

What has been said above gives the Christian the theological and philosophical basis for the curriculum. God has not limited His provision, however, to this. He moves in still closer to human personality by His very presence in the teaching-learning process. This we call the *divine element* in Christian education. We have already commented on this fact in a previous chapter. Therefore, repetition is not necessary at this point. Instead, it will suffice merely to list the facets involved in the divine element for the sake of completion at this point and to show how they fit into the philosophy of the curriculum. The divine element in the curriculum includes the presence and power of the Holy Spirit, the inherent power of the written Word of God which is "the sword of the Spirit," the capacities of the *regenerated* self to learn, and the impact of the Christian personality of the teacher. These factors in themselves provide tremendous teaching atmosphere and power for the Christian teacher and learner. Still another factor, however, is what we call atmosphere or the structure of Christian education. The philosophy of Christian structure has been clearly defined by Jaarsma.[1] Structure has been defined as that which holds a matter together, much as steel is the framework of a building. The history of education shows that education in every age has had an inner structure to provide coherent power. For the Greeks, it was loyalty and eloquence; for the Hebrews, it was knowledge of the law and obedience; in the Middle Ages, it was knowledge and discipline. The structure of education, therefore, is that which gives coherence. For the Christian, the structure of education is found in the threefold provision of love, faith, and obedience. In chart form it looks something like the following:

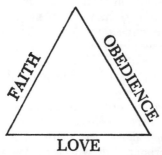

In this view, love is the foundation of it all. God is love. The love of God is imparted by the Holy Spirit to the transformed hearts of saved men that they may love God and men. To love is to love from the heart but with the whole man. Sin prohibits love, but a transformed heart can love. Love forms a coherent motivation which directs redeemed man's life. Love is, therefore, basic to Christian education and without it there is no true Christian education. Love is, further, basic to the curriculum, for it involves the whole man.

Faith is also necessary. Since love fastens the whole man in God, the capacity of faith is turned toward God. The whole man with a new heart of love lays hold by faith upon God and His Word. Faith opens the way to true knowledge and understanding. Unsaved men believe but their faith is in self and social adjustment. Consequently, any integration that takes place is temporary and mis-directed hellward.

[1]Cornelius Jaarsma, *Fundamentals in Christian Education* (Grand Rapids, Mich., Wm. B. Eerdmans Pub. Co., 1953), pp. 249, 289, and 316.

Obedience is also part of the structure. There is surrender in love. No longer does self rule; instead the ego is turned Godward. Thus, we see the framework of the structure of Christian education. Such a process has not directed curriculum construction in the past and very little is present today.

The implications of this view are clear. It becomes the clear duty of educators to build structure into the life of the pupil. This provides coherence for child development; it provides the Christian ideal to strive for. It shows what kind of person the Christian should be and how he should act — in love, faith, and obedience. Thus, Christlikeness is the goal. Love, faith, and obedience guide the pupil toward that goal. The teacher cannot commit the child to these factors but he can exemplify them and motivate the child in this kind of atmosphere. The child must develop *in* this atmosphere and commit *himself* to it. The curriculum, therefore, presents the truth to which the child should commit himself. The teaching process includes inspiration, instruction, and discipline in that truth.

Moving still closer to the pupil in the curriculum, we are now concerned with the subject matter itself. The Christian view of subject matter is determined primarily by the view of culture itself from which subject matter is abstracted.

A popular conception of culture and subject matter from the secular point of view is represented by Smith, Stanley, and Shores.[2] Culture consists of facts, principles, social norms, and an infinitude of meanings plus tools, machines, institutions, and modes of individual and social action. Subject matter is a part of this total culture and consists primarily of what men know and believe and of their valuations and loyalties. In the Scriptures, the Christian view of culture is connected directly with the creation of the world by God. Through creation God gave definite responsibilities to man by means of a cultural mandate when He said, "Be fruitful and multiply, and replenish the earth, and subdue it: and have dominion over it" (Genesis 1:28). Man was thus charged with the task of mastering and developing the cultural setting under God and in His service. But sin brought tragedy and selfishness! In his heart man accepted the world without God and his capacity for his God-given task was seriously affected. God's curse rests upon the world.

In the face of this, God set in motion the process of redemption. His plan is that through regenerated hearts the kind of people will result who will carry out His original mandate. However, God had to change His procedure somewhat to accomplish this.

[2]B. Othanel Smith, William O. Stanley, and J. Harlan Shores, *Fundamentals of Curriculum Development* (Yonkers-on-Hudson, N. Y., World Book Co., 1950), p. 273.

The gospel witness has priority over the cultural mandate, although the latter has not been revoked. Now Christians exercise the cultural mandate in the light of the Gospel.

Thus man and his cultural product constitute the culture milieu or setting. This constitutes the curriculum or educational medium. The natural man accepts life as he finds it; he directs his life according to human needs. For him the curriculum will help to accept life intelligently and meaningfully in *this* setting. For the Christian, regeneration gives him another approach and another end. Rather than being dominated by the cultural setting, he evaluates it for the new life lived out of the Scriptures. For him, the curriculum should help him to live this new life to God's glory and praise. The heart of the curriculum, therefore, is the new life in Christ. The cultural product becomes a medium, a means to an end, and under constant appraisal for the regenerated life.

Still another factor enters into the Christian view of the curriculum — the concept of learning. The Christian leans definitely toward the Gestalt theory of learning. The "whole" concept certainly fits into the emphasis placed by the Christian on the whole man. For him, the whole man is involved in learning. Some people today say that learning is a heart matter, though they do not use the Scriptural meaning of the term. The Scriptures support the heart theory. "Thy word have I hid in my heart, that I might not sin against thee" (Psalm 119:11). Nothing is really learned until it is accepted in the heart. The Scriptures do not deny that certain psychosomatic behavior is acquired by conditioning and trial and error nor that insight gives intellectual comprehension, but only the Holy Spirit can help a child accept truth in his heart. It is beyond doubt, nonetheless, that the learning process demands that curriculum content be definitely related to pupil capacity and interest.

At this point we are ready to summarize the Christian view of the curriculum into a definite pattern. In chart form it appears as follows:

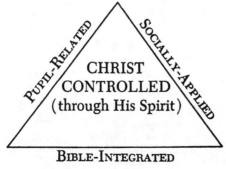

4. Sources of Authority in Curriculum Building

The question of authority has a marked bearing on curriculum building. Such authority rests in general upon a twofold basis. First, there is the legal basis which is derived from the state, giving the legal right to build a curriculum in the school system. The second basis is moral where authority is derived from fundamental principles.

More specifically, there are four possible sources of authority for curriculum building: (1) in the divine will, (2) in eternal truth, which is the humanistic position, (3) in science, and (4) in society. The humanistic conception of curriculum authority has been sponsored largely by Robert M. Hutchins in his *Higher Learning in America*.[3] Reason is at the basis of this view. It is claimed that reason rises above thinking and attaches itself to principles of eternal truth which never change. This eternal truth forms both the core and criteria for knowledge. The Christian must object to this view for a number of reasons. It is too subjective. It leaves God out as the source of eternal truth. Reason quite often disagrees on what truth is. It tends to separate the ideal from practice.

The *scientific* concept of curriculum authority likewise takes the position that truth is the source of authority in education. The primary emphasis, however, is placed on *method*. Method is both the source of authority and the only reliable means of establishing truth. The Christian likewise objects to this view. First, while the scientific method is recognized in some respects as a reliable method, the Christian maintains that this method is only *one* way to get truth. The scientific method cannot deal adequately with moral truth, and education is primarily moral and intellectual. Values are philosophical and are not subject to objective analysis. Furthermore, scientists have often deliberately disregarded moral values. This is unscientific. Others try to be neutral but this, too, is unacceptable. Still others use values held *presently* by society, but these constantly change. There is no real security in this approach.

The *social* concept maintains that the school finds its source of authority for curriculum building in society itself. Schools are set up by society to prepare pupils to live in society. Thus authority is found in the fundamental moral and intellectual commitments constituting the core of society. The democratic tradition, they say, best represents this view. The Christian again must object to this view because it is fragmentary. Society does not tell the *whole* story, for man is more than a social being. Divine society is a part of the total social structure and culture. The spiritual

3New Haven, Yale University Press, 1936.

aspects of man's nature are paramount. Furthermore, educators do not always practice the democratic spirit. In fact, some of them are quite authoritarian about the democratic spirit. Still further, social theory is based too much on the now. The Christian believes that the past and the future are important too. In this view, values are based on human judgment and this often is erroneous and incomplete. While it is recognized that changes are constantly occurring in society, this does not preclude the possibility of unchangeable principles. There can be changes of *application* of principles without changes in the principles themselves. Neither does a sharp distinction *have* to be made between the ideal and practical as is often contended by the advocates of the social group who criticize the Christian position in this regard.

The basis for the *Christian* concept of curriculum authority is found in the revealed will of God. Divine revelation forms the basis for knowing the purposes and objectives by which such authority is guided. This provides both a philosophical and practical basis for authority, theory and practice.

Diversity of *sectarian* opinion does not disqualify the educator from a moral obligation to be guided by the Creator. Separation of church and state is not *separation from* religion. The Christian viewpoint, thus, will redeem the educator from the present value-crisis with its consequent confusion now prevalent. A changing society cannot formulate the criteria by which the whole process is judged. This can be found only in the Word of God.

5. *Underlying Principles for Curriculum Building*

The progressive development of the Christian philosophy of education to this point brings us to the place where it is possible to formulate the basic principles for curriculum construction and development. These principles, of course, will follow the pattern provided in the Scriptural basis for the curriculum considered in the last section: i.e., the Christian curriculum is Christ-controlled, Bible-integrated, pupil-related, and socially applied. It is evident also that these principles will serve both for church-related education and day-school education. Still further, they are applicable at each and every level of the school system: primary, secondary, and higher education.

CHRIST-CONTROLLED

1. The Triune God is at the center of the curriculum; the fear of God is the beginning of wisdom.
2. Creation and Revelation provide the foundations of curriculum construction and development.
3. Christ, as Redeemer and Mediator, is the Person of the Godhead who meets the pupil, through His Spirit, in the educative process.

4. Christ is the center of the life and message of Christian education; He is the Head of the Church, the body of Christ.
5. The presence and power of the Holy Spirit must be depended upon in the whole process of Christian education; He brings conviction, regeneration, and instruction as the Spirit of Truth, Life, and Holiness.
6. Christlikeness through the regenerating and sanctifying power of the Spirit is the goal for both the individual and society.
7. Worship is foundational in Christian education, for it is here that direct contact, both individually and collectively, is made with God through Christ; this provides both inspiration and instruction.
8. All content for Christian education must be in harmony with the life and teachings of Jesus Christ; the great doctrines of the faith will center in Him; this provides the basis for integration and correlation of subject matter.
9. All materials should be evaluated by His standards of life and ministry and should be used to achieve the objectives of Christion education.

Bible-integrated

1. The curriculum recognizes the Bible as the inspired Word of God; it is the primary source of truth about God, man, and the world.
2. The curriculum will recognize that redemption is the main theme of the Bible.
3. The total Christian heritage of history and doctrine will be Bible-related and used in the curriculum.
4. The Bible will be recognized as the record of man's highest ethical values; it is the rule for both faith and practice.
5. The ethical principles contained in the Scriptures should be applied to all areas of man's experience in everyday life (home, school, work, play, social relations, etc.).
6. The *total* Bible truth should be directed at the various problems of curriculum content.
7. The curriculum should stress the origin and development of the Bible record.
8. The learner should be guided in the use of the Bible as the Divine Revelation; as such, its values for both personal and group worship will be recognized.
9. The mechanics of Bible construction and organization should not be neglected.
10. Extra-biblical materials will supplement Bible materials; as far as possible the entire cultural and religious heritage will enrich the curriculum.
11. The principle of gradation will be recognized in the application of Bible truth to the various grade and age levels in the school system.

Pupil-related

1. In the curriculum, the pupil will be viewed from the standpoint of creation, fall, and redemption.
2. The purpose of the curriculum, therefore, is to contribute toward the goal of Christlike personality in the pupil.

3. The curriculum will attempt to build the structure of love, faith, and obedience into the life of the pupil.
4. Pupils will be motivated and urged to commit themselves to the will of God and to a life of communion with Him.
5. The total nature of the pupil is to be developed in relation to his total environment.
6. As a part of the Church, the body of Christ, pupils will be urged to participate in the program of the Church which is engaged in building the Kingdom of Christ.
7. The curriculum will recognize the needs and experiences of pupils in the following areas of personal and social relationships:
   a. The individual's relation to God through Christ
   b. The individual's relation to human society
   c. The individual's relation to his life vocation
   d. The individual's relation to the ministry of witnessing
   e. The individual's relation to the Church
   f. The individual's relation to the universe
8. The curriculum will provide guidance in the use of home experiences in the program of Christian education.
   a. The home is the first and greatest teacher; these teaching values will be recognized.
   b. The curriculum will also provide guidance for the home.
   c. The curriculum will recognize the perils to the home.
9. The vocational problem of each individual will be cared for in the curriculum.
10. Curriculum construction and development will be directed by the best known psychological and educational principles.
    a. The laws of learning will be faithfully observed.
    b. Materials, methods, and experiences will be adapted to the various levels of maturity. This is the principle of gradation.
    c. Learning must be related to the needs, interests, and capacities of the learner.
    d. Individual differences will be recognized.
    e. The principle of apperception will be observed and practiced in production and in the teaching-learning process.
    f. Pupil motivation will be necessary.
    g. The curriculum will possess the qualities of comprehensiveness, balance, sequence, and integration.
    h. Man's relation to God will control the choice of subject matter.
    i. Learning takes place when truth is accepted in the heart.
    j. Flexibility and variety are necessary.
11. Materials which are attractive, practical, and of high quality should be provided.
    a. Suggestions for teacher and pupil planning will be present.
    b. Guidance on teaching methods.
    c. The literary style will be simple, clear, and interesting.

SOCIALLY-APPLIED

1. The needs held in common by mankind will be stressed in the curriculum:
   a. A sense of security
   b. A sense of belonging
   c. Clear, moral guidance
   d. Christian motivation

     e. Knowledge of the truth
     f. Redemption
     g. A place of service in God's Kingdom

2. A comprehensive program of evangelism and outreach will be provided by the curriculum.
3. The missionary outreach and imperative as the dynamic motivation for the individual and the church will be stressed.
4. The curriculum will orient the learner in a world of rapid social change, of science and technology, and give him a sense of God as Absolute and consequent security in His fellowship.
5. The curriculum will be related to the problems of the present day; it will interpret the facts of present day society.
6. The Christian ideal for society — the Kingdom — will be exalted in the curriculum along with its implications for social relations, economics, labor, finances, etc.
7. The curriculum will offer Christian suggestions for the solution of social issues.
8. The curriculum will be realistic in placing stress on the fact that the present day social setting is characterized by sin and apostasy.
9. The curriculum will stress the fact that redeemed men are co-workers with Christ; participation, therefore, in community improvement and redemption will be urged.
10. Christian education is accomplished through the Christian institutions of society — the home, the school, and the church.

B. FACTORS WHICH AFFECT CURRICULUM CONSTRUCTION

1. *Educational Aims and Objectives*

Of all the factors which have a direct bearing on curriculum building, aims and objectives are the most influential. This is true because they reflect the basic philosophical outlook on life. They are formal expressions of one's world view. Furthermore, they provide guide lines for educational procedures and methods. They are also means whereby evaluation of methods and materials is made possible. A full discussion of aims and purposes was given in a previous chapter and it is not necessary to repeat them at this point. It is important, however, to point out the strategic position which they have in the educative process with particular reference to the subject matter curriculum.

2. *The Nature of the Pupil*

The pupil is the focal point in the teaching-learning process. A right understanding of the pupil is basic to teaching. How to teach is largely determined by the learning process. In turn, the learning process is determined by the nature of the pupil which is ordained by God. The nature of the pupil was discussed at some length in the chapter on psychology. It is not necessary to repeat that discussion here. It is important again, however, to understand the relationship of the nature of the pupil in curriculum construction. Since the pupil is central in the educative process, it becomes necessary to gear the materials and methods of the curriculum to the nature of the pupil. It is extremely important for the Christian to bear in mind that basically man is religious in nature. The pupil, consequently, must be viewed in the light of his creation, fall, and redemption. The need for redemption is the primary need. In meeting this need, education finds both unity and integration in teaching and learning. The second major factor of pupil nature which affects the curriculum is the unity of the personality. Although man's original unity is now expressed in disharmony because of the effect of sin, man still retains essential unity as a framework for his personality. Therefore it is necessary that man be viewed in the curriculum in the *totality* of his personality. Learning and teaching involve the whole child in his whole environment. Still further, the psychological characteristics of the pupil should be borne in mind at each age level. They are manifested in the following areas at each level: physical, mental, social, and spiritual. The needs of man to be met through the curriculum are likewise to be focused upon these same areas. Another factor involved here is the learning process itself. The preparation of curriculum materials as well as suggestions for teaching methods are directly related to the nature of the learning process.

3. *Other Factors*

Other factors which affect the curriculum include tradition, professional leadership, public demand, the influence of secular education, and the use of the scientific method. *Tradition* is a force which safeguards society from radical changes. It operates according to the laws of habit. It is the easiest course to follow generally, so that new lines of procedure are slow in coming. In spite of new advances in theory, tradition still plays a large part in both the fields of secular education and Christian education. For example, for centuries Hebrew, Greek, and Latin were held in the curriculum by tradition. Now there is a movement away from this practice.

Another factor is *professional leadership.* In secular education the influence of this factor is manifested in the part played by professional organizations of education, such as the N.E.A., departments of education in colleges and universities, and publications. In Christian education it can be seen in the influence exerted by clergymen, various professional organizations in the church, such as the National Council of Churches of Christ in America, the various denominational boards, the schools, colleges, seminaries, and departments of religious education. There is no doubt that such leadership is imperative for the field of education in providing technical knowledge of materials, scientific knowledge of pupils, and accurate information on the problems and needs of society. But there are dangers, too, dangers of losing touch with the people and of formulating aims which do not actually meet the needs.

Public demand is also a large factor to be considered in curriculum construction. Evidence for this is found in the fact that great reform movements have often come up from the people. Changes are often demanded by many people working together. This is particularly effective in secular education. An example of this is the change from the methods of mental discipline so long used in the public school system. Public pressure through the school boards in demanding that courses be liberalized and modernized was sufficient to make the change in the long run. The same is true in politics and government. Although the methods of procedure perhaps would be a little different in the church, yet it is possible that group pressure can result in curriculum changes in Christian education. This is particularly true in church-related schools.

The *influence of public education* on Christian education has clearly affected curriculum construction. Through research and experimentation public education has made great strides. Backed financially by the state, public education has set up standards and demanded adherence to them, whereas Christian education is largely voluntary, unpaid, and, in too many instances, fragmentary. In spite of this, curriculum experts in the church have been deeply affected by the viewpoints of secular educators. Evidence of this can be seen in a number of places represented by the following list: (1) the child is the central factor in curriculum planning, (2) the socialized curriculum aids the school in fulfilling its function, (3) the curriculum must be graded, (4) the materials of the curriculum must come from many sources, (5) the curriculum must be as broad as the interests, relations, and activities of the pupils in school, and (6) teacher training is imperative.

One last factor to be mentioned is the *influence of the scientific method.* The effect of this method has been largely present more so among liberal religious educators than among evangelicals. It must be admitted, however, that many evangelicals have come to appreciate the values of this method more in recent years. To them, however, it is not a means of discovering God's truth, but it serves rather in the area of the application of that truth. It is useful in implementing the improvement of methods as well.

4. *Organization of the Curriculum*

Still another outstanding factor which affects curriculum construction is that of organization. Organization refers to the plan or arrangement of materials for the teaching-learning process. Organization becomes pertinent at three levels of manipulation by the teacher: (1) it can refer to the curriculum as a whole, (2) to individual units or courses within the curriculum, and (3) to lessons within the individual units and courses. At this point, we are interested in the curriculum as a whole.

In meeting this problem, *secular education* has formulated three general approaches. In essence, these approaches are three *pure* forms of organization. While it is recognized that in actual practice, no pure form exists, in general all forms of organization are evaluated by them. As listed by Smith, Stanley, and Shores, the three pure forms of curriculum organization are: (1) subject, (2) activity, and (3) core.[4] Each of these forms has distinctive characteristics of its own. The *subject organization* restricts the learning process to indoctrination. The *activity organization* has been sponsored largely by John Dewey and emphasizes learning through activities characterized by saying, making, finding out, and creating. The method stressed here is that of problem solving. The *core organization* places emphasis on social values with the solution of social problems forming the method. This form of organization has had a variety of developments in recent years, chief of which include the following approaches: (1) unified courses as primary categories, (2) the cultural-history core, (3) the adolescent needs core, (4) the children's needs and interest core, (5) the social-functions core, (6) the social-problems core, (7) the community school, and (8) the experimental approach. Perhaps the latest development has been that of the social-reconstruction approach.

In the field of *religious education,* the problem of organization has been deeply affected by the various approaches in secular education. In general, however, there have been four major theories of curriculum organization used in this field: (1) haphazard organization, (2) chronological organization, (3) logical organization, and (4) psychological organization. In the *haphazard* plan, it is quite evident that there is no fixed formula. In fact, there is no plan at all. No consideration is given to the needs of the pupil, nor to the quality of materials produced. Any organization realized takes place accidentally. In the *chronological* plan, the historical development of Christian truth is followed. The facts are mastered as we go along. In the *logical* plan of organization, the importance of materials is stressed. Deductive analysis guides the whole procedure. In the *psychological* plan, the point of view and needs of the learner are the important items. Psychological organization starts with that which is nearest the learner in interest, need, grasp, and perhaps proximity. The psychological approach tends to become more logical as the mind matures.

⁴Smith, Stanley and Shores, *Op. Cit.,* p. 373.

In general, there are certain *spiritual factors* which directly affect the organization of a genuine Christian curriculum. First and foremost is the strategic position of the Word of God. The true Bibliocentric approach, however, is not to be narrowly conceived in intellectual terms. Broadly considered, it includes both the cultural and spiritual aspects of Christian experience. It includes subject matter and pupil experience. It provides balance by recognizing the factors inherent in curriculum theory which are genuinely Christian. These factors include the Bible, the pupil, society, and Jesus Christ. It also observes that the great objective is the whole-person-in-life obeying God and living for Him on this basis. Still further, it recognizes the New Testament Pattern provided by the Church as embracing four major factors which should be inherent in the pattern of organization: (1) evangelism, which includes Christian experience, (2) education, which embraces knowledge and instruction, (3) edification, which includes worship, and (4) enthusiasm, which embraces the social aspects to be manifested by fellowship, social life, and recreation.

More specifically, curriculum organization takes the form of a *bibliocentric pattern*. Here the courses of study are organized around the core of Biblical truth to realize the ideal of integration and correlation. This view will be more adequately dealt with in a section which follows.

C. The Content of the Curriculum

1. *Subject Matter — a Definition*

In secular education, subject matter is thought of as a part of the culture. It consists of what men know and believe, their values and loyalties, not things or objects but knowledge *about* them.[5]

Smith has classified subject matter into four general categories: (1) general and specialized, referring to group life, (2) descriptive, consisting of facts and principles, (3) normative, providing norms and standards, and (4) subject content, the organization of core ideas for instruction.[6]

The *Christian* concept is comprehensive enough to embrace both cultural *and* spiritual elements of society. Subject matter, therefore, consists of both the cultural and spiritual products of man in organized form. These products are the fruit of the cultural and spiritual activities of men through the ages. They are used as mediums of instruction. Thus, the various bodies of knowledge are variously organized to become the curriculum content of the schools. This is the result of man's *cultural activity*.

The spiritual is also a source for subject matter materials. The

[5]*Ibid.*, p. 273.
[6]*Ibid.*, p. 274-78.

spiritual products have come to man through creation by God. They are composed of His Word, the life and ministry of Jesus Christ, the Bible, and the Work of the Holy Spirit. The responses of man to these spiritual products compose his *spiritual activity.*

Thus, the Christian engages in both cultural and spiritual activity. He is *in* the world and involved in its activities, but he is not *of* the world. His spiritual activity gives direction to his cultural activity. However, it is the cultivation of spiritual activity in the midst of cultural activity which provides the primary problem for the Christian educator in formulating the Christian curriculum.

2. *Objectives of Curriculum Materials*

In secular education, the ultimate goal of subject matter is social adjustment and reconstruction. To the Christian this is fragmentary. To him, both cultural and spiritual activities have a common end for the pupil. This end is twofold in its application: (1) to realize and manifest the authority of Christ, and (2) to realize the end of Christian or heavenly citizenship. The purpose of subject matter, then, to the Christian is to accomplish this twofold end: (1) to help the Christian fill his place in the *cultural world* and to make Christ effective in it, and (2) to help the Christian in his *spiritual activity* to have fellowship with God. The great overall objective in the whole process is "that the man of God may be perfect, throughly furnished unto all good works" (II Timothy 3:17). Here it is at once apparent just how practical lesson materials can be. To the teacher, they provide the basis for being selective from the vast range of Christian experience as recorded in the Bible. They also provide him with a sound basis for interpretation. Another advantage is the fact that they are often organized into teaching units, having comprehensiveness, balance, sequence, and age-group gradation. They provide guide lines for the teacher, thus making him far more efficient in preparation and presentation than otherwise. They also promote teacher growth. In addition, there are many advantages for the pupil which include information, motivation, direction, and appreciation.

3. *Criteria for Subject Matter Selection*

In *secular education,* the criteria for content selection are of necessity confined *within* the culture situation. Smith, Stanley and Shores have offered the following criteria for the selection of subject matter.

1. Is the subject matter significant to an organized field of knowledge?
2. Does the subject matter stand the test of survival?
3. Is the subject matter useful?

4. Is the subject matter interesting to the learner?
5. Does the subject matter contribute to social reconstruction?
6. Is the subject matter in line with the democratic ideal?[7]

The *Christian* does not rely entirely on such criteria as listed above. The primary criterion to him is that of heavenly citizenship as recorded in the Bible. Materials should be selected which will cultivate this citizenship. He takes from the cultural and spiritual products those things which energize, direct, and form the learner on his level unto the citizenship of heaven. Without this citizenship-destiny, the curriculum cannot truly be educational. Without a consideration of the level on which it is to be given, it cannot take into account the whole man. Furthermore, curriculum materials should be selected to insure for the Christian a victory over evil in the culture setting, and a victory which is freely chosen. Still further, as heavenly citizens *here*, pupils are called upon to be workers. Therefore, the curriculum materials are to be chosen in view of the various callings of life.

4. *Procedure for Selection*

In *secular education*, the procedure for the selection of materials for subject matter is directed by the aims of education, also through a process of experimentation, or by a job analysis, and quite often by consensus.

In *religious education*, such principles have been clearly formulated by the Special Committee on the Curriculum Guide of the Division of Christian Education of the National Council of Churches of Christ in the U.S.A.

The following principles should govern the choice, adaptation, or creation of curriculum materials in the local church:

1. Curriculum decisions should be made subject to the approval of the Committee on Christian Education, the Workers' Conference, or some other responsible and authoritative group in the local church, not by individual teachers or superintendents acting independently of the rest of the church school.
2. Suggested adaptations or variations from the denominational curriculum pattern should be carefully studied in the light of the total purpose and plan of the curriculum and its comprehensiveness, balance, and sequence of courses.
3. Resource materials should be selected because of their effectiveness in helping teachers to lead their pupils into appropriate experiences in terms of the ultimate objectives for Christian education, as adopted by the local church.
4. Before deciding on variations from the approved denominational curriculum, and its particular resource materials, care should be taken to determine whether the greater need may not be for:

[7]*Ibid.*, Ch. 12.

a. more help to teachers in planning their class procedures;
b. more help to teachers in relating lesson content to the actual needs, interests, and experiences of their pupils;
c. more supplementary materials for pupils and teachers.

5. Keep careful records of all adaptations and variations from the basic curriculum plan so that important phases of development will not be neglected.[8]

In the final analysis, the true *Christian approach* must be governed by Christian aims and objectives, by the needs of the *whole* man, and be judged by Biblical criteria.

5. *Areas of Subject Matter Content in Secular Education*

In the beginning the subject matter content of the average school curriculum was comparatively simple. The history of the American school curriculum, however, reveals the vast expansion in that regard at the present time. Pupils cannot hope to cover the fields of knowledge now at their disposal in the short time given to school work. Instead, there must now be of necessity limitation of consideration to minimum essentials plus areas of specialization. An example of this is found in the average high school curriculum today. Pupils may choose a terminal course in vocational education, or pursue a college-preparatory course. In some places now a course in general education has been added.

The ramifications of the curriculum on the college and university level are so vast at the present time that it would not be practical to give an example. One has only to consult one of the thousands of catalogs and bulletins of present day schools of higher education to get an indication of the development of the curriculum at this level. Provided below, however, are two examples of the typical situation to be found in a present day elementary and high school curriculum.

The content of the average elementary school in this country may be seen from the typical grade placement of subjects used in many schools today as follows:

Grade 1	Grade 2	Grade 3	Grade 4
Reading	Reading	Reading	Reading
Numbers	Numbers	Arithmetic	Arithmetic
Writing	Writing	Writing	Writing
Music	Music	Music	Music
Art	Art	Art	Art
Physical Ed. and Health	Physical Ed. and Health	Physical Ed. and Health	Physical Ed. and Health
Social Studies and Science	Spelling	Spelling	Spelling
	Social Studies and Science	Social Studies and Sciences	History
			Science
			English
			Civics

[8]Quoted from *A Guide to Curriculum in Christian Education*, p. 84, published by the National Council of Churches. Copyright 1955. Used with permission.

Grade 5	Grade 6	Grade 7	Grade 8
Reading	Reading	Reading	Reading
Arithmetic	Arithmetic	Arithmetic	Arithmetic
Writing	Writing	Writing	Writing
Music	Music	Music	Music
Art	Art	Art	Art
Physical Ed. and Health	Physical Ed. and Health	Physical Ed. and Health	Physical Ed. and Health
Spelling	Spelling	Spelling	Spelling
History	History	Science	Science
English	Science	English	English
Science	English	Geography	Geography
Geography	Geography	Literature	Literature
		State or Local History	State or Local History
		Home Ec.	Home Ec.
		Shop	Shop

In a *typical high school* the grade placement of subjects today looks like the following:

Freshman	Sophomore	Junior	Senior
Physical Ed.	Physical Ed.	Physical Ed.	Physical Ed.
Music	Music	Music	Music
English I	English II	English III	English IV
Gen. Math.	Foreign Language	Foreign Language	Geometry II
Algebra I	Algebra I & II	Geometry I	Trigonometry
General Science	Biology	Chemistry	Physics
Home Ec. I	Home Ec. II	Home Ec. III	Social and Ec. World problems
Community Civics	World History	American History	Gen. Shop III
	Geography	World History	Voc. Courses
	General Shop I	General Shop II	Shorthand II
	Typing I	Vocational Courses	Typing II
		Typing I & II	
		Shorthand I	

In some high schools pupils have access to elective subjects organized around a core program.

6. *Areas of Subject Matter Content in Christian Education*

In the field of Christian education related to the *church school*, the following areas of content have been suggested as the composition of a good curriculum:

   a. The Bible
      (1) Origin and nature of the Bible
      (2) Old Testament
      (3) New Testament
      (4) Methods of study, devotional use, and how to teach the Bible
   b. Faith or Beliefs — regarding:
      (1) God
      (2) Jesus Christ
      (3) Nature of man
      (4) Meaning of the church
      (5) Bible as source book of faith
      (6) Christianity and competing world philosophies
      (7) Christian interpretation of the universe

   c. Personal Experiences in Christian Living — such as:
     (1) Worship — personal and corporate
     (2) Health — mental and physical
     (3) Stewardship
     (4) Personal evangelism
     (5) Leisure time and recreation
     (6) Vocation — Christian approach and preparation, also challenge to church vocations
     (7) Friendship
     (8) Educational and cultural development
   d. Christian Family
     (1) Christian interpretation of sex
     (2) Preparation for marriage
     (3) Establishing Christian homes
     (4) Parenthood
     (5) Christian relationships in the home
     (6) Families in relation to the community
   e. Church Life and Outreach
     (1) Church history
     (2) Nature and program of the church
     (3) Church membership
     (4) Service in and through the church
     (5) Missionary outreach
   f. Social Problems
     (1) Amusements
     (2) Liquor and other narcotics, gambling, delinquency and crime
     (3) Race, group, and interfaith relations
     (4) Christian principles in relation to community life, the economic order, policies of business and labor, government, education, citizenship, and world order
   g. World Relations
     (1) Opportunities
     (2) World Missions
     (3) World citizenship
     (4) Ecumenical movement
   h. Service and Christian Leadership
     (1) Opportunities
     (2) Measures and preparation
     (3) Principles and objectives
     (4) Skills and methods[9]

Moving into the area of *Christian day schools,* perhaps the best statement of curriculum organization has been formulated by the Educational Committee of the National Union of Christian Schools. Here the course of study for the *elementary* school has been organized into the following subject-matter areas: Bible study, Mathematics, Language Arts, Social Science, Science, Physical Education, and the Fine Arts. The *High School* courses are very largely extension and outgrowths of the same kind of organization.[10]

[9]*Ibid.,* pp. 46-47.
[10]National Union of Christian Schools, *Course of Study for Christian Schools,* rev. ed., (Grand Rapids, Mich., Wm. B. Eerdmans Pub. Co., 1953).

In a typical *Christian Liberal Arts College,* the divisional organization of a midwestern school serves as an example.

Division I — Biblical Education and Apologetics
  Departments
    Bible and Philosophy
    Christian Education
    Archaeology
Division II — Education
  Departments
    Education and Psychology
    Home Economics
    Health and Physical Education
    Military Science
Division III — Languages and Literature
  Departments
    English
    Speech
    Foreign Languages
Division IV — Science
  Departments
    Biology
    Chemistry and Geology
    Mathematics, Physics, and Astronomy
Division V — Social Sciences
  Departments
    Economics and Business Administration
    History
    Political Science and Geography
    Sociology and Anthropology
Division VI — Fine Arts
  Departments of Music and Art
Division VII — Graduate School of Theology and Christian Education

The author discovered in a survey of Bible schools and colleges that the same typical situation prevails. Most of these schools follow the pattern laid out by secular organization.[11]

7. *Evaluation*

By application of the criteria contained in the Bible, the Christian takes the position that subject matter in the secular school is largely socially related. This is good as far as it goes, but the *whole* man is not dealt with in this situation. There are moral and

[11]Herbert W. Byrne, "A Study of Administrative Practices in Selected Bible Institutions," an unpublished doctoral dissertation in the Library of Bradley University, 1952.

spiritual aspects of truth which must be included in subject matter before it can be genuinely Christian.

In the Christian liberal arts schools and Bible schools, attempts are made to relate the subject matter content to generalizations of Christian truth. Little effort, however, has been made thus far to develop a real Bible philosophy of Christian education. The efforts that have been made may be described as *Christian-secular education*. This simply means that Christian teachers are teaching their subject matter in a secular frame of reference. Where the problem becomes most acute is in the classroom situation in the teaching process. Few Christian teachers have learned to use the implications of the Christian philosophy of life as contained in the Bible as a direct guide in the teaching-learning process. A real *Bibliocentric* course of study has yet to be developed for higher education, particularly on the college level.

8. *Steps in Course of Study Construction*

The science of education has demanded efficiency in constructing courses of study for American schools. The science of curriculum construction, therefore, has been given great consideration in recent years. Typical of secular efforts in this regard is that of Professor Nelson Bossing of the University of Minnesota, who suggested a series of steps to be followed in curriculum construction.

Step   1. A clearly Defined Conception of the Curriculum
Step   2. Statement of a Social and Educational Philosophy
Step   3. Statement of the Accepted Basic Principles of Learning
Step   4. Statement of the Aims of Education
Step   5. Scope and Areas of Curriculum and Course of Study
Step   6. Sequence and Time Allotment
Step   7. Determination of Content Materials and Activities
Step   8. Organization of Materials and Activities
Step   9. Teaching Procedures
Step 10. Evaluation Procedures
Step 11. Pupil-teacher Reference Materials
Step 12. Mechanical Makeup of the Course of Study[12]

In the field of *religious education*, the problem of curriculum construction has been met through cooperative efforts on the part of the denominations. Some denominations have united in informal cooperative efforts at planning curriculum materials. Others have worked in inter-denominational organizations. The best illustration of this is the more than 30 denominations in the United States and Canada which cooperate in making of curriculum outlines through the Commission on General Christian Education of the Division of Christian Education of the National Council of the Churches

---

[12]Nelson Bossing, *The High School Curriculum* (New York, Ronald Press), chapter 15.

of Christ. In this group, cooperation is purely voluntary and each denomination is responsible for its own curriculum. In some instances such cooperation goes beyond the creation of outlines to actual production of materials on a cooperative basis. In the case of the outlines two committees are employed for this work: (1) the Committee on the Uniform Series, and (2) the Committee on the Graded Series.

The steps through which the various committees go are outlined below in a typical process.

1. Formulation of course of study outlines from the Bible
2. The editorial process which includes:
   a. Detailed planning of materials, including quality, cost, number, etc.
   b. Selection of writers
   c. Conferences with writers
   d. Policies regarding the use of copyrighted materials
   e. Writing the curriculum units or courses
   f. Review of manuscripts
   g. Revision of manuscripts
   h. Experimentation with materials
   i. Editing for accuracy
   j. Layout
   k. Printing
3. Audio-visual additions[13]

In other areas of Christian education, the efforts at building a true bibliocentric curriculum have been few.

SUGGESTED CLASS ACTIVITIES AND PROJECTS FOR CHAPTER VI

1. Make a comparative chart which shows the various theories on the nature of the curriculum.
2. Outline the Scriptural theory of the curriculum.
3. Draw a chart to show the Christian theory of the curriculum.
4. List the various factors which must be considered in curriculum construction.
5. Draw a chart to show how you would organize subject matter according to the bibliocentric pattern.
6. Discuss the concept and problem of integration in curriculum building.
7. What is the difference between natural and supernatural interpretation?
8. Draw a chart to show the various steps necessary to construct a bibliocentric curriculum.

[13]National Council of Churches, *Op. Cit.*, Chapter 9.

THE EDUCATIVE PROCESS – METHODS

OUTLINE FOR CHAPTER 7

A. THE NATURE AND PURPOSE OF METHOD IN SECULAR EDUCATION
   1. Definition
   2. The Nature and Purpose of Methods

B. METHODS HISTORICALLY RECORDED
   1. Representative Methods of the Past
   2. Trends of the Present Day
   3. Some Present Day Methods in Secular Education

C. SECULAR METHOD PHILOSOPHICALLY CONCEIVED
   1. Naturalism
   2. Realism
   3. Pragmatism
   4. Idealism

D. THE CHRISTIAN PHILOSOPHY OF METHOD
   1. The Nature and Purpose of Method
   2. The Christian Philosophy of Method in Relation to Secular Method
   3. The Christian Concept of Method
   4. The Christian Approach to Truth
   5. Method in Religious Education
   6. Method in Christian Education

E. NEWER WAYS OF TEACHING
   1. Problems in Bible Study and Teaching
   2. The Inductive-Deductive Method
   3. Newer Ways of Teaching

F. EVALUATION OF PUPIL PROGRESS IN EDUCATION
   1. In Secular Education
   2. In Religious Education
   3. In Christian Education

7 | THE EDUCATIVE PROCESS — METHODS

A. The Nature and Purpose of Method in Secular Education

1. Definition

There are many definitions of method. This is true because one's philosophy determines his definition. Because there are varying philosophies, there are various definitions of method. Simply stated, method is an orderly, systematic procedure employed to carry out some purpose or to gain some preconceived goal. In the educational world, method involves the use of educative procedures in attaining educational goals. Such procedures fall into two main categories, administrative and instructional.

2. The Nature and Purpose of Methods

Administrative methods include those devices and processes by which classes are grouped, advanced, and dealt with in regard to abilities and capacities. Instructional methods include those devices and processes which facilitate the teaching-learning process, culminating in knowledge, habits, attitudes, and ideals. Primary emphasis, however, is given to instructional methods when dealing with methodology.

The basic problem of method concerns the shape and form in which the curriculum should be cast in order to accomplish the goals in mind. One's concept of the curriculum then largely determines his concept of the method to be employed.

There is a difference of opinion among secular educators regarding the relationship of method and curriculum. Some think that method is something which exists quite distinctly and separately from content. Others believe that the two are inseparable. For them, separation can be made only in concept, but not in practice.

The primary purpose of method in secular education is to vary the environment of the pupil with the hope that modification of the stimuli which impinge on the pupil's mind and personality will produce favorable responses in his reactions. Such a purpose is not to be conceived mechanically. Instead, the teacher must try

185

to enlist the voluntary cooperation of the pupil who does his own learning. Thus, the teacher is a guide and inspirer of the pupil.

B. Methods Historically Recorded

1. *Representative Methods of the Past*

One of the oldest and most revered of the methods is the *Socratic Method*. For a long time this method was considered an ideal one. It gets its name from the Greek philosopher Socrates who lived in the Fifth Century B.C. He employed the use of question and answer in his teaching method. He did not approach the instructional situation with answers already worked out but rather he used many questions. Once having obtained an answer he would proceed to ask more questions to test the validity of the first answer. Even when he gave answers himself Socrates generally put them in the form of questions. Thus, he became a learner along with the pupil. He believed that the function of the teacher was to help the pupil discover whatever truth he possessed. Later on, the method became known as the dialectic method.

For many years, even up through the Middle Ages, perhaps the outstanding method employed in the schools was that of *imitation and memory*. It is self-evident that this method requires a reproduction on the part of the pupil of that which is handed out to him by the teacher.

The *lecture* method arose out of the custom of the professors of medieval universities to pour out information to their students. This was necessary, of course, due to the scarcity of books. The few books which were in existence were generally in the possession of the teachers. The result was that pupils had to take notes as their teachers read or lectured from the books.

These methods largely prevailed until Erasmus began to advocate a tieing in of the subject matter with the natural interests of the pupil. He tried to motivate the curriculum by coupling it to drives already spontaneously operating. Thus, he frequently used informal talking. It was a long time, however, before this method became popular.

In the Sixteenth and Seventeeth Centuries harsh discipline was often used to ensure learning. This took two forms. One was the use of severe punishment of some sort to coerce study and learning. The second form required the student to master difficult and often disagreeable lessons, by holding him strictly to their accomplishment. It was not so important *what* the pupil learned as *how* he learned it. John Locke is said to have advocated this method.

Modern methods perhaps started with Comenius (1592-1670). He was among the first to advocate methods which appealed to the five senses. For example, he advocated the use of pictures and object lessons. His theory was based on the psychological principle of apperception which demands that the teaching process should proceed from the known to the unknown. He demanded that the known should be concrete things; it was "things" before words and examples before rules. This method had a profound influence on educators in the centuries to follow.

Rousseau (1712-1778) accepted the method of Comenius but he insisted that true education consisted less in knowing than in doing. Hence, he went on to include feelings in his method; he introduced a romantic element into method. His premise consisted of getting the pupil to want to learn. This, of course, demanded pupil freedom.

Where Comenius emphasized the physical senses and Rousseau the child's native tendencies, it remained for Pestalozzi (1746-1827) to show the teacher how to use these concepts. He stressed pupil activity through the use of object lessons and physical objects as the best way to learn and teach. The pupil must have first-hand experience with that which he is trying to learn. Thus, the pupil progressed from objects to definitions and then on to principles.

It remained, however, for Herbart (1776-1841) to place the greatest stress on the proper steps for a teacher to take in the teaching process. His method was based on association psychology and became known as the doctrine of apperception mentioned above. To ensure that apperception takes place Herbart advocated five distinct steps for the teacher to follow. The first step is *preparation* in which the teacher commences the lesson with something familiar to the class. The second step involves *presentation* of the new material to be learned. The third step is *association* which involves a comparison on the part of the pupil of the materials in the first two steps. When the pupil sees the relationships involved, he will be able to advance to a higher level represented by the new material. The fourth step involves *systematization* or *generalization* in which the teacher presents the class with similar instances involved in step three. Thus, the class is able to generalize what has been learned in that step. The fifth and final step involves *application*. This involves assignment in which the pupils are expected to practice what was learned in the first four steps.

At the dawn of the Twentieth Century there were marked tendencies to adopt some of the newer European procedures which had been developed at that time.[1] This was particularly true of the methods of Pestalozzi which were highly recommended by Horace Mann. Pupil appeal in his methods was sufficient to gain

[1] John S. Brubacher, *A History of the Problems of Education* (New York, McGraw-Hill Book Co., Inc., 1947), p. 230.

him much popularity. Some of the practices in American schools included object lessons, school museums, field trips, shop and farm work, and the inductive lesson.

Returning graduate students from German universities promulgated the Herbartian five steps as general method. Edward Thorndike adopted the Herbartian method and combined it with his scientific study of psychology. This method became a practical opportunity to translate his scientific conclusions into a practical classroom method.

Froebel's ideas on method were brought here by Germans who emigrated following the revolution of 1848. They were sponsored here very largely through the efforts of William T. Harris, one time United States Commissioner of Education. For a while this method of self-activity was limited to pre-primary education but it soon became adaptable to the manual training movement. Francis Parker advocated the use of this method in the primary and intermediate grades but with some modifications of his own. It remained, however, for self-expression and self-activity as a pedagogical method to be most strongly recommended in this century by the members of the progressive education association. Here it found expression in their educational philosophy in various forms, such as the activity school, child activity, and the activity curriculum. Freedom-loving America was the ideal setting for this emphasis on pupil freedom.

At the outset of this century new movements and developments in education began to affect methods in a new way. They included the rise of dynamic concepts of educational psychology and psychoanalysis. Gradually the effect of old world views was dissipated and American educators began to formulate their own distinctive ideas on methodology. Mann, Parker, and John Dewey began to criticize the methods arising out of German educational tradition.

2. Trends of the Present Day

At the present time, faith in any universal method in secular education seems to have waned. Some of the old methods have lost their influence. There seems to be a tendency to synthesize the best elements of those methods which have been considered the most practical. An illustration of this is the inductive-deductive method. At the present time, almost all logicians are agreed that deduction and induction are inseparable, and that the application of the one always at the same time involves the application of the other. Furthermore, it is now doubted that method can really be separated from the personality of the individual teacher. Methods are conceived as related to subject matter, the pupils, and even to the community background and viewpoints of all concerned in the method.

In the past several decades, therefore, in this country we have witnessed a marked tendency to improve the specific techniques in methods by the application of scientific methods of research and social emphases. At the present time, social reconstruction has led to an emphasis on *living* democracy instead of merely talking about it. The philosophy of experimentalism under John Dewey conceives of method as a means to this end. The "reconstruction of experience" makes method a means; but this reconstruction has no other end than "the continuous reconstruction of experience," therefore method becomes an end. This latter view is certainly definitely opposed to the Christian concept of method.

Some of the factors responsible for the present day emphasis on method have included new views on the learning process, more knowledge of the pupil, greater appreciation for individual differences, and a larger view of society. Consequently, the scientific method has played a large part in the development of these newer views on method. Now there is no one method deemed best, in spite of definite leanings toward problem-solving through the use of scientific techniques.

3. *Some Present Day Methods in Secular Education*

Some of the methods which are advocated at the present time and emphasized above others include the problem method, the project method, the unit plan, the socialized recitation, individualized instruction, supervised study, and audio-visual aids.

The problem method was submitted by John Dewey. In this method he advocated learning by doing but it was doing toward some end, not merely busy work. The consequences and outcomes of such doing were important to Dewey. Therefore, the problem method involved the systematic and intelligent and active solving of some difficulty for a specific purpose. The whole procedure will be subject to careful evaluation. This method is really another way of looking at the scientific method. Starting with a felt difficulty, the student begins to gather, organize and evaluate the facts, seeking to formulate an hypothesis, all of which is subject to evaluation of whatever conclusions might be drawn.

William Kilpatrick introduced the problem method into educational circles through emphasis on the project. This method enlarged the scope of activity beyond that of mere problem-solving and also gave greater emphasis to emotional development and appreciation. The primary difference between this method and that of problem-solving lies in the fact that the project involves a problem located in a concrete natural setting so that "the learner had to size up the situation, conceive a plan of what needed to be done, devise ways and means of manipulating materials to execute his plan, and check the results."

The unit method was advocated by Henry C. Morrison. Here stress was placed on "what" the pupil studies as well as "how." He combined the elements of Dewey and Herbart. Based on the premise that children need to master what they were studying, Morrison's formula consisted of pretesting, teaching, testing the results, making adjustments, teaching and then testing again until actual learning took place. Subject matter for study of this kind was divided into units in which concrete problems or areas of interest were present.

To overcome the tendency in the other methods to suppress the pupil and overstress the teacher, the socialized recitation was designed to develop the qualities of initiative and cooperation in a democratic and socialized setting. Informal class discussions and group activities lie at the heart of this method.

The plan for individualized instruction is based on the need for recognizing individual differences. The Dalton Plan is the outstanding example of this method. Here the student is allowed to advance at his own rate through individual study. Group activities are not neglected, but the primary emphasis lies in individual initiative and progress. Under this plan classrooms become laboratories and conference rooms and teachers become consultants.

Supervised study also recognizes individual differences and stresses the importance of study habits and techniques. Here pupils are guided individually by the teacher, both using the problem-solving ideas.

At present there is great emphasis on the use of audio-visual materials and methods. Although relatively new, the practical consequences of their use are quite apparent. These methods seem destined to remain.

C. SECULAR METHOD PHILOSOPHICALLY CONCEIVED

1. *Naturalism*

The method of naturalism is the inductive method of the natural sciences. To the naturalist this is the only method. Nature is our teacher. This method involves going from the simple to the complex, from the known to the unknown, and from the concrete to the abstract. Self-expression, self-activity, and self-discovery are at the heart of this method. Parents and teachers, therefore, must not interfere with the child so that he can grow and develop in complete freedom. To the Christian, there are values in self-denial, self-control and discipline as well as in self-expression and self-activity.

2. Realism

This view is closely related to that above. The realist virtually has no method as such. His method is the method of nature. The teacher should stick to the facts of nature. Lecturing is merely the natural way of imparting the facts of nature. He can vary his methods, but the primary aim is to induce the student to remove all subjective barriers and to throw his nervous system wide open to the objective influence of physical facts.

3. Pragmatism

The method of the pragmatist is essentially one of trial and error through the use of the scientific technique of problem solving. The aim is to turn out men who do things, not primarily placing emphasis on knowledge or contemplation. What they do is empirical, is of biological and social significance, and plays its part in influencing the course of events in the actual world.

4. Idealism

The method of the idealist is transcendental, not empirical. The method is primarily one of discussion, but lectures and experiments are found useful, all of which helps pupils share experiences with the teacher, and assists them in developing their own personalities and achieving deeper insights. Thus, idealism has a broader concept of method by asserting that it is possible to learn through other methods than the experiment. Reflection, says the idealist, on problems which cannot be proved by the experiment also have educational significance. Philosophical methods, therefore, are supplementary to the scientific techniques.

D. THE CHRISTIAN PHILOSOPHY OF METHOD

1. The Nature and Purpose of Method

To the Christian, method is the means by which the goal of Christian education is achieved. The goal of Christian education is Christlike character. In approaching this goal, the Christian educator is concerned with two facets of approach. On the *ethical* side of method, *moral discipline* is required in accomplishing the character-goal set up. On the *intellectual* side of method, *instruction* in the truth of the Gospel is required to accomplish the goal. We are using the term method in this latter sense. The purpose of Christian methodology, therefore, is to bring the pupil to a realization and experience of Christlike character and to a revelation of God. The aim of Christian education is to see God revealed; the goal of Christian education is to qualify man to reveal God. Method is the means by which these are accomplished. It is a way of doing things. Consideration of method requires one to view method from the standpoint (1) of its philosophical basis and (2) of instructional techniques.

2. *The Christian Philosophy of Method in Relation to Secular Method*

Dr. Mark Fakkema pointed out that secular education is directed in its methodology by means of natural interpretation which is manifested in two ways: (1) pupil *acquisition* through a "pouring in" process, and (2) pupil *growth* through a "drawing out" process.[2] The "pouring in" process refers to the impartation of factual knowledge on the part of the teacher who seeks to fill the mind with educational information. The "drawing out" process is consistent, Fakkema says, with the evolutionary process which emphasizes the needs of growing children. In this view, the child is given complete freedom and education is largely stimulative in character. Self-expression is encouraged. "Education should be cast in the mold of experience for experience' sake rather than experience for the sake of achievement." Advocated by John Dewey, the latter view is the dominating one at the present time. Such education, says Fakkema, leads to subjectivism, relativism, and moral delinquency.

On the one hand, the Christian observes that these methods stress *some* needs. For example, the first method emphasizes the importance of knowledge. The latter method emphasizes the importance of the child and the need for knowing the child's nature. It is quite obvious, however, that the kind of philosophy which embraces the good points of both methods is lacking.

On the other hand, there are serious objections to both of these views. The first method overstresses subject matter to the neglect of the pupil. Furthermore, the scope of this method is inherently restricted. Fakkema says that the "pouring in" process is a direct implication of the philosophy of materialism which operates completely outside the realm of morality. Ideas, he says, moral or otherwise, do not necessarily insure moral character.

The "drawing out" method has a tendency to neglect content. Fakkema says that this method underrates the values of objective truths by virtually denying their existence. Furthermore, the advocates of this theory proceed on the assumption that child nature is good. Because child nature, in reality, is not naturally good, the "drawing out" method simply projects the manifestation of evil by encouraging it. Virtually, then, this method is immoral.

The Christian educator should reject both of these views of method. The former is materialistic in nature, while the latter is

[2]Mark Fakkema, *Christian Philosophy: Its Educational Implications* (Chicago, The National Association of Christian Schools, 1952), p. 97-T.

naturalistic. Both of these philosophies are in direct opposition to the Christian Theistic World View. In doing this, both of these views deny a God-centered pattern of educational philosophy.

3. *The Christian Concept of Method*

The Christian view of method is based on supernatural interpretation. With God central in the universe, the Creator and Source of all truth, all method must also center in Him. All truth is a revelation of God, we have seen, whether it comes through general revelation (in nature) or special revelation (in the Scriptures). God is therefore directly connected with subject matter because through subject matter God is revealed. The pupil also is expected to be a revelation of God. He is to reveal God in life, experience, and conduct. Fakkema says that "educational methodology is the manner in which . . . (a) the objective revelation of God in school content (*and*) (b) the subjective revelation of God in the pupil . . . is stepped up from the nonrational level to the rational . . . level of the subject who studies."[3] This whole process is a matter of the teacher cooperating with the Holy Spirit to accomplish this glorious end. The business of the Holy Spirit is to regenerate the human heart through the work of Jesus Christ upon the cross. The teachers' responsibility is to witness by both precept and example to the God-revealing character of the subject and object. Thus, this method comprehends the good points of the two secular methods mentioned above: the importance of the subject matter and the pupil.

The Scriptural term used to describe the method explained above is that of "bringing up." Where secular education emphasizes either "pouring in" or "drawing out," Christian education stresses the values of "bringing up" the child in the nurture and admonition of the Lord. Such a view does not preclude the possibility of using various instructional procedures to accomplish this "bringing up" process. To this problem we now turn our attention.

4. *The Christian Approach to Truth*

Several ways of determining truth have been suggested. In fact, there are four possible approaches: (1) revelation alone, (2) revelation plus reason, (3) reason alone, and (4) revelation plus reason plus experimentation. Where revelation is used alone, the danger of suppressing the God-given faculty of reason is present, leading to irrationalism. Here there is no tendency to manifest a lack of faith in divine revelation. Rather, reason must supplement revelation in apprehending the revelation and applying it. Reason alone is rejected because it neglects revelation. Revelation plus reason is acceptable as far as it goes. Here the Christian bases

[3]*Ibid.*, p. 103-T.

his views on divine revelation. Faith joins with reason in accepting and using this revelation. But there are instances where experimentation has revealed truth totally beyond both reason and faith. An illustration of this is seen in the way some inventions have come to man. The principle of the steam engine came as a result of pure accident when it was observed how steam in the kettle spewed from the spout and rattled the lid. Experimentation does not *originate* truth; it merely *discovers* it. The Christian educator must maintain his confidence in revelation and reason, but he should not blind himself to the possibilities of discovering God's truth through experimentation and the use of the deductive-inductive approach to truth.

5. Method in Religious Education

In religious education, liberal educators have very largely adopted and adapted the methods advocated by the philosophy of John Dewey and experimentalism. Here problem solving and socialized instruction along with the project method have been most useful.

The adoption of both pragmatic philosophy and method in fact led to a new method in the field of religious education. This new method became known as the "growth theory." The substance of this theory is as follows. When a child is physically born, he is already in the kingdom of God. God is all of nature and the process of evolution is but His eternal working. Hence, the child, as a part of nature, is a part of God, and the proper function of religious education is so to environ the child that he may make his own unique contribution to the eternal process of which he is a part.

Thus the whole business of the child in life is "to grow"; no change of nature is necessary. The function of the teacher is simply that of a gardener, to provide food for the tender plants to grow. The child should not be bound by old dogmas, old teachings, or even old commandments. Horace Bushnell and George A. Coe advocated this theory for religious education. Coe particularly compromised with John Dewey, and as a leading advocate led the way in the use of the methods of naturalism and pragmatism.

6. Method in Christian Education

In Christian education, the deductive method was used for a long time. Today practically all the popular methods in Christian education are inductive and developmental. Actually, the approach is deductive-inductive in nature, leading toward the character development of individuals along with the acquisition of information.

Much of the inspiration for and guidance in the use of methods in Christian education was given by Jesus Christ. He used the objective method, the analytical-synthetic method, the inductive-deductive method, the method of suggestion, the Socratic method, and discipline. Other methods used today in Christian schools include memory, recitation, discussion, lecture, project, drama, and storytelling. This by no means exhausts the list. Audio-visual aids illustrate this. To the Christian, there is no one best method. A combination of methods seems to be the best overall approach.

The objective or illustrative method, as employed by Jesus, involves more than the use of object lessons as such. Where lessons in the object are confined largely to the object itself, the objective method starts with the concrete but truths derived therefrom may be either psychical or physical. It may be used for illustration or not; it may be used to deepen appreciations, or it may throw light on some deeper abstract truth. Jesus used this method to objectify spiritual truth and thereby practiced well-known psychological principles. Examples of this method as used by Jesus can be seen in His employment of current events, parables, allegories, and metaphors. He also illustrated through many other figures, such as similes, hyperboles, irony, etc. Perhaps the outstanding example He employed was when He objectified the meaning of His love for the lost by His death on Calvary's cross.

The analytic-synthetic method involves acquisition and assimilation of information. In acquisition information is received through perception, conception, and retention; in assimilation it is compared, related, and generalized. Actually, both processes are one in operation, although each may be employed separately. In dealing with the concepts of the kingdom of God, Jesus employed this method.

The inductive method of teaching proceeds from particular facts to general principles derived from the facts. Deduction begins where induction stops; it leads from the generalization to new particulars or to the application of general principles to new data. Jesus used both methods. This method will be more fully discussed in a section to follow.

Jesus employed the popular Socratic method. This, as formerly pointed out, involved the use of questions and answers. Jesus was a master in the art of questioning.

The *selection* of methods is determined by a variety of measures. The aims and objectives, the needs and ages of the pupils, the time and skill at the teacher's command, and many other factors play their part. The teacher should select methods carefully in the light of his best judgment as to how best he can deal with the subject matter, the pupil, and objectives.

Variety and correlation should direct the *use* of methods.

Again, it is the combination of methods which results in greatest fruitage. This allows for adaptability and flexibility.

E. NEWER WAYS OF TEACHING

1. *Problems in Bible Study and Teaching*

Every Christian teacher, whether he works in a Christian day school, college, or Sunday school, is anxious to teach the Word of God most effectively. We are assuming that such teachers know the Lord and the truth of the Word. We are also assuming that each comes to his task in the right spirit, with the proper concept of the task. In spite of these things, the study and teaching of the Bible is a gigantic task and there are problems to be faced. Until such problems are overcome the task of the teacher is only partially complete.

Some of the more obvious problems for the teacher include the mastery of extensive Biblical content and translations, not so much of content, as transference of exact thought. For children, there are problems of language, geography, time, grading of content to pupil level of understanding, and application of truth to life.

2. *The Inductive-Deductive Method*

Many teachers of Bible are shallow in both study and teaching techniques. A major reason for this seems to be that many of such teachers are "spoon-fed." They depend too much on commentaries, Sunday school quarterlies, and other prepared materials and thus fail to study for themselves.

The inductive-deductive method is designed to help Bible students discover truths for themselves. The principles of induction and deduction are used in correct thinking. The adaptation of scientific methods to Bible study was made by Dr. Robert A. Traina, currently professor of English Bible at Asbury Theological Seminary.[4]

The steps of this method, as listed by Professor Traina, are (1) observation, (2) interpretation, (3) evaluation and application, and (4) correlation.[5]

3. *Newer Ways of Teaching*

Because of the new developments in methods of teaching and learning, particularly in the field of early childhood development and education, our attitudes toward the ability of children to learn are changing. There is now a strong recognition that the

---

[4]Robert A. Traina, *Methodical Bible Study* (New York, The Biblical Seminary of New York, 1952).
[5]*Ibid.*, see Table of Contents.

learning capacity of the person begins at an early age — the first two years of the child's life are most significant.

Some implications of these findings are that children learn most at home from parents, and that the ways of teaching in the past have not always been compatible with the real ways that children learn. It may be helpful at this point to contrast the more traditional ways of teaching with those of the more creative ones:

Traditional	Creative
1. The teacher is teller	1. The teacher is guide
2. The pupil listens	2. The pupil discovers
3. Content — stresses facts	3. Stresses principles
4. Methods — story-telling and lecture	4. Methods — discussion, play, many activities, groupings
5. Physical arrangement — in rows	5. Variety — small and large groups; circle arrangements; activities

The utilization of the newer methodologies calls for restructuring organizational patterns, developing leadership skills, improving organizational units, expanding leadership and teacher-training programs.

F. Evaluation of Pupil Progress in Education

1. *In Secular Education*

Both teachers and pupils are interested in knowing about their progress. The teacher is particularly interested in finding out if goals are being achieved, if the quality of the pupil's work is acceptable, and if the quantity of work done is sufficient. Other reasons for evaluation include the teacher's knowledge of the areas in which student growth and development have been adequate, the places where difficulties have arisen, and motivation.

Some forms of measurement have been used all along in education. Methods have progressed through the stages of oral and written examinations to the modern testing movement. With the rise of scientific and educational psychology, quantitative measurements came into use, beginning about 1880. The Twentieth Century has witnessed the greatest development of educational tests. Gradually the emphasis has shifted from testing to evaluation. Where tests placed emphasis primarily on knowledge, evaluation is more concerned with progress toward desirable goals. Tests are included in evaluation but the teacher is not limited to their uses. Pupil responses can be observed and judged by the teacher. Where tests are objective, pupil responses are subjective. Other techniques of evaluation include teacher observation of the pupil's reaction to work and fellow students, questions, and general observation on attitudes, habits, appreciations, etc.

The general *principles* of evaluation include (1) observation of the amount, quality, and direction of pupil progress toward the goals of education, (2) evaluation is a continuous process, and (3) evaluation should embrace the *whole* pupil.

The various *aids* to evaluation include tests, both written and oral, daily participation and recitation, anecdotal records, oral and written reports, notebooks, and score cards.

The various *types* of tests include mental tests, educational tests, embracing achievement tests, survey tests, diagnostic tests, and aptitude tests. The latter are available in the fields of mathematics, stenography, and mechanics. "Interest" tests are used to aid vocational choices.

Tests of mental capacity attempt to discover the degree of potential ability or native ability which an individual possesses. General intelligence tests fall into this category, as do more specific tests of psychological functions such as memory tests, tests of observation, tests of imagery, and many others. The purpose of such tests is to secure a cross section view of the individual's powers at the present time.

Aptitude tests attempt to secure information concerning actual skills, knowledges, and interests which, together with knowledge of specific potentialities, may aid in guiding the individual in his life's work.

Achievement tests are illustrated by tests given in the various subject matter areas. In other words, they are tests of mastery, how much a person has achieved in a certain field of endeavor. Some of these tests are tests of speed and quality. For example, both speed of work and quality of work in arithmetic, reading, handwriting, and similar skills may be tested.

General survey tests are used to discover a person's general potentiality in the light of his success with specific items in a field of study or his intelligence as a whole. A general intelligence test is one illustration of this. Similarly, an arithmetic test which covers the whole field is another illustration.

Diagnostic tests are designed to make intensive analyses of specific habits or abilities. They not only reveal whether a person is good or poor but also exactly where his excellence or deficiency lies. Prognostic tests are similar tests but used for purposes of predicting a person's success or failure in a certain field.

The characteristics of a good evaluation instrument include validity, reliability, objectivity, ease of scoring, and ease of administration. Validity refers to the ability of a test to measure well what it is supposed to measure. Reliability reveals the consistency with which a test measures its accuracy. When human judgment and opinion are absent from test scores, test makers call this objectivity. Miscellaneous characteristics of good tests include good norms, good appearance, good materials, quality of paper and print.

There are a variety of test forms which a teacher can use. These include short-answer items, long-answer items, true-false tests, completion items, multiple-choice items, and matching items.

Several methods of reporting evaluations are used in secular schools. One is the percentage plan based on a maximum of 100 points. Here the teacher is faced with making the distinctions, such as an 85 or 86, when assigning pupil marks. A second method is grading by letters, such as A, B, and C, where the *position* of students in relation to fellow students is used. A third procedure is called individual evaluation. Here the pupil's work is not compared with an arbitrary standard or the average achievement of his fellows. Instead, the question is asked: "To what extent is the pupil working up to his full capacity?" If the pupil is doing what is expected of him, his marks will likely be high. Others receive relative marks according to their efforts. Marks may be in terms of letters or written statements. The tendency at the present is to discard the use of symbols. Obviously, there are advantages and disadvantages to all of these methods. It is quite evident, too, that there is a great deal of subjectivity on the part of teachers in awarding the marks. Today, efforts to measure the whole child are being stressed. There is much to be done in this field, however.

Philosophically conceived, the *realist* is interested in objective results. All methods of measurement and evaluation to him must be objective. Since the *idealist* is interested in subjectivity, his methods will combine both emphases, giving primary concern to the latter. To him, qualities of mind are more important than exact reproduction of facts. The *pragmatist* will generally agree with the realist in practice. In theory, however, he does not place as much importance on measurement. He is interested in problem solving. The total situation is more important to him than one facet of it as expressed through tests and measurements.

2. *In Religious Education*

The advocates of religious education have stressed the importance of measurements and evaluation. Led by liberal theologians, who were members of the Religious Education Association and more recently of the National Council of the Churches of Christ in America, this group has had more to say in this regard than any other group perhaps in religious circles. While they recognized the difficulties involved in the use of objective tests in the realm of religion and character education, nevertheless they have made a definite effort to use the techniques. They have been guided largely by the advances in the field of secular education. The latest ideas were published recently by the Division of Christian Education of the National Council of Churches of Christ of America in the booklet entitled *Evaluation and Christian Education.* To test factual information about the Bible and Christianity, the usual objective tests as developed in secular education directed the pattern of testing. These include true-false, multiple choice, completion, essays, etc. Now more subjective methods are undergoing experimentation.

To test beyond factual information it is not possible to use objective tests. Instead, evaluative questions are designed for use by teachers and pupils to ascertain attitudes, appreciations, habits, personality development and growth, personal and social relations. Through observation, conversation, and counsel with the pupils, friends, and families, some kind of evaluation may be indicated and information provided which will help pupils and teachers chart the progress which is made. Although one may question just how reliable and valuable such information may be, yet this is certainly to be commended as an effort in the right direction.

3. *In Christian Education*

Measurement and evaluation in the ranks of Christian education has been and is a "weak sister." Most of the practices which are used at present follow the procedures listed in the fields of secular education and religious education. This is a vast field of research for evangelical scholars. It is certainly an area which provides a prime example that the area of experimentation gives one an opportunity to discover many of God's great truths. Where there *are* practices in evangelical Christian education, the general characteristic to be observed is the fact that most of the testing stays close to the Bible. Little work, if any, in the field of personality and character development has been sponsored by this group.

There are many good reasons why Christian educators need to test their teaching. First, they should be interested in whether or not they have reached their objectives (Galatians 6:4; I Thessalonians 5:2). Second, testing, used correctly, can be used to stimulate pupils to a greater interest in learning. In the third place, the Christian teacher is interested in the quality of work done. The greatest reason, however, lodges in the fact that the Christian teacher is interested above all in what the pupil does with Christian truth after he leaves the classroom, whether or not it issues in Christian character and conduct. The forms of testing may well follow those listed in the sections above. The areas in which testing should be used are in the realm of content, Bible knowledge, comprehension, attitudes, choices, conduct and character. Such a program can be justified in the light of the need of improvement which now exists in our ranks, the dearth of Bible and spiritual knowledge, and the seriousness of the task at hand. Until such time as improvements and changes are made, the traditional pattern of reporting evaluations by grades and marks will continue.

The Christian educator recognizes the value of tests and measurements, but in the final analysis the interests of the pupil himself are paramount. Teachers, therefore, will supplement test results with personal judgments and will be careful to evaluate pupils beyond the scope of mental accomplishment. Tests can be used as means to an end, as leads, as evidence of trends, but not as final determinants. The Christian teacher should not blind himself to the fact that life itself provides an education.

SUGGESTED CLASS ACTIVITIES AND PROJECTS FOR CHAPTER VII

1. List the methods employed by great teachers of the past.
2. List some of the new methods developed within this century.
3. Make a chart to show the position of the various philosophies on method.
4. Discuss the implications of the terms "pouring in," "drawing out," and "bringing up."
5. Discuss the relation between reason and revelation in the Christian approach to truth.
6. Outline the concept of the "growth theory" as practiced in religious educational circles.
7. Write a paper or give an oral report on the "Methods of Jesus."
8. Discuss fully the nature and implications of the inductive-deductive method in Christian education.
9. Discuss the comparative values of objective and essay examinations.
10. What tests are suitable for religious education?

THE SCHOOL SYSTEM

OUTLINE FOR CHAPTER 8

A. THE ORGANIZATION OF SECULAR EDUCATION
  1. National Organization of Education
  2. State Systems of Education
  3. Local Systems of Organization
  4. Higher Education

B. THE ORGANIZATION OF CHRISTIAN EDUCATION
  1. The Home
  2. The Church
  3. The School
  4. The Christian Day School
  5. Higher Education

C. THE NATURE AND FUNCTION OF SECULAR SCHOOL ADMINISTRATION
  1. Definition
  2. Function

D. ADMINISTRATION PHILOSOPHICALLY CONCEIVED
  1. Realism
  2. Idealism
  3. Pragmatism
  4. Christian Theism

E. A BIBLIOCENTRIC PATTERN FOR SCHOOL ADMINISTRATION
  1. Philosophical Basis
  2. General Administration and Control
  3. Business and Finances
  4. Academic Administration
  5. Personnel Administration
  6. Student Personnel
  7. Public Relations
  8. Worship

8 | THE SCHOOL SYSTEM

A. The Organization of Secular Education

1. National Organization of Education

Four major governmental divisions participate in the organization and administration of American education. First is the role of the *federal* government. The United States does not have a national system of education because the present policy is to make the second division, the *States,* dominantly responsible for education within their borders. Within the state are *county* and *township* types of organizations. In some states, the county is the smallest unit; in others there are even smaller units within the county which control local units of education.

Although it has been the tendency to place responsibility primarily for education at the local level, there has always been federal concern for education. This is seen first of all by the mention of education in the Constitution which provides for State control. In spite of this, however, the national government has participated at great length both legally and financially in the development of American education.

The chief centralizing agency in education on the national level is the United States Office of Education. The primary purposes of this department are to gather information about the nation's schools, disseminate this information, and promote the general cause of education throughout the land. Recently in 1951 this office was re-organized into three divisions: (1) State and local school systems, (2) vocational education, and (3) higher education.

The United States Commissioner of Education is appointed by the President on a bipartisan basis. The duties of this officer are to see that the above functions of the Office of Education are carried out and to make an annual report to the Congress.

The national government has provided federal aid to education from time to time. Such aid has taken the form of federal land grants for education, money grants to states, and various acts of Congress to facilitate the work of education across the country. Special areas which have been given attention include agriculture, vocational education, handicapped persons, home economics, teacher training, etc. The school lunch program is another prime example. There is an increasing tendency in the present day for more federal participation in education, but there is evident opposition from many sources.

2. *State Systems of Education*

The Constitution makes the States responsible for the education of the people. There is marked variety, however, in the ways the states carry out this responsibility. There are certain general patterns of organization to be noted, however.

Most of the states have what they call State Boards of Education. The major purposes of this group are to coordinate, supervise, and administer the state program of education. It is the central body for the promotion of education within the state and is subject to the state legislature.

The duties of these boards are various and many. Sometimes they include general supervision of the entire public school system. In other instances their duties are restricted to certain types of education and to higher education. In many states, this board appoints the state superintendent of education. Budgets are prepared by the State superintendent, approved by the board, and then sent on to the legislature for approval.

The work of the State superintendent is to gather and compile educational statistics. He may assist the legislature with proposed school measures. Publications are issued from his office on school matters and problems. State funds for schools are allocated and often distributed through his office. He meets with various state boards and attends conferences. In some states, teacher certification is a responsibility of this officer. In others the county superintendent has delegated power to perform this function.

The superintendent also works as head of the state department of education in many states. The department is made up of various divisions which represent elementary, secondary, higher education, and a staff. The primary concern of the department is instruction. A great many responsibilities concern the work of the superintendent.

3. *Local Systems of Organization*

Education began as a local institution, and in spite of state and national developments, the local units have not ceased to operate. Most of the states have *county* units of organization. Where the county acts, it usually does so through a county Board of Education. This board exercises general control over the schools within its bounds. In many of these instances there is a county superintendent. Through his office the money for county schools flows. In some states teacher certification for the county is located here. His duties include the interpretation of school laws, technical advisor to local boards, supervisor of the accrediting program, and representative of the state department.

Townships embrace a geographical area of 36 square miles. In densely populated areas the township is a practical unit for school administration. A township board of education performs much the same function as a county board.

Local school boards see that the laws of the state are applied to the local schools. Members are elected by the voters of the district. A board of seven members seems typical. The local superintendent is the executive officer of the board. He has the responsibility of the general administration, organization, and supervision of the local school system including teacher selection, supplies, and equipment. The organization of the local school is made complete by the principals, teachers, and staffs.

4. *Higher Education*

Traditionally, the scope of higher education embraces four years of college or university beyond high school and from one to three years of graduate work. There is a tendency today to regard the scope of secondary education as inclusive to the first two years in college, with the senior college years and graduate work considered in the bracket of higher education. There is also a trend toward additional work after the doctor's degree in some of the professional areas of study such as medicine and dentistry.

Schools in the bracket of higher education are controlled by both public and private sources. The marked tendency, however, is to lean toward private control, certainly freedom of sponsorship. Although the number of private institutions has exceeded that of the public institutions, the enrollments have been about the same. The G.I. bills for veterans helped to increase sharply the enrollments of colleges and universities. There is still expected a sharp increase all along the line in this bracket in the years to come.

Accreditation is an important factor in higher education. The entire United States is covered by a network of state and regional associations, which have six geographical divisions: New England, Middle States, Southern, North Central, Northwest, and Western. More than 100 nationwide organizations, such as the National Commission for Accreditation of Teacher Education, and the National Commission on Accrediting certify institutions in all states. The present tendency among accrediting bodies is to shift from quantitative to qualitative standards, or a synthesis of both, in evaluating the various institutions.

Beside public and private institutions there are many classifications of institutions of higher education in this country. In the main, however, the following institutions are most prevalent: (1) junior colleges, (2) liberal arts colleges, (3) municipal colleges and universities, (4) community or technical colleges, (5) general colleges, (6) universities, (7) land-grant colleges and universities, (8) professional schools, (9) graduate schools, and (10) other institutions of higher learning. Generally speaking, a college is an institution with a four-year general course leading to A.B. or B.S. degrees. A university has, in addition to the undergraduate non-specialized division, a graduate program and specialized professional schools on the graduate level. Obviously, there are many variations within these levels. Other institutions of higher education in this country include such federal institutions as the Military Academy at West Point, New York, the Naval Academy at Annapolis, and the Coast Guard Academy at New London, Conn. Other types of schools include summer schools, extension schools, and correspondence schools.

B. The Organization of Christian Education

1. *The Home*

Christian education begins in the home as the basic unit of society. The Christian believes that education is not restricted to the public school system. The Bible points to the home as the basic educational institution (Deuteronomy 11:18, 19; Ephesians 6:4). Parents have been obligated by God to see that their children are properly cared for and educated. There are four agencies which bear the responsibility of educating the child — the home, the church, the school, and the state. Actually, there is only one agency — the home — while the others are assistants in this responsibility. Teachers stand in the position of *loco parentis* and thereby have delegated responsibility to assist parents in the great task of educating the children.

In spite of delegated responsibility, the school still stands secondary to the home in providing advantages for the education of children. The early years of child life are the most impressionable ones. The influence of the parents provides an unmatched teaching situation. The attitudes of the family members make deep impressions. The natural teaching situations of the home make learning both natural and easy. The security and love of the parents make learning assured.

To carry out its primary responsibility, parents must make sure that the home is really Christian. This calls for Christian experience and conduct on the part of the parents. The Bible and prayer must be central in home teachings on religion. Evangelism must be a definite part of the teaching process. There must be Christian service and training for all members of the family.

Some of the specific responsibilities borne by the Christian home in the moral and spiritual education of its children include the manifestation of Christian attitudes, the sharing of duties in Christian living, Christian conversation, family worship as expressed in grace at the table, bedside prayers, and general prayer periods, and guidance in Bible study. Attendance at public worship services and Sunday school services are also additional avenues of training and service.

The home must look to other institutions as allies in the great task of education. The first one, and most important in many respects, is the Christian church.

2. *The Church*

Although the Scriptures place primary responsibility for the children's welfare upon the parents, nevertheless they do not prohibit the church from engaging in both theological and general education. The church becomes the ally to the home in the education of children.

First among the institutions sponsored by the church is that of the *Sunday school.* While it is recognized that the Sunday school has some weaknesses, this institution has played a tremendous part in the Christian education of children. Perhaps the most outstanding function of the Sunday school, overlooked by many church members, is that of evangelism. It is common knowledge now that the great majority of church members and conversions take place in the ranks of the Sunday school. Furthermore, it is a place for growth in Christian knowledge and character. It is a training station, preparing its membership for service in building the Kingdom of God. Through its various classroom procedures, expressional activities, and official functions, it provides many worthwhile situations for both personal and social growth and development. One can note the testimonies of thousands of people to the effect that the Bible and the Sunday school have meant much in the shaping of their character. By establishing right attitudes toward the total environment and by facilitating the individual's adjustment to the will of God, the Sunday school makes it possible for the individual to develop a Christian philosophy of life. Thus, the Sunday school has the function of developing the spiritual nature of its pupils from the standpoint of psychology, sociology, ethics, and theology.

The pattern by which the Sunday school works in setting up and operating its program, as indeed the whole church does, is recorded for us in Acts 2:41, 42 — evangelism, education, worship, and fellowship. Here is a comprehensive program which includes the seeking and the saving of souls, the instruction of those souls in the Christian life and viewpoint, the guidance of souls in worship, and the development of souls in Christian service and fellowship. Here the educational function is broader than instruction. It also includes training, organization, administration, and supervision. The evangelistic function embraces missions and outreach as well as soul winning. Educationally, the church is not only interested in its internal affairs and pupils. It also seeks to extend the influence of its teachings to the community. It is interested in its membership living the things which are taught. The program of Christian education and the Gospel must be relevant to local conditions.

The church also educates through its various organizations. These include the choirs, men's groups, women's groups, children's groups, the youth fellowship, vacation Bible school, weekday religious education, social and recreational groups. Actually, all groups educate. The various committees, the staff, and various promotional techniques all contribute to the instructional situation. The entire organization and all the activity should be guided by a consistent, Scriptural, and comprehensive philosophy of Christian education.

The Church should be organized not only that it may be comprehensive in the *content* of its program as mentioned above, but it should also include the *entire* congregation and *all groups* within the congregation in its scope. At the denominational level there will be a special Board of Christian education. At the local congregational level there will be the same kind of a Board. The work of this Board will be integrated and correlated with the various other boards of the church. A unified program of Christian education will be provided under the leadership of this Board. Its primary responsibility is to create and see that the educational policies of the church are carried out.

Branching out beyond the confines of the local church and denomination, there are national groups and associations which are engaged in Christian education. Representing the *liberals* and *neo-orthodox* groups are the Division of Christian Education of the National Council of Churches of Christ in America, and the character education movement sponsored by Ernest M. Ligon of Union College. Among *evangelicals* the Evangelical Teacher Training Association and the National Sunday School Association are being widely used in bringing about a real Sunday school revival. In addition to the preaching ministry, the Bible Conference movement throughout the world has made great contributions to Evangelical Christian education. Various youth movements, such as

Youth for Christ, the Inter-Varsity Christian Fellowship, Child Evangelism Fellowship, Incorporated, and Young Life Crusade have made significant contributions. In spite of these developments, there is still much ground to cover.

3. *The School*

The Christian thinks of the school as an ally of the home in Christian education. The reason for this is the fact that the process of education has become so vast and extensive that it is not possible for parents to accomplish the results desired. The teacher, therefore, stands in *loco parentis*. The school helps the home. Today evangelical Christians are facing a crisis in education. There are three possible avenues through which they may have their children educated. They are (1) the public school, (2) parochial schools, and (3) private schools.

The Christian recognizes the importance of the public school and its strategic place in a democracy. He decries, however, the secularism and naturalism which have permeated the total structure of this system of education. He laments the fact that the Bible and its teaching are left out of his child's education in the public school. He desires, in many cases, to turn elsewhere for what he considers the right kind of education. Where Christian parents are depending upon the public school system, they have to take particular pains at home and in the church to supplement this education with spiritual training. The danger involved is that the influence of the home will be overwhelmed by the social pressure and secular tendencies of the public school. The program of the public school in itself is not too bad but it is what is left out that counts.

Parochial schools are popular with Catholics and Lutherans. It is doubtful, however, if these schools will ever be widely supported among Protestants and Evangelical Christians.

The third alternative for Christians is the private school of the independent type, either of the boarding school nature or the parent-controlled day school patterned after the public school. The boarding school has been influential in the past, but at the present time such schools are few in number.

4. *The Christian Day School*

Background and Trends. A relatively new educational development has taken place in America in the rise of the Christian Day School Movement. These schools made their appearance around World War II.

A report from Mr. Robert L. Lamborn, Executive Director of the Council for American Private Education, indicates that there are about 20,250 private elementary and secondary schools in this country, half of which are Catholic. All told, they enroll about four and one-half million students. Most of these schools are to be found in the heavily populated areas of the country where most supporting churches are located. California, New York, Pennsylvania, Illinois, and Michigan are leading states in enrollment. Nationally, such schools enroll more students than colleges and universities.

Elmer Towns in an article entitled "Explosion of Christian Day Schools" in *Christian Life* magazine, June 1973 issue, pointed out the large growth of Protestant Christian day schools, with expansion particularly noted in the South. While enrollment in Catholic schools has decreased about one million in the past ten years, Protestant schools are expanding rapidly based upon deep convictions about the importance of the Bible and evangelism.

Growth of the Christian Day School Movement has been extensive. In 1973 the U.S. Office of Education released a statement that showed the number of Protestant schools increasing 66% during the decade of the sixties. Expansion continues as people grow more dissatisfied with school conditions resulting from continued secularization of the public schools, busing and racial issues.

No one organization or individual speaks with absolute authority on the scope and direction of the entire Christian Day School movement. Among the organizations which sponsor and direct these schools are the National Association of Christian Schools, Wheaton, Illinois; National Union of Christian Schools, Grand Rapids, Michigan; National Christian Education Association, Newton Square, Pennsylvania; Accelerated Christian Education, Garland, Texas; and the American Association of Christian Schools, Hialeah, Florida. The Council for American Private Eduation, Washington, D.C., is also a source of more information on these and other types of private schools. There are several regional associations, such as the Western Association of Christian Schools, Whittier, California; the Eastern Association of Christian Schools, Upper Marlboro, Maryland; and the Christian Education Association of the Southeast, Milton, Florida.

Dr. Al Janey, president of the American Association of Christian Schools, Miami, Florida, reports between six and seven thousand Protestant Christian day schools with an enrollment of about one million. It is reported that Southern Baptists have more than 400 schools in Florida. In the Dallas-Fort Worth area there are about 200 schools, 100 in Houston and 85 in Memphis, 20 of which are run by churches. In the fall of 1972, Pensacola Christian Schools reported an enrollment of 2000, the largest of its kind.

The National Association of Christian Schools reports a beginning figure of 76 schools and 10,000 pupils in 1920 to a current figure of 285 schools and 62,000 students. Some of these schools are small; others are large multi-unit systems. This organization provides services for its membership in business and financial guidance, curriculum, government relationships, general school operation, and promotion. It is concerned with basic principles. It encourages study, research and writing which embody these principles. It sponsors conferences, meetings, workshops, and seminars.

The American Association of Christian Schools in 1973 reported 120 schools and an enrollment of 50-60,000 pupils distributed over 30 states. The National Association of Christian Schools reported 311 schools with about 60,000 enrolled. The National Union of Christian Schools reported 300 schools with 650,000 pupils in 26 states and Canada. From 1965 to 1973 the California Association of Christian Schools grew from 68 to 350 member schools, increasing enrollment from 11,388 to 46,032 pupils.

These developments are confirmed further by an article in the *US News and World Report*, October 8, 1973, entitled "Boom in Protestant Schools." It was recognized that Protestant schools are spreading across the nation in some 30 states, ranging in size from 100 to 200 students, with tuition ranging from $400 to $1,000 per year. Busing and racial issues are not the sole reasons for this development. Rising alarm of parents over academic laxity in public schools, along with rampant misbehavior, robbery, drug abuse, and classroom disruption are cited as reasons for development. Many parents are seeking a learning environment characterized by better discipline and more religion. The future looks bright for Christian Day Schools.

Motivation. It is commonly accepted that Christian Day Schools were originated as a protest movement against the deficiencies and secular humanistic religion of the public schools. However, it must be recognized also that these schools exist in their own right and on completely defensible Biblical and Christian bases.

Many good reasons can be cited for the development of Christian Day Schools. To help meet the needs of the national life the Christian school will not only help to eliminate many of the evils of society but will also help to educate America's young in the things of God and thus bring Him into the center of our lives.

There is no greater tragedy than the breakdown of the American home, so evident in today's society. By helping to educate children and parents in God's will and Word the Christian school strengthens the foundations of the home, contributes to the up-bringing of mature Christian people, and assists the home in meeting its supreme responsibility.

To be really blessed, children need a spiritual center to their lives, giving direction and meaning to everyday life. By pointing children to God the Christian school assists the home and church in this great work. "Every daily interest must be related to God." It is the Christian school that provides relationships which will directly contribute to these ends.

Tax supported schools cannot be expected to provide the motives listed above. Christian schools were established to give children of Christian homes and church congregations an education that fully supports their spiritual position.

Some schools have been established as a missionary outreach of local churches. Through the prayers of the people and the program of the school pupils are reached, taught and evangelized. Thus the school is able not only to serve children of Christian but also of non-Christian homes.

While the overall purpose of Christian Day Schools has been to help children live Christian lives, they have also come into existence as a protest movement against evil forces in society. Great concern is expressed over the moral depravity so prevalent in our society, the use of drugs and violence in the schools, the low academic standards there, as well as the lack of discipline.

The ultimate objective and motive is to bring up children in the nurture and admonition of the Lord. Thus the primacy of spiritual values is emphasized. People are trained to minister in and witness to every phase of human endeavor.

Program. Generally speaking, there are only two kinds of Christian Day Schools: (1) those that are sponsored, supported and controlled by some *institution,* such as a church, and (2) those that are sponsored, supported and controlled by *individuals.* If individuals maintain the school for others, it is known as a "private school." If local individual parents and others cooperate as a social group to establish, maintain, and control the education of their own children, then it is usually called a "parent-society school."

Schools sponsored by churches, also known as parochial schools, are classified according to sponsoring churches, such as Roman Catholics, Lutherans, or Seventh Day Adventists. The schools of individual initiative can also be designated as non-parochial and are classified on the basis of their religious emphases, such as Reformed, Mennonite, and other evangelical groups.

Most of these non-parochial Christian schools are unique. They stress the importance of knowing the Bible as the Word of

God. They show the educational effectiveness of the Bible by pointing up the importance of such matters as creation, divine providence, the source of all truth in God, the relevance of God in present day life, the spiritual nature of man, the effectual presence of God to enrich life and give hope for life after death. No education is complete until the *totality* of truth is revealed to students.

It is apparent, therefore, that current Christian Day Schools differ rather significantly from typical parochial schools. Not limited to a local church or sponsoring denomination, they are Christ-centered, rather than church-centered. Most parochial schools are sponsored by churches or denominations strictly for their own members and constituency.

Programs in these schools emphasize not only Bible instruction but also worship and devotional life. There is close cooperation with parents and home needs and interests. Great value is placed on authority and discipline. Respect for both God and country is inculcated. Thus, there is a patriotic element.

Christian schools strive for academic excellence as well as spiritual quality. Their philosophy is based on God's mandate to care for, rule over, and sustain all creation. Overall, there is a concern on the part of parents and other supporters that God's will be done.

5. *Higher Education*

The Christian college stands high among the important agencies of Christian education. Beyond high school we find that Christians have developed Bible schools and colleges and denominational and inter-denominational Christian liberal arts colleges. We have yet to see a Christian evangelical university.

The denominational school is a child of the Reformation. This movement was quick to seize upon education as a means of perpetuating its Christian principles. Luther and Calvin urged the founding and maintenance of Christian schools and colleges. The same was true in the early years of the history of this country. Education at that time was the servant of the church. The culture of that time was religion-centered and church-dominated. The period of 1830 to 1850 saw the greatest development of denominational colleges in this country. Most of these schools were motivated and directed by religious purposes. At the present time the philosophy of naturalism is dominating the average secular college and university. It has even permeated many of the church-related colleges. The Christian should not merely bemoan this fact but should make an attempt to do something about it. The truth of the matter is that evangelical Christians have failed to produce the scholars, the textbooks, and curriculum materials sufficient to meet the rising tides of secularism and naturalism on the college level. The time has come for evangelicals to rise to the great demands placed upon them and to the challenge presented to them.

The distinctiveness of a Christian college lies in its world view which is based on the Bible and the Gospel of Jesus Christ. It is to be expected, naturally, that the administration, faculty, curriculum, student body, and constituency should reflect this point of view. To be Christian, therefore, an evangelical Christian college should have the following characteristics:

1. A Christian world view based on the Gospel of Jesus Christ as contained in the Holy Scriptures
2. Christian aims, purposes, and objectives based on this world view and abstracted from it
3. A Christian administration and faculty fully committed to these objectives in life and teaching
4. A Christian spirit and atmosphere and school life
5. A Christian curriculum and program-bibliocentric
6. A Christian motivation and product

Besides being characterized by Christian evidences, the Christian college is expected to be Christian in all of its functions. Frank Gaebelein has listed five cardinal functions which Christian higher education as a whole should fulfill.

1. Christian higher education should provide balanced programs of liberal and professional education that are Biblically centered and are designed to prepare selected young people for leadership — either as full-time Christian workers or as consecrated members of other professions and occupations.
2. It should afford general education and various types of vocational training in a distinctively Christian setting to young people from Christian homes who, while not suited for liberal arts and professional training, would profit from at least two years of post-high-school education.
3. It should foster scientific and creative study in major areas of scholarly endeavor with the special aim of relating to the Christian faith the findings of this study, producing books and articles that will make the results of Christian scholarship more widely known.
4. It should offer systematic instruction in Christian learning to adults through evening and extension courses and through special institutes, workshops, and conferences.
5. It should give counsel and support to community, regional, national, and world-wide agencies committed to the extension of the Gospel of Christ.[1]

---

[1] Frank E. Gaebelein, *Christian Education in a Democracy* (New York, Oxford University Press, 1951), pp. 137-38.

This section on evangelical higher education would not be complete without mentioning a new kind of higher education which has arisen in the late Nineteenth and first half of the Twentieth Century. In the first part of the Twentieth Century more than 150 Bible Institutes and colleges have enrolled over 25,000 students. These schools have been and still are the citadels of evangelical Christian education. There are three groups of these schools: (1) Bible schools below the college level; (2) Bible institutes, which offer diploma courses on the college level, and (3) Bible colleges which offer courses culminating in recognized baccalaureate degrees. Such schools offer three, four, and five-year programs with specialization in such areas as missions, Bible and theology, Christian education, pastoral work, and sacred music. The most outstanding characteristic of these schools is the distinctive place given to the study of the English Bible. Other distinct emphases include practical training in Christian work and the stress placed on deep spirituality in matters of faith, prayer, vision, and consecration. In the past these schools have not been too academic, but there is a remarkable tendency and practice today which leads many to stress and work toward the importance of quality, accreditation, and the inclusion of courses in general education, humanities, social sciences, and natural sciences in their programs. Today, particularly at the college level, there are definite attempts on the part of Bible college administrators to raise the level of the quality of these schools. Following the establishment of the Accrediting Association of Bible Institutes and Bible Colleges and the North American Association of Bible Institutes and Bible Colleges, new emphasis on quality and accreditation have borne great weight in lifting the standards of these schools.

C. The Nature and Function of Secular School Administration

1. Definition

The term *administer* means to manage, conduct, or direct. The administration of the school system, then, means to manage the affairs of the school. The administrator is the person who administers, who has executive work and ability.

2. Function

Education is a gigantic enterprise. Every business must be properly managed if it is to pay dividends in money or service. In education, likewise, there is a multitude of details to which attention must be given if the school is to operate efficiently. Plans must be made, policies adopted and executed, information must be secured and dispensed, budgets must be built, monies must be spent, school buildings and equipment must be cared for, teaching staffs must be secured, the program organized, etc. Simply stated, leadership must be given to the total school organization.

Essentially, school adiministration is a means to an end. Schools are provided and maintained as a means of education. Administration exists, therefore, for the benefit of the pupil. Some of the primary responsibilities connected with school administration include the following:

1. Selection, placement, and supervision of teachers
2. Preparation and certification of teachers
3. Administration of all instructional employees, including substitute workers, salaries, pensions, and evaluation of efficiency
4. Administration of the school plant, including planning, construction, finances, use, operation, and maintenance
5. Administration of school business affairs, including budgetary procedures, supplies, transportation, insurance
6. Administration of pupil personnel, including attendance, census, classification, progress, guidance, health and evaluation
7. Administration of instructional materials, including curriculum construction, textbooks, extracurricular activities, and library
8. Special phases of school administration, including accounting, publicity, and office administration

D. ADMINISTRATION PHILOSOPHICALLY CONCEIVED

1. Realism

To the *realist*, the purpose of administration is functional. The administrator should organize material and personnel. The first is by far the easier of the two skills. In all administration, the administrator is to be guided by the *facts*. Objective experimentation is the determining factor in all organization. Tests, teachers, buildings, and equipment are all dealt with according to the latest views of experimental science. The chief motivations used are tangible in the form of rewards and penalties. Thus, materialistic goals are considered the chief motivating factors for graduating classes. *Naturalists* will concur with most of these positions.

2. Idealism

The purpose of education for the idealist administrator is the development of inner spiritual growth, the selfhood. Consequently, he will expect both teachers and pupils to operate constantly at their best in the school situation. The purpose of the school is to help each pupil develop to the best of his capacity. This, of course, is performed in the greatest possible democratic spirit and environment. He constantly holds up his concept of the ideal situation to both the school and the community.

3. *Pragmatism*

The pragmatist administrator is not so much interested in ideals as he is in solving problems that arise in the school situation. He has deep sympathy for the needs and interests of teachers, pupils, and the community. Although the pragmatist has no hard and fast theory of education, he is prone to follow the results of experimental research in pedagogical principles. He depends on scientific conclusions rather than opinion. These conclusions must be used in a social setting and for social purposes.

4. *Christian Theism*

The evangelical Christian educator has a philosophy of school administration. His job is to show the relevance of the Bible and Christian philosophy to each and every phase of school life. This view is developed in the section which follows.

E. A BIBLIOCENTRIC PATTERN FOR SCHOOL ADMINISTRATION

1. *Philosophical Basis*

The Christian conceives of school administration, along with the secular educator, as a means to an end. He is able to concur in general with the nature and function of school administration as now practiced in secular education. He hastens to add, however, that all in which the Christian educator engages is used for the glory of God and for the further purposes of realizing the Kingdom objectives now and in the future (I Corinthians 10:31).

A bibliocentric pattern for the administration of Christian schools demands that the Christian philosophy of life, as recorded for us in the Scriptures, be the guiding factor. From this, philosophical principles, ethical conduct, and social concepts are abstracted. Here is where curriculum principles also demand that the whole school environment be used to further the educative process which issues in the glory of God. Because the Christian educator is interested in the development of the whole man in his whole environment, he realizes that the school community has spiritual, academic, social, and physical implications, all of which contribute in some measure to the development of the student.

The implications of this position affect every phase of the organization and administration of the Christian school. Biblical principles and content should permeate the life and practices of the school at all levels. This is seen in the chart form on page 220.

The example of Jesus as a Leader of men and an Administrator of the Church has relevance for school administration today. This was brought out admirably by Paul F. Douglass, president of The American University, in an unusual little booklet entitled *Spiritual Experience in Administration*.

1. Formulate your goals in clear purpose and achievable ways — Luke 4:1-26
2. Recruit a team to achieve your goals — Matthew 4:18-22
3. Inspire the team with a single purpose — Matthew 5, 6, 7
4. Play the other's role and look at yourself — Matthew 7:12
5. Huddle to plan the next play — Luke 5:4-9
6. Use the resources of humble people — John 6:1-14
7. Be frank with associates — Matthew 18:15-17
8. See human values beyond official red tape — Luke 10:29-37
9. Retreat to your own private world for renewal — Luke 11:1
10. Rekindle the aspiration of the staff — Luke 11:1-4
11. Work for other people as well as with them — Matthew 20:20-29

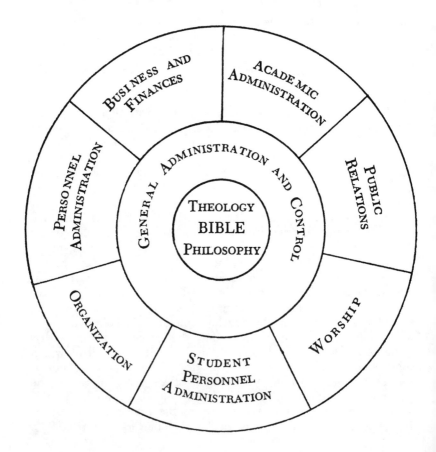

12. Perform to the limits of ability — Mark 11:41-44
13. Express appreciation — Matthew 26:6-13
14. Expect a Judas on your team — Matthew 26:14-25
15. Understand that a leader faces Gethsemane alone — Mark 14:37
16. Persist until purpose is realized — Acts 2:17[2]

2. General Administration and Control

General control in administration is accomplished through some kind of Board of Control. The members of these boards should be men and women of high purpose and proved Christian character. These Boards are normally policy-making bodies. Duties are legislative and judicial rather than executive. They hold ultimate authority over the institution. All the policies and duties of such boards should be directed by Christian and Biblical principles. The purposes of Christian schools should be clearly outlined. The Christian philosophy of life should be the motivating factor.

Authority for internal administration is given to the chief executive from the Board. Such an officer is generally the President or Principal of the Institution. Strict adherence to the best that is known in business principles should be practiced by all personnel. Accountability accompanies responsibility (I Corinthians 4:2; Romans 14:12).

It is the primary responsibility of the President or Principal to gather around him a team of workers best fitted according to qualification and ability to carry forward the program of the institution in an effort to realize the objectives set up. All such personnel should feel the call of God upon them for the great work of His kingdom (I Corinthians 3:9; 12:4-7).

The Scriptural principle of law, order, and decency demands that all faculty and business meetings be organized and operated in the best possible way and in accord with the highest ethical principles. As far as possible a "team spirit" should pervade the relations of the entire staff, for in the multiplicity of counsel there is wisdom (Proverbs 15:22).

3. Business and Finances

Best policy seems to indicate that all business functions should be centralized in one office, that of the business manager who is under the general supervision of the President. The functions of this office include purchasing, collections, accounting, bookkeeping, giving budget assistance, payment of bills, supervision of student finances, operation and maintenance. In the handling of monies Christian ethics demands the strictest adherence to the require-

[2]Paul F. Douglass, *Spiritual Experience in Administration* (Washington, D. C., The American University Press, 1951), Chapter 3.

ments of honesty and integrity. Christian schools should not overlook the training values in the demands of Christian stewardship and payment of school costs on the part of the students. Wherever possible the Good Samaritan principle should be exercised, but not at the expense of student initiative and character. All staff members should be treated on the basis of the Golden Rule (Matthew 7:12).

4. Academic Administration

There should be one officer in every institution definitely charged with the responsibility of academic leadership. Although the President may function in the presiding capacity, the logical one to assume all other leadership functions in the educational program is the Dean or Principal. Proper departments and divisions of the faculty, staff, and materials of instruction should follow the best known academic procedures. In fact, the Christian school should strive for the highest academic excellence while at the same time preserving its Bible and theological heritage.

The methods of instruction in the classroom should be in accord with the latest and best pedagogical theory. Constant efforts on the part of the faculty should be made to improve teaching-learning processes. Spirituality demands the highest quality at all levels of the school life (Colossians 3:23).

Curriculum construction should be directed by bibliocentric principles and direct efforts to integrate and correlate the Christian philosophy of education with all school subjects should be a matter of constant study and application. Careful formulations of objectives should direct the use of materials and methods at all levels of instruction.

5. Personnel Administration

Faculty and staff members should be carefully selected on the basis of competence, maturity of Christian character, and professional skill. It should be considered an ethical responsibility for an institution to provide adequate salaries. An agreement should be formalized by a written contract which stipulates such major items as tenure, salary, and duties.

It is good practice for a school to make provision for hospitalization and accident insurance, preferably group insurance, and for a retirement plan on mutual participation. Faculty and staff housing should be made a matter of chief concern because living conditions are vitally related to morale and accomplishment. Teaching and work loads should be based on demands which are commensurate with the task and abilities of the workers (Colossians 4:1).

6. *Student Personnel Administration*

Christian schools need to give particular attention to this area of school life because of the impact of secularism and irreligion of our day. The lack of Christian training in the home along with the superficiality of much church life make it imperative that students receive Christian training, instruction, and counseling in the Christian school. The services demanded in this area merit the employment of a single director or administrator.

A good counseling program is necessary. A personal interest should be taken in each student. All phases of the student's welfare should be considered — personal, spiritual, physical, social, academic, vocational, and financial.

It is a good practice to set aside a definite period at the beginning of the school year for student orientation and adjustment. Emphasis should be placed on the spiritual life, wholesome social activities, a testing program, and early attention to all student problems.

An organized counseling program will include such factors as the selection of curricula and courses, diagnosis of academic difficulties, the choice of a vocation, the formulation of standards of conduct, promotion of scholarship, adjustment of personal difficulties, and spiritual counsel.

Social life and discipline should be under the overall supervision of the faculty. A student social committee is effective in both planning and initiating social events. Discipline was discussed more fully in a previous chapter. Health services on a limited scale should be provided. Wide latitude can be given to students by the faculty in planning, organizing, and operating student organizations, but ultimate authority should be retained by the faculty. Guidance by a faculty adviser is preferred to control by detailed regulations.

Although competitive athletics may not be engaged in to a great extent, a well-organized and supervised program of intramural athletics can make definite contributions to health as a wholesome recreational activity. Recreational facilities and a physical education program for both men and women is imperative.

The spiritual life should be wholesome and vital. It should be more than a philosophy or part of the academic program. It should pervade all of the school's activities. There should be, however a balance of emphasis which avoids both formalism and fanaticism. The spiritual life should help to achieve other valid objectives and be broad enough to include the fellowship of other evangelical groups.

Where a Christian service program exists in the school program, it should be in charge of a director who implements the policies of the faculty. Assignments will be made on the basis of a student's aptitudes, abilities, and degree of maturity. Training will be intelligently coordinated with theoretical instruction on the one hand and with the organizations which engage student assistants on the other. Counsel and direction shall be given to the students in this work and regular reports and evaluation will be expected.

While it is readily admitted that extra-curricular activities have many contributions to make to the student's personal, mental, spiritual, and social development, the Christian school should strive to go beyond these values. In all of these activities the glory of God should be paramount. Students should seek to practice and witness to their faith through such activities. They will be careful to manifest Christlikeness in all their activities. Jesus "increased in wisdom and in stature, and in favor with God and man" (Luke 2:52).

7. *Public Relations*

Biblical principles and philosophy should direct the course of public relations in the Christian school. All promotional features should be characterized by complete honesty and sincerity. The sensational methods of worldly promotion and high pressure salesmanship should be avoided by the Christian school. Only those methods which will glorify God and truthfully present the needs and program of the school should be tolerated. At the same time those procedures which are used should be characterized by quality no less evident than that found anywhere else. Here, too, is where a real opportunity for Christian witness and instruction to the public is found.

Where genuine Christlikeness is manifested in the school system, and where the Spirit of God is honored, the Christian public will be attracted and led of the Spirit to support the school in prayer and by finances. They must be led to see that the school is truly dedicated to the task of kingdom building, that the Christian school is a place where God selects, trains, and prepares His servants for the great task of world evangelism.

8. *Worship*

Perhaps there is no better place to draw this chapter to a conclusion than at this point. As the Christian Philosophy of Life and Education represented in the bibliocentric view provides integration for the instructional program of the school, so the matter of worship unifies the spiritual life and devotion of the school. Here is the place where the objective presence of God can be realized; here is where the subjective elements of personal experience can be centered in God. Here is where the whole spiritual atmosphere of the school can hit a high point. Here, too, is where all else that goes on in the life of the school can be integrated in a social and spiritual situation.

Worship has an *evangelistic* function. In this the sinner is converted, the backslider is reclaimed, and the believer is sanctified. It has a *pastoral* function in that the call to service is issued, the saints encouraged, the weak protected, the wayward corrected, and Christian fellowship deepened. The *devotional* function is supplied through united praise, adoration, and thanksgiving. The *intellectual* function of worship brings again to the attention of the student the Christian world view, the Christian clues to life and knowledge. Worship is designed to complete and give meaning to all other activities in the school. As such, it becomes the climax of Christian education.

SUGGESTED CLASS ACTIVITIES AND PROJECTS FOR CHAPTER VIII

1. If possible secure or draw charts which show how the various systems of secular education are organized.
2. Outline the duties of a school board.
3. Make a study of the importance of the home as a teaching agency in the Scriptures.
4. Show from the Scriptures why parents have the first responsibility in teaching children.
5. Show the importance of the Sunday school as the main teaching agency in the church.
6. From Acts 2 show the divine pattern of education.
7. What is the significance of the term, *loco parentis?*
8. Discuss the advantages and disadvantages of the parochial school systems.
9. What are the distinctive marks of a Christian school?
10. Outline the general duties of a school administrator.
11. Draw a chart which shows the theory of bibliocentric school administration.
12. What principles of administration did Jesus employ?
13. Secure and discuss the criteria of good school administration used by accrediting agencies.
14. Where does worship fit into the Christian school?

Section Three

THE CONTENT OF A CHRISTIAN PHILOSOPHY OF EDUCATION

The content of a Christian Philosophy of Education is concerned primarily with the truth-content organized into forms called subject matter disciplines. These disciplines can be organized into areas of truth as well as separate and individual subjects. Section Three is devoted to the consideration of how the various areas of truth are integrated, organized, and prepared for use in the classroom. Each of these areas is defined with the scope of studies involved clearly indicated. In addition short sketches of the historical development of the subjects in each area are given to provide background material and orientation, values to the student are suggested and indications regarding the clues to integration, interpretation, and the development of general objectives are provided. Following a statement of the Christian view of truth for each area is a list of the particular disciplines comprising the areas together with introductory discussions on each discipline.

THE CHRISTIAN PHILOSOPHY OF BIBLICAL STUDIES

OUTLINE FOR CHAPTER 9

A. REVELATION
   1. The Primacy of Revelation
   2. General Revelation
   3. Special Revelation

B. BIBLICAL STUDIES
   1. Definition and Scope
   2. Values
   3. Function
   4. Integration and Interpretation
   5. General Objectives for Biblical Studies

C. THE BIBLE
   1. Nature and Purpose
   2. General Objectives for Bible
   3. Education in the Bible
   4. The Bible in Education
   5. Jesus Christ and Education

D. CHRISTIAN THEOLOGY
   1. Nature and Purpose
   2. General Objectives for Christian Theology
   3. Relation of Philosophy and Theology
   4. Philosophical Concepts of God
   5. Theological Content
   6. The Contemporary Theological Situation
   7. Secular Education and Theology
   8. Theology and Education
   9. Some Implications of Theology for Education

E. CHRISTIAN PHILOSOPHY
   1. Nature and Purpose
   2. General Objectives for Christian Philosophy
   3. Problems of Philosophy in the Present
   4. Problems of Philosophy in the Past
   5. Problems of Philosophy in the Future
   6. A World View and Education

9 | THE CHRISTIAN PHILOSOPHY OF BIBLICAL STUDIES

A. REVELATION

1. *The Primacy of Revelation*

No thinker can devoid himself of an absolute. Either he will give allegiance to some man-projected absolute or he will begin his philosophy with a revelational absolute. The Christian philosophy begins with the latter, for he believes that God has chosen to reveal Himself to man. All truth to the Christian is the reflection into the soul of the truth that is in God. This was stated clearly by Claude Thompson who said:

> Since all truth is ultimately God's truth, the related truths of each and all human interests will be measured in terms of Revelation. This is not to say that Theology will attempt to dictate the *findings* of any discipline. It does mean that the *interpretations*, the *meanings*, will be found in Theology. The position taken is, briefly, this: all truth is revealed truth; that instead of there being "degrees of knowledge" (to use Maritain's phrase) it were better to say "degrees of revelation."
>
> It means that, in a very real sense, it is incorrect to speak of knowledge being discoverable by man's "unaided reason." Since God is the *a priori* of man and since God has nowhere left Himself "without witness": all knowledge is revealed knowledge.
>
> In philosophy and the sciences, it is revelation in terms of *ideas;* in ethics, politics, and all human relations, it is revelation as a *practical guide;* in aesthetics, it is revelation as *appreciation;* in religion, it is revelation as *divine action.* This illustrates what we mean by "degrees of revelation" — all knowledge being revealed knowledge.[1]

The Bible teaches that God has revealed Himself to man in two ways: through General Revelation in nature (Psalm 19:1) and man's conscience (Romans 2:14-16), and through Special Revelation in the Bible and His Son Jesus Christ (Hebrews 1:1, 2). The terms, "general" and "special" revelation, reveal the extent and purpose of God's revelation. God has revealed Himself both in what He has created and what He has spoken. Christians are expected to be diligent in understanding both of these sources

[1]Claude H. Thompson, "The Queen of the Sciences," *Asbury Seminarian*, Vol. 4, No. 4, Winter, 1949, p. 135.

of revelation. Biblical revelation does not pretend to answer all questions but theology does provide one with a guide to the understanding of all other channels of revelation.

The special disclosure of God's grace in providing His revelation came not as an inner obligation nor did it rise primarily from the transcendent power of God. It came rather as a display of His unmerited favor and because of the fall of man into sin. Through the fall of Adam into sin man was cut off from direct communion with God and from His truth, but God has bridged the gap through special revelation. Special revelation, however, does not comprehend the entirety of God's revelation. Christianity does not deny that God is everywhere revealed in the space-time universe and internally in the very mind and conscience of man as well. This is called general revelation. The actual revelation of God in nature, history, and man, therefore, is a central Biblical affirmation.

A comprehensive view of revelation depends on the contributions of both general and special revelation. Without special revelation, general revelation is incomplete for sinful man. Without general revelation, special revelation lacks a demonstration of the character and actions of God by which one comes to a greater appreciation and understanding of His work of redemption.

2. General Revelation

By virtue of the creation general revelation preceded special revelation in point of time. According to Wiley this term means "that disclosure of Himself which God makes to all men — in nature, in the constitution of the mind, and in the progress of human history."[2]

In nature we find a revelation of God through the physical universe (Psalm 19:1-4). This is largely supported in the New Testament by the Apostle Paul (Acts 14:15-17; 17:22-34), where he shows that nature reveals God sufficiently to lead men to seek after Him and worship Him. In Romans 1:19-21, Paul shows how nature is a revelation of the existence and personality of God. General revelation, however, is limited because only through the added revelation of His Word can men find God's plan of salvation. Although nature is filled with the evidences of God's presence, sin has darkened the intellect and dulled man's sensibilities so much that it is difficult for men to read such evidences. The substitution of a sensory experience by which man comes to a knowledge of God is not as sufficient as direct personal experience of Him through grace and regeneration.

[2]H. Orton Wiley, *Christian Theology,* Vol. I, p. 16 (Kansas City, Mo., Beacon Hill Press, 1941).

By creation man is both a creature of nature and a personal being above nature. The powers of thought, feeling, and willing are personality factors which reveal man as a spiritual being. Thus man through the body is a participant in a physical environment. Just as the physical world makes itself known to man through the senses, so the spiritual environment is revealed in his consciousness through his spiritual sensibilities. Thus, God has generally revealed Himself to mankind through man's spiritual sensibilities and conscience.

A third means by which God has used general revelation to reveal Himself is in history. History is a record of the actions of men. God, too, has been and is active in man's affairs. He is an inner directing Presence in history and an Authoritative Will above it, directing life toward the goal He has in mind. To the Christian, that ultimate goal is the Kingdom of God.

3. *Special Revelation*

Special revelation is a higher form of revelation by which God has revealed His redemptive purposes in His Son, Jesus Christ. While general revelation provides man with a manifestation of the power and presence of God in His creative works, special revelation has revealed particularly the character and will of God.

Special revelation was made necessary for several reasons. First, it is to be expected that a physical demonstration of God would be insufficient for complete satisfaction of man as a spiritual being. Second, since man was created a spiritual being for fellowship with God it is reasonable to suppose that God would supplement general revelation with a disclosure of Himself through personality beyond that possible through impersonal and abstract nature. Third, the entrance of sin into the world and its effects upon man made it imperative that man be given assistance in his efforts to overcome the consequent evils and aversions resulting therefrom. In this provision God would make known His aversion for sin and His plans for man's redemption. God had to contend with the abnormal consequences of sin as discovered in the apathy, perversity, and spiritual darkness which characterize the minds of men. Through Jesus Christ, therefore, the spiritual nature of man becomes the particular sphere of divine activity in special revelation.

The modes through which special revelation has come to man are twofold: (1) through the life and ministry of Jesus Christ and (2) the Bible. Christ is the living Word and the Bible is the written Word, both of which form the basis of the special revelation.

One other reason for special revelation must be pointed out. Not only has sin destroyed communion with God and obscured a knowledge of Him derived from nature, but a special *written* revelation, objective in nature, is demanded by which the moral development of man as a being and of men as a family might be secured. In other words, the moral constitution of man implies for its development a written revelation. This was argued brilliantly by Walker as follows:

> Man is created conscious of imperfection and capable of culture.
>
> Man can receive moral culture only by the aid of signs of moral truth embodied in written language.
>
> Man may have by nature an intuition of the being of God, but he has no knowledge of the *character of God;* but that character has been revealed in accordance with the process of linguistic developments and in adaptation to man's nature and wants, in the Old and New Testaments.
>
> Man is a being of Faith, and can be affected by the character and will of God only by the exercise of faith. Faith naturally looks out of self for its objects. The past, the future, God and the spiritual world are without the soul, as revealed by faith.
>
> Man is a being of Conscience; but the character of conscience is determined by faith. Unless faith sees God in truth, conscience will not enforce it on the soul. But it will enforce whatever faith dictates as the character and will of God, whether right or wrong.
>
> Faith is in itself blind. It does not know truth from error; and reason has never had power without revelation to correct its false affirmations. The highest effort of reason is to produce doubt. It can not substitute truth for falsehood.
>
> Conscience is blind. It is a potential force, but it follows faith, right or wrong; and when faith is false it enforces falsehood in the soul.
>
> Both faith and conscience look to God for authority; and until faith sees God in Truth, Conscience will not convict the soul of guilt for disobedience.
>
> Hence, in the moral culture of the soul, everything depends on the revelation of truth. But this truth must come to the soul, not as human opinion, or as the utterances of philosophy, but as Truth which Faith and Conscience recognize as rendered obligatory upon man, by the will and authority of God. *Without* revealed Truth, *Reason has no data. Faith is false and Conscience is corrupt.* The erring nature of man's moral powers, without Revealed Truth, requires a revelation from the Maker. As there can be no moral culture with a false faith and a corrupt or dead conscience, hence a revelation of objective Truth, rendered efficient by the perceived presence and authority of God is a moral necessity, in order to the culture of the human soul.[3]

B. BIBLICAL STUDIES

1. *Definition and Scope*

Biblical Studies are those branches of learning and departments of knowledge which draw their content primarily from the

[3]James B. Walker, *Philosophy of the Plan of Salvation* (New York, Chautauqua Press, 1887), pp. 256-57.

Holy Scriptures. The field includes the disciplines of Bible, Christian Theology, and Christian Philosophy. The field of Bible embraces the study of the Bible both as a whole and in part through survey, analysis, and synthesis. The field of Christian Theology embraces studies of doctrinal truths organized and systematized from Biblical and natural sources. The field of Christian Philosophy embraces the Christian interpretation of reality, of knowledge and truth, and of moral and aesthetic values.

2. Values

Biblical studies provide the thought structures for all education and the principles whereby all truth is recognized and evaluated. They lay the foundation and provide opportunity for the student to obtain a factual knowledge of the Scriptures — a knowledge which should lead to:

1. A deeper personal experience with Christ
2. Growth into Christian maturity
3. An ability to interpret the Word correctly
4. A Christian theistic world view
5. A life of consecrated Christian service in cooperation with the fellow-members of the body of Christ

3. Function

The Christian educator believes that he has God-given integrative means based on the presuppositions of Christian theism. These means are provided to him through what is called synoptic studies which are studies aware of their own distinctiveness but also functionally providing a perspective for seeing things in connected wholes. These studies are the Biblical Studies. The primary function, therefore, of these disciplines is to provide a source and basis for formulating a Christian world view and guide lines for organizing subject matter into meaningful wholes and relationships.

4. Integration and Interpretation

Biblical studies provide the synoptic basis and wholistic approach by which integration and interpretation of the total curriculum are made possible. This was pointed out in Chapter III.

In addition to observing the practical value of Biblical studies in integrating the curriculum as a whole, each of the separate disciplines within the area of Biblical studies must be integrated. This is evidenced by the chart form on page 236.

The Christian Philosophy of Revelation provides the Christian educator with his basic assumptions. The Revelation of God forms the heart of all truth for him. The formal written expression of this Revelation, both Special and General, has been preserved in the three studies comprising the area as a whole — Bible, Christian Theology and Christian Philosophy. All three of these disciplines form the complete unity of God's revelation.

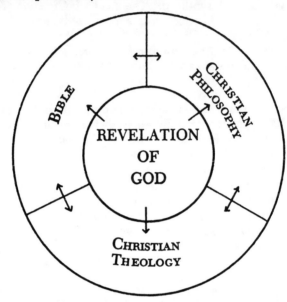

Interpretation is accomplished in this area, as in all others, through the application of the inductive principles of thinking as described in the section on "interpretation" in Chapter III.

5. *General Objectives for Biblical Studies*

From the foregoing discussion it is now possible to summarize the philosophy of Biblical Studies in the form of general objectives for the total area. Such objectives may well serve as guide lines for both teaching and learning.

1. To give the student a working knowledge of the Bible as a divine revelation and to give him an understanding of Christian theology
2. To lead the student to a full commitment and loyalty to the Christian faith
3. To help the student form a Christian world view
4. To guide the student in the development of Christian character
5. To lead the student to an appreciation of the place of the Bible in his growth into spiritual maturity
6. To deepen and enrich the student's whole personality — intellectually, emotionally, and volitionally: to secure as his supreme motivation the glory of God and the good of men
7. To help the student derive from Bible studies the principles of critical thinking, whereby he will be able to evaluate concepts and discriminate between truth and error

8. To create in the student an appreciation for the place of Biblical Studies as the integrating factor in the total curriculum, including student life, school administration, and academic studies[4]

C. THE BIBLE

1. Nature and Purpose

The Bible, as a whole, is God's Special Self-Revelation communicating to man His sovereign will in human language to the end that man might be regenerated through grace and conformed to the image of God's Son.

Structurally and historically, the Bible is divided into two parts, the Old Testament and the New Testament. The Old Testament is a progressive, historical, ethical, and prophetic record of God's Self-revelation, which anticipates and culminates in redemption through Jesus Christ. The New Testament continues God's self-revelation through His Son, the Lord Jesus Christ, and through the work of the Holy Spirit in the Church, the body of Christ. God's ultimate goal here is His own glory through the reconciliation of all things.

The Bible stands alone in its own right as a subject of study, but it also operates synoptically by providing a service function to all other disciplines in the subject matter curriculum and even to school administration as a whole. The following suggestions reveal somewhat the strategic place that the Bible has in the curriculum.

1. It provides the historical record of God's Revelation
2. It provides much content for study
3. It tests and measures all truth by its principles
4. It releases great principles by which thinking can be guided
5. It provides the thought-structures which form the substance of Christian Theology
6. It provides the bases whereby integration and correlation are made possible in the curriculum as a whole

2. General Objectives for Bible

The nature and purpose of the Bible reveal certain general objectives which serve as guide lines for the teacher and student in the teaching-learning process. Some are listed as follows:

1. To impart to the student (for the most part deductively) an understanding of the historical and teleological structure of the Bible and an acquaintance with the facts which constitute it
2. To train the student in the various proven methods of Bible study:
   a. By a brief presentation of each method in class, leaving the

[4]Statement of the Committee on Biblical Studies of Fort Wayne Bible College, 1959.

more comprehensive treatment of it for the course in hermeneutics

  b. By periodic demonstrations of its use in connection with specific passages by the professor during the course of the semester
  c. By periodic assignments given the student in which he will be compelled by the very nature of the assignments to utilize the principles of a given method of study in order to complete the assignment

3. To develop in the student the ability to make the Bible relevant for current problems and needs, both social and individual:
  a. By the periodic application, on the part of the professor, of Bible truths to present-day problems as the occasion arises
  b. By periodic assignments which demand that the student search out for himself Biblical truths, and then make them relevant for the present-day situation.[5]

3. *Education in the Bible*

Essentially, the Bible is an educational code and its history is the history of education. From its opening pages in Genesis to the closing chapter of Revelation, the God of Light and Truth has sought to bring light, truth, and life to mankind.

The Bible shows that God is the first and great Educator. The very essence of wisdom is to know Him. The very content of education comes from Him. All creation is an expression of God.

The whole content of the educational curriculum stems from the creation by God. In chapters one and two of Genesis is given the Scriptural account of the origin of education. There God is pictured as the source of creation and knowledge (Genesis 1:1). God created and instructed man (Genesis 1:27, 28; 2:16, 17). There in Eden was the first school: God was the Teacher and man was the pupil. Instruction was a process of religious education and the method was one of indoctrination. The account is in marked contrast to the mythological one which pictures man as a product of natural organic evolution, who was first concerned with the educational processes involved in hunting and fishing, and whose religion arose as a result of dream interpretation and the worship of fire and mystery.

In the beginning the purpose of God's education was the maintenance of a perfect relationship between Himself and man. When man first sinned against God, this brought an altered situation. God's purpose became one of restoration and then maintenance. His method, however, remained the same — positive and authoritative. The responsibility of the pupil was to learn in and by obedience and through faith.

We note also that God has made known where the responsibility lies for the education of the child. It lies in the home with

[5]*Ibid.*

the parents. This principle was adopted, but not thoroughly practiced, by the Greeks and Romans. The home rather than the school was the center of their educational systems. Even heathen people have recognized this principle. Children are born of the parents and education becomes the natural thing for them.

The centrality of the home in God's educational plans cannot be seen more clearly than in His dealings with the early Hebrews. Even though God dealt nationally with these people He always spoke in individual terms when speaking of the education of the children. Classic passages in the Old Testament which testify to this fact are found in Deuteronomy, Proverbs, and Psalm 78 where the parents are the responsible educators of the children. The New Testament teachings bear on the same subject (Ephesians 6:4). Where the burden of the educational problem became great and beyond the resources of the home, all others who were brought in to assist the parents were thought of as *loco parentis*.

The Bible is concerned with the *religious character* of education. Education in Biblical terms is not considered complete without primary emphasis being given to religion, to the religious and moral needs of mankind. All subjects were to be taught from this point of view.

Because man has been created in the image of God, he is of necessity in his very nature religious. It is not possible to separate man from this fact. Because the child bears the image of God, it is not possible to ignore this fact in education.

The Patriarchal period was one of individualism. The Magna Charta of Hebrew education was Genesis 18:19, "For I know him, that he will command his children and his household after him, and they shall keep the way of the Lord, to do justice and judgment; that the Lord may bring upon Abraham that which he hath spoken of him." God's ultimate purpose through Abraham was to bless all people through him and to do this by sending the promised Saviour. Abraham was commanded to train his household to act righteously and justly. The education of this period was domestic, inclusive, and comprehensive.

The period embracing the experiences of Israel from Egypt to Babylon was one of nationalism. During this era the Golden Age of Hebrew history witnessed the development of a remarkable system of Hebrew education. During this time the Bible books of the law, the prophets, books of history, Psalms, and Proverbs were written. Moses, Joshua, Samuel, David, Solomon, Isaiah, Josiah, and Jeremiah were among the illustrious leaders. Solomon's Temple was erected and the people enjoyed a high degree of culture. The literature itself apart from any educational formulae was a splendid example of the fruitage of the Hebrew system of education. The education of this period also was largely domestic although there were certain exceptions, such as the assembly of the congregation for instruction (Joshua 8:30 ff; 24:1 ff), Jehoshaphat's traveling institute (II Chronicles 17:7-10), the Schools of the Prophets, and scattered examples of the use of tutors.

A great nation came into being which necessitated a more complex and organized system of education (Deuteronomy 6:7; 11:9; 4:44; Proverbs 6:23; 3:1; 4:2). Laws of hygiene, domestic relations, civil and criminal procedure were developed. The rituals of the tabernacle and temple services were written. The great sacrificial system was meaningless apart from the educational value of its symbolism.

Few people have appreciated the high degree of advancement made by the Hebrew educational system during this period. The curricula were broad and deep; the scope was wider than at first thought. The Scriptures, of course, formed the core curriculum and were carefully and intimately studied. Outside the field of the Bible many fields of knowledge were included. Solomon is the prime example. In the field of the natural sciences, plant and animal life were studied, embracing what today in the subject matter areas are known as botany, zoology, ornithology, entomology, and ichthyology. Physical education, including emphases on health, disease, and their relations to holiness of life, was stressed particularly as it regarded spiritual development. Great emphasis was placed on Hebrew industrial life, including business principles. Great value was placed on history and prophecy. Other books besides the Sacred Writings were used. From the standpoint of literature the Bible has no equal. The musical arts occupied a prominent portion as evidenced by the brief but numerous Bible references. When it comes to art and architecture the Tabernacle and Solomon's Temple rank with the world's masterpieces. Philosophy played a great part in' the Hebrew educational system. The books of Job, Proverbs, and Ecclesiastes are devoted almost exclusively to this subject. The wise men and seers were numerous although Solomon is known as the greatest of Hebrew philosophers.

One great factor which led to the captivity of Israel was the almost complete secularization of the educational curricula. Morality and religion were divorced from culture. Materialism led to lowered morals and a religious degeneracy, all of which resulted in a devitalized education. People lost a personal sense of obligation to aspire to the divine ideal in character; they therefore quit practicing morality. The problem of the great prophets was to get the people to raise their ideals to God again, but they failed. They failed to educate their children to listen.

The Synagogue Period was one of professionalism. The reading and expounding of the Scripture with their commentaries were carried to the people in the synagogues and were developed under Ezra and Nehemiah (Ezra 7:10, 25). Soon after, a professional spirit captured the teachers. The synagogue replaced the home and the scribes became stereotyped in their teaching methods. They became engrossed in the letter, not the spirit, of the law. Conformity meant more than life. It took the coming of Jesus to rectify the errors of this system and to lay the groundwork for something better.

Jesus was the best educated man the world has known. He was the very embodiment of God's plan. He was a lifelong student of nature and human nature. He lived in constant communion with God. Such was the preparation of Jesus. With regard to the practice of the Jews, He was primarily a teacher. He provided a model in content and method. He gave His disciples the content and commissioned them to evangelize and educate. The educational ideal was the perfect man of God in Christ. Following closely His pattern, the early Christian Church placed primary emphasis on teaching. Paul became an educational evangelist (Colossians 1:28, 29; Ephesians 1:17, 18; 4:11 f). He and the early apostles, however, used an individual approach primarily. The institutionalization of the schools was to remain as a later development. Although valuable ground was lost through the failure to institutionalize Christian education, the rapid spread of Christianity over the Medieval world is the religious miracle of the ages. Furthermore, social foundations were laid in the character, methods, and curricula content provided by Jesus which are sufficient to build an adequate philosophy of Christian education and a successful system of education.

4. The Bible in Education

From what has been said above it can be readily observed that the Bible is basic in Christian education. It is formative in its educational influence. This can be seen from several standpoints. First, the Bible brings *spiritual enlightenment* to the heart and mind of the pupil. Here it ministers to the deepest need of human nature. In this respect it is redemptive, but it also has educational discipline. Having led the pupil to the source of his life, it also leads him in the kind of life-discipline required for satisfactory living. After all, this latter reason is at the very heart of every true educational purpose.

A second basic reason for placing the Bible at the central position in the curriculum is to be found in the fact that it provides the historical record of *representative human and Christian experience.* The Book exhausts the possibilities in this category by pointing out all shades of righteousness and unrighteousness in the conduct of men. The record in this instance is both national and individual experiences. Generally speaking, the Bible traces the experience of man from his origin through the fall of man into sin to his recovery through God's plan of redemption. The Bible is a vast compendium of materials on man in his individual and social relationships. This emphasis on personal and social experience has direct implications for education today.

Still further, the Bible has *literary* value. No other book in the English speaking world offers the possibilities for study in the English from the literary point of view as does the Bible. Almost every conceivable type of literary expression is to be found within its pages. Its materials are easily adaptable in many places for children to read and study. Its combination of a variety of literary styles with a multiplicity of types of literature — stories, prose, poetry, drama, etc. — qualifies this inspired book for a place in all educational curricula. It is rather paradoxical to think that this great book is comparatively neglected among school subjects.

Perhaps the greatest reason, second only to revelation itself, why the Bible is basic is found in the service which it supplies to the curriculum through *integration and correlation.* Integration provides unity by bringing all parts into a whole. Correlation shows the implications of mutual relationships. In the case of subject matter, correlation would reveal how subjects compare, overlap, and correspond with one another. Revealing as it does the centrality of God as the source of all truth, the Bible transcends all other books in showing the essential unity and correlation of truth. As possible in no other book, the Bible correlates history, geography, literature, and religion. The present-day confusion and lack of integration in the American system of education lies in the failure to have a unifying core, realized only in the Word of God. The history of education reveals that in the beginning the major educational institutions of this country had such a core, but have wandered away from it. To say this, however, is not to overlook the condition also prevalent in many so-called Christian schools and colleges of this country. Curricula in many of the latter schools have been developed in a humanistic frame of reference rather than in a Christian and Biblical one. The time has come for all schools to re-evaluate their theories and practices in the light of Scriptural integration to effect both spiritual and academic excellence. The task before us is to follow the pattern supplied in the Bible whereby it is possible to correlate Christ and the Bible with all subjects of study, with all administrative practices and student activity. The truth of the matter is that an institution does not necessarily achieve Christian education by simply providing for chapel services, prayer meetings, and similar activities. These activities can be enjoyed by students without having the semblance of a Christ- and Bible-centered education in the classroom. Instead, Biblical and spiritual principles should be the directing influences in every subject.

The whole matter of integration can be summed up by saying that all truth comes from God. This does not directly imply that all truth has equal status. Some truth is natural truth; it is truth about creation, but not revelation. To the Christian the truth of revelation is more important than the truth of creation. The purpose of creation is revelation. All truth reveals God; all creation reveals God. Spiritual truths are, therefore, more to be emphasized than natural truths. At the same time, however, we should emphasize the fact that natural truth *does* reveal God. As such, it has an important place in the curriculum and essentially is not secular but sacred. Every subject, to be properly integrated and correlated, should be taught within a Biblical frame of reference. The Bible is basic to Christian education.

One final reason why the Bible is basic in Christian education should be mentioned. The Bible contains truth which has *inherent capacity* to regenerate men and society. Jesus said, "The words that I speak unto you, they are spirit and they are life" (John 6:63). In conjunction with the Holy Spirit the truth of Scripture becomes a leavening influence for good in the heart of him who will accept the truth and believe it. It is with confidence in the Word that every Christian teacher can approach his task with the assurance that there is every chance for fruitfulness. Herein lies the secret of the formative influence of the Bible. The Bible is basic to Christian education.

5. Jesus Christ and Education

One of the greatest books on Jesus as a teacher was written by Dr. Herman Harrell Horne entitled *Jesus — The Master Teacher*. Dr. Horne concluded that Jesus' place in educational history was central and greatest on the basis of the following objective facts, as he listed them:

1. His followers outnumber those of any other teacher
2. The nations that profess His name, though following Him afar off, lead the world's civilization
3. He lived and taught the solution of man's greatest problem: the adjustment of the claims of the individual to those of society
4. He taught the highest moral and spiritual truths
5. He taught these truths simply, using effectively the pedagogic arts
6. He committed His teachings wholly to a choice few whom He trained as His witnesses

7. He taught them from highest motives — love, sympathy, compassion, and the sense of divine mission
8. He had the five essential qualifications of a world-teacher, namely, a world-view, knowledge of His subject-matter, knowledge of His pupils, aptness at teaching, and a character worthy of imitation in all respects. He lived what He taught.[6]

In addition to these general observations regarding the place Jesus has in education, there are at least three specific contributions which He made to the educational world that we should mention. The first is intellectual. Jesus was interested in reaching and persuading the minds of men. He did not divorce the intellect from the whole nature of man. To Him intellect, emotions and will were so inextricably interwoven and unified that "what comes to Him as knowledge is pressed and gathered into every part of Him, and fills His entire nature as truth." The fact that Jesus was concerned with truth, and that truth is concerned with the whole man, gives pertinent evidence to show that Jesus helped to lay the foundation for present-day emphasis on educating the whole man.

Two additional intellectual contributions are good habits of thinking, particularly the inductive, and stress laid upon the affinity of Christianity for democracy. Where the source of all man's knowledge is in God, and when such knowledge is closely connected to character which is found in God, then all men have a right to education. Where truth is related to the whole man, freedom is demanded to achieve the development of Christian character.

The second major contribution made by Jesus was in the realm of content. He was the Master Teacher. As an Educator He awakened new potentiality and power in His followers. His purpose was to incarnate truth in life, to arouse and cultivate the spiritual nature of men to righteousness, freedom, and perfection. The substance of this content led to the creation and development of new life. The content of the teachings of Jesus, therefore, was rich, comprehensive and thorough. The substance of the content which Jesus provided for the field of education to some people would seem limited. As far as so-called secular truth is concerned, that is perhaps true, but in the realm of the moral and spiritual, and particularly as this kind of content touches the secular, Jesus' contribution has never been matched. In view of the supremacy of the spiritual, of values over facts, His teachings provide the kind of content which gives meaning and guidance to all other truth. "Never man so spake" (John 7:46).

The development of personality lies at the heart of the educa-

[6]Herman H. Horne, *The Master Teacher* (New York, Association Press, 1942), pp. 202-03.

tional process. Jesus Christ has been called the "Prophet of Personality" and herein lies His great significance for education. The way Jesus as a living personality dealt with life's realities has given to men the highest example of the development of personality and the achievements of personality. By triumphant living Jesus charted a course which leads men to an appreciation of the capacities of personality for higher experiences. Psychology has done much to describe the manifestations of mental processes and consequent behavior but it has yet to find a way to delve into the hidden and latent resources of the mind and personality. The power to touch the inner man not only reveals the originality of Jesus' teachings but the very power to create and develop personality. "In him was life and the life was the light of men" (John 1:4).

The third major contribution made by Jesus to education lies in the area of methodology. This is clearly evidenced by His knowledge of men, His strategy in dealing with men, and His teaching methods. The latter was dealt with in a preceding chapter.

The early church and the Apostle Paul took up the philosophy and methods of Jesus and perpetuated them into later centuries. From that day until this, formal methods and institutions of instruction have been originated and sponsored by the Christian Church.

Today the Bible continues to bear great influence in the world. Its influence has been marked on our language, our literature, art, civil and national life, social reforms, and particularly in the lives of countless people.

D. CHRISTIAN THEOLOGY

1. Nature and Purpose

Next to Bible, Christian Theology is a strategic part of the area of Biblical Studies. Christian Theology is concerned with the whole of reality as reality is particularly concerned with and related to its source — God. It is concerned with the relation of God to the reality which He has created and vice versa and especially with the purpose of man within reality. It looks to revelation for its source of knowledge and thereby adds a dimension to thought not present in other disciplines. This discipline focuses particularly on the relation of our faith to the Church, but its contributions are sufficiently important to education as a whole to merit a peculiar place in the area of Biblical Studies.

For a formal definition perhaps Wiley's is acceptable generally: "Christian Theology, or Dogmatics as the term is often used technically, is that branch of theological science which aims to set forth in a systematic manner the doctrines of the Christian faith." Drawing heavily upon Divine Revelation, Christian Theology embraces a study of God as the source, subject and end of all theology, a study of religion, the church and the work of the Holy Spirit within its life, and the relation of theology to contemporaneous thought. Four main divisions of this subject have been used traditionally. They include exegetical theology, historical theology, systematic theology and practical theology. Where emphasis is placed primarily on Bible, exegetical theology is the study of the contents of Scripture, exegetically ascertained and classified according to doctrine.

Some of the contributions made by this area of study include the following:

1. Theology provides a frame of reference for all knowledge, all truth, and all being. It shows that all truth, sacred and secular, is one in God.
2. The various spheres of life are coordinated according to the dictates of Christian faith expressed in Christian Theology. In this it guides Christian Philosophy.
3. It specializes in a description and explanation of the nature of God — the Source of reality.
4. In revealing the nature of God, it discloses the clues by which truth can be properly interpreted.
5. It provides structures of thought, such as creation, immanence, and transcendence by which truth can be interpreted.
6. In relation to history, it furnishes the categories of purpose, providence, incarnation, redemption, and destiny.
7. It provides an integrating center for knowledge, expressed through great principles and focused in the Person of God.
8. It discloses God's will for men, thereby providing both a sense of purpose and destiny.
9. It guides thought life along the lines of God's thought life.
10. It measures curriculum content through the spiritual generalizations of revelation.

2. General Objectives for Christian Theology

A sample of some of the more general objectives for Christian Theology is that which is found at Fort Wayne Bible College, as follows:

1. To help the student to acquire a personal and practical knowledge of the Bible through the systematic study of the fundamental doctrines which are implicit in God's divine revelation.

2. To help the student to correlate the fundamental truths thus ascertained into an orderly, systematic, well-balanced theological pattern as the basis of his own Christian experience and philosophy of life.

3. To aid the student in acquiring a clear, sound, authoritative and comprehensive understanding of Christian doctrine as a whole, together with an appreciation for, and thorough grasp of, the basic elements of each major doctrine, as the necessary basis of all effective preaching, teaching, and witnessing.

4. To help the student to discover and understand the Bible's supreme message of redemption, as embodied in systematized truth and centered in Jesus Christ, and thus prepare him to proclaim the Christian Gospel effectively in the world of today.

5. To develop, crystallize, and organize the student's doctrinal thinking, to stabilize his Christian experience, and to help him to become a good minister of Jesus Christ, a competent and skillful interpreter of divine truth, a trustworthy guide to things eternal.

3. Relation of Philosophy and Theology

Philosophy and theology occupy much common ground in that they strive for ultimate truth concerning God, the universe, man, and all their relations. They differ in their methods. Philosophy seeks knowledge through reason, speculation, and induction. Theology relies upon the authority of God's Word; it begins with revelation. Both of these methods are legitimate. Christians do not deny the use of reason as a reliable informant as far as it goes, but revelation provides the basis for the Word of God, which, in the final analysis, is of a higher authority. Philosophy, on the other hand, does have definite value for the theologian. It furnishes him support for the Christian position. It reveals the limitations of reason because careful study shows that essentially philosophy has no real theory of origin and no explanations of sin, death, etc. Fragmentary answers to those questions do not provide a satisfactory philosophy of life. Philosophy also serves the theologian by acquainting him with unchristian views.

Philosophers and theologians should work together. Neither should ignore the works of the other. Certainly there is no need for warfare. If God is the Author of all truth, and He is, then philosophers and theologians should press research for truth without hesitation.

4. *Philosophical Concepts of God*

Before getting into the heart of the matter regarding the teachings of theology on the doctrine of God, perhaps it would be wise and profitable to list in outline form the philosophical positions of the representative philosophies on the nature of God. A comparative study in outline form is provided following:

THE NATURE OF GOD

A. NATURALISM
1. The term "God" has no supernatural connotation.
2. Religious experience *is* the experience of God.
3. Wieman — God is the supreme value-producing factor in the world.
4. God is impersonal and wholly *within* the process of Nature.
5. God is within Nature and therefore not infinite.
6. God is good because He is the power in Nature which makes good possible.

B. PRAGMATISM
1. There is no personal God.
2. Purely a naturalistic conception of God.
3. God is the realization of ideal values.
4. The God-idea works, therefore it is useful.
5. God is emerging as the universe moves toward Him.
6. God is good, but not ultimate in goodness nor power.

C. REALISM
1. Virtually the same as the naturalistic concept.
2. But it also believes in objective existence, so God is not identical with nature. Instead God has personal character, either natural or supernatural.
3. God is the source of and the greatest of all values.
4. The will of God is perfectly good, but has not yet been fully realized in man and the world.
5. No metaphysical consistency among realists.

D. NEO-SCHOLASTICISM
1. God is not extended, but is immanent in His creation.
2. God is absolutely subsistent; in Him essence and existence are identical.
3. God is pure and perfect actuality; there is no potentiality in Him.
4. The goodness of God and the being of God are identical.
5. God is infinite in goodness and perfection.
6. The eternity of God transcends all time limitations and measures.

7. God is one, not two, nor many; all other individuals are excluded from being what He is by virtue of what He is.

E. IDEALISM
1. Ultimate Reality is Spirit
2. The Ultimate Spirit is an Absolute Self who is mental and conscious.
3. All other selves are really parts of the Absolute Self.
4. Two views on the power and goodness of God.
   a. Majority view — God is all-power and all-goodness.
   b. E. S. Brightman — God is good, but finite.

5. *Theological Content*

Many methods of systematization are used to organize the content of theology. Analysis reveals that doctrines most commonly are arranged in local order as follows:

Theism: The existence of a personal God, Creator, Preservor, and Ruler of all things

Theology: The attributes of God; the Trinity; creation and providence — in the fuller light of revelation

Anthropology: The origin of man; his primitive state and fall; the results of the fall for the race

Christology: The incarnation of the Son; the person of Christ

Soteriology: The atonement in Christ; the salvation in Christ

Ecclesiology: The Church; the ministry; the sacraments; means of grace

Pneumatology: The Person and work of the Holy Spirit

Eschatology: The intermediate state; the second advent; the resurrection; the judgment; the final destinies

The reader is referred to Chapter Two for more information on content.

6. *The Contemporary Theological Situation*

It is common knowledge that present-day theology and philosophy have felt the deep impact of German thought. Kant, Hegel, Schleiermacher, Ritschl, and Troeltsch brought certain concepts philosophically into focus. Among those concepts were (1) God is immanent, (2) Christianity is just another religion, but of course, the highest developed expression of religion, (3) Christian experience can be fully explained by modern psychology without Biblical reference, and (4) revelation means human insight and discovery. Along with these, of course, was the emphasis given to evolution. British theologians also lined up with these views. Eminent among the American thinkers affected by German thought were Parker and Bushnell. Along with the philosophical views, and evolution as a method, was added the weight of Biblical criticism.

Thus, this century began with the inroads of idealistic immanentism.

For the first 25 years of this century, classical liberalism held sway. The authority and inspiration of the Scriptures were rejected; the fact of sin and the provision of a blood atonement were opposed. The evangelical forces retreated from a mighty onslaught of unbelief and the liberal forces took charge of the academic and literary worlds. The whole church rocked and reeled before the attack. Evangelical theology was ridiculed and considered outmoded and in many instances was the brunt of a direct frontal attack.

The last 25 years has witnessed a remarkable revolution in theological thought. This revolution has been marked by internal revolt among the liberals, external pressure from other philosophies, and a counter-attack from evangelicals. Shortly after World War I, the new theology of crisis struck Germany from Switzerland. The leaders of neo-orthodoxy were Karl Barth, Emil Brunner, and Eduard Thurneysen. Soren Kierkegaard's writings also entered the battle. The inevitable result was that liberalism began to totter, so much so that it was said that a new Protestantism had replaced Schleiermacher, Ritschl, and Troeltsch. Neo-orthodoxy stressed the sinfulness of man, the transcendence of God, the necessity of Christology, but retained many tenets of evolution and watered down the doctrine of divine inspiration. In America signs of revolt came from philosophers outside evangelical circles who began to reject Hegelianism. The pragmatists rallied around John Dewey and William James, and the humanists gathered force at the University of Chicago around such men as Shailer, Mathews, Ames, Hayden, and Wieman. Although this school of thought remained essentially naturalistic, nevertheless, humanistic reinterpretations of Christianity made large inroads into American Protestantism through secular and religious educators. The period of about 1925 to 1935 witnessed a period of controversy in the theological world. The optimistic tenets of liberalism were rudely shaken by two mighty world wars and a great deal of social disintegration. A series of controversies arose which ultimately meant the complete downfall of liberalism. What is known as the fundamentalist controversy, better thought of as an evangelical counter-attack, began to take place. The scholarship of such evangelicals as J. Gresham Machen, B. B. Warfield, Vos, and Mullins proved conclusively that the theology of liberalism was not Biblical, neither was its gospel the Gospel of the New Testament. When humanism added its voice in pointing out the marked inconsistencies of liberalism, the inevitable result was retreat for the liberals. Instead of embracing humanism, however, there was a reaction against it, too.

A period of readjustment and alignment then followed for

several years. It appeared that a strong central bloc was formed, on the one hand opposed to humanism and on the other opposed to fundamentalism. The term "realism" was coined to cover a multitude of differences. In the early thirties the writings of neo-orthodoxy began slowly to make their impact.

Recent years have seen a marked resurgence of evangelical forces. The rise of the National Association of Evangelicals, through which the forces of evangelicalism are formally organized for fellowship, study, and service, and the publications of a number of aggressive evangelical scholars, including such men as Bernard Ramm, Gordon H. Clark, Edward Carnell, Warren C. Young, Carl F. H. Henry, Mark Fakkema and Wilbur Smith, are evidences of this. Fundamentalism has become known now as *evangelicalism.* The movement is marked with a new openness of mind toward science, a willingness to unite on theological issues and doctrines, new scholarship, and greater tolerance.

Liberalism finds itself in a state of controversy. The cleavage in liberal ranks has been sufficient to divide them into three strong parties: (1) neo-orthodox, (2) neo-liberal, and (3) neo-naturalist. Some advocates of these veiws are swinging back to orthodox and fundamental doctrines of the Scriptures, to an acceptance of conversion and the supernatural in Christianity. However, they have a long way to go before they reveal a complete swing back to New Testament Christianity.

It is evident that confusion is a major characteristic of theological thinking today. A simple comparison of views on major issues was made by Carl Henry.[7]

I. GOD
  1. Evangelical view
     God is eternal supernatural personal Being, Triune, Revealer, Creator and free
  2. Roman Catholic view
     Virtually same as the Evangelical view, except that it is primarily philosophically conceived rather than Biblically
  3. Liberal view
     No uniformity in this view; unitarian, primarily as to personality
  4. Neo-orthodox view
     God is triune personal activity and transcendent
  5. View of Humanism
     Adopted naturalistic view that God is the moving front of evolution; personality is symbolical

II. REVELATION
  1. Evangelical View
     Bible is the Written Word of God, inspired of the Holy Spirit, originally without error

[7]Carl F. H. Henry, *The Drift of Western Thought* (Grand Rapids, Mich., Wm. B. Eerdmans Pub. Co., 1951), ch. 4.

2. Roman Catholic view
   Equal value is assigned to the Bible and Church; revelation is the infallible interpretation of the church and pope
3. Liberal view
   Special revelation is subordinate to general revelation; revelation is human insight
4. Neo-orthodox view
   The Bible is "witness" to revelation; it contains the Word of God but is not literally the word of God
5. View of Humanism
   Denies the supernatural; relies instead on the scientific method; revelation is human insight subject to revision

III. MAN

1. Evangelical view
   Man is a distinct species, created by God, originally holy, now fallen into sin, but redeemed through Jesus Christ
2. Roman Catholic view
   Retains creation, original holiness, and the fall, but a mild depravity; salvation comes by faith and works
3. Liberal view
   Virtually the evolutionary point of view; essential goodness of man with no need of blood atonement
4. Neo-orthodox view
   Man's existence due to evolution; man fell symbolically; the fall is the story of us all
5. View of Humanism
   Man stands at the apex of the animal realm by virtue of craftiness, not essential difference in nature; sin is a cultural lag.

IV. REDEMPTION

1. Evangelical view
   Man, as a sinner, needs salvation through repentance and faith by which he receives a new nature and forgiveness through the propitiation of Jesus Christ and the work of the Holy Spirit.
2. Liberal view
   There is no need of rebirth through blood atonement; redemption comes through following the ethical example of Jesus Christ by which man is delivered from inner tensions and frustrations which leads to perfect adjustment
3. Neo-orthodox view
   Crisis experience is normative; redemption comes through commitment to Christ's law of love; through men, God is made personal in the world
4. Roman Catholic view
   Salvation comes by faith and works
5. View of Humanism
   Redemption is the deliverance from inner tensions and discord by which personality is integrated and unified; whatever achieves this is considered divine

7. Secular Education and Theology

Most secular philosophies of education are based on naturalistic suppositions and are the result of human reasoning. It is surprising and offensive to many educators to receive the suggestion that there might be such a thing as a theology of education. Even among evangelicals this concept is strange because they have been taught for so long the tenets of secular education in the atmosphere of Christian surroundings. The thought of direct connection is entirely foreign to many. Secular education by-passes many issues in the life situation which have theological implications, such as sin, death, destiny, etc. The absence of a common basis for thinking as well as a common language have made it difficult for Christian concepts to be acceptable in secular ranks.

For many years, according to the history of education, theological concepts played a large part in education. In fact, Christian theism was the dominating idea which moulded society from Christ through the Reformation. Because the sad tendency was to divorce faith from practice, as well as to neglect the social implications of the Gospel, naturalistic and secular emphasis became dominant. In spite of this, many outstanding educators through the centuries, illustrated by Comenius, have couched many of their educational concepts in theological language. Furthermore, the historical record of the American educational system is replete with one instance after another of religious references. In spite of denials, it is apparent that secular education essentially has a theology, though a negative one. By making a deliberate effort to suppress the teaching of Biblical truths in public education, educators are expressing a negative theology. By leaving God unmentioned, they virtually testify to their unbelief.

8. *Theology and Education*

The past several years has witnessed a great interest in the relation of theology to education. Books, pamphlets, panel discussions, and magazine articles have been devoted to theological relations to education. The failure of liberalism and the contemporary crises in the social world have focused attention on spiritual issues and values. It is now evident that philosophical discussions cannot possibly be adequate and comprehensive without seriously considering the religious implications of life. Theology helps to supply the lack involved and at the same time provides integration from the religious standpoint.

The Christian believes that his theology has relevance to all Christian activity and life. Since education is inextricably concerned with life, it cannot escape theological issues and values. Since Christian theology is the repository of God's revelation in systematized form, and since that revelation is the wisdom of Christian life and thought, it *must* have vital relation to Christian education and all education.

A theology of education will save Christian education from the experiences of secular education, characterized by fragmentariness and confusion, and at the same time deliver it from a secular framework. Modern secular education has no integrating core. By raising the integration of subject matter from the natural science level to that of the philosophical level, Christian theology will bring unity, integration, purpose, and worthy objective to the field of education.

9. *Some Implications of Theology for Education*

The short survey of the great doctrines of the faith brings us to the point where it is now possible and profitable to summarize their implications for theory and practice in the field of education.

I. THE DOCTRINE OF GOD

A. God exists and is central, providing unity and ultimate being.

B. True philosophical unity is found only in the *Christian* God of Revelation.

C. All things are related understandingly to and are derived from God through creation.

D. To know God is the essence of wisdom.

E. The essence of education is a revelation of a personal God.

F. The doctrine of God systematizes the divine attributes so that we are provided with a guide to the revelation of the Divine Person in subject matter.

G. The Creation by God provides the basis for the curriculum and the subject matter in the curriculum; essentially therefore, there are no such things as secular school subjects.

H. The fundamental problems of education are theological in nature and require the wisdom of theology for understanding. The natural sciences are greatly helpful in this regard but they must also be interpreted against the background of theological wisdom.

I. Since theology provides guidance for education, there should be mutual assistance between theologians and educators.

J. It is possible to be a teacher, philosopher, or scientist without studying theology, but without Christian theology it is not possible to be Christian in any of these areas.

K. Theology shows the way out of educational confusion by clearing up the uncertainty about the nature and destiny of man and by revealing the nature of God, man, society, and the universe.

L. Theology reveals the limitation of education. Christian education can sow the seed, but only God the Holy Spirit can give the increase.

M. The Holy Spirit is the Administrative Agent by which the revelation of God is made known to man and the redemption of God is made actual in man's heart and life.

II. THE DOCTRINE OF REVELATION

   A. Christian Education becomes a matter of the interpretation of God's revelation.

   B. The purpose of education is to show God revealed; the objective of education is to qualify man to reveal God.

   C. The content of education is provided through a curriculum which is directly God-related and God-revealing.

   D. Theology provides a systematization of the attributes of God which students and teachers should expect to see revealed in all truth.

   E. God has revealed Himself in three ways: (1) General Self-revelation through nature; (2) Personal Self-revelation through His Son, and (3) Special Self-revelation through the Bible.

   F. The Bible provides the integrating and correlating factor in the curriculum.

III. THE DOCTRINE OF MAN

   A. Man is not a product of evolution, but was created by God, in the image of God.

   B. Man is dependent upon God. The best interests of the child, the pupil, therefore, cannot be served outside of the love, mercy, and provision of God.

   C. The pupil is the focus of education. The theological concept of man should be the view of man held in education.

   D. The problem of sin has made education more difficult.
      1. Sin blinds man; Jesus Christ brings light. This is education.
      2. Sin cripples man; Jesus Christ heals, restores, and corrects. This, too, is education.
      3. Sin corrupts the mind; Jesus Christ and the Holy Spirit regenerate and purify the mind. This, also, is education. Thus, regeneration makes possible a better kind of education.
      4. Sin disintegrates the truth.
      5. Sin makes man egocentric.
      6. Sin blurs man's concept of the educational objective.

   E. The whole-pupil-in-his-environment should be considered in all education.

   F. Theology provides the answer with regard to man's purpose on earth and his destiny to come. This should be the controlling factor in educational theory and practice. All other purposes, such as citizenship, character development, and cultivation of personality, are secondary purposes and find meaning only in the light of the ultimate.

   G. Education should be a universal privilege for all men.

   H. Man is a rational creature created in the image of God with moral responsibility in freedom. Man must not, therefore, be approached by the educator as an animal which has reached the peak of development.

IV. The Doctrine of Redemption

    A. Jesus Christ should be at the center of Education.
        1. He provides eternal life.
        2. The Incarnation is the supreme example of perfect humanity.
        3. It is also the supreme example of educational method.
    B. True education is redemptive in character.
    C. The provision of redemption has made education necessary and adequate in Jesus Christ.
    D. The essential element in the educational process with regard to method is life itself with the living thereof. Living at its best comes through redemption. We learn by doing.

E. Christian Philosophy

1. *Nature and Purpose*

Christian philosophy constitutes the third discipline in the area of Biblical Studies. Generally conceived, Christian philosophy is the Christian approach to wisdom. More specifically, it embraces the Christian interpretation of reality, of knowledge and truth, and of moral and aesthetic values.

In general the function of philosophy is to achieve synoptic integration by relating things systematically. Philosophy is all-inclusive, for it deals with total meanings, questions of purpose and value, and consults data from all experience. In all of this it seeks the organization of all knowledge and experience into a coherent explanation of reality, or a world view. It is also more narrowly concerned with ontological and epistemological problems particularly as they relate to each other separate discipline in the curriculum. This it accomplishes through an examination of the basic presuppositions, methods, and basic concepts of those disciplines. The contributions of Christian philosophy may be summarized as follows:

    1. It coordinates the various spheres of life as a whole.
    2. It relates knowledge systematically.
    3. It examines the presuppositions, methods and basic concepts of each discipline and group of disciplines.
    4. It strives for coherence, the formulation of a world view.
    5. Its method is to consult data from total experience.

2. *General Objectives for Christian Philosophy*

From the foregoing considerations, it is possible to formulate a set of general objectives for use in teaching and learning as follows:

    1. To lead the student into an understanding of the basic concepts of Christian thought, the first principles that are active in it, and the presuppositions that underlie it.

2. To develop in the student the ability to think deeply and critically.
3. To guide the student in making Christian thought relevant to everyday living.

3. Problems of Philosophy in the Present

Man stands in the present, then he looks backward and forward. Present problems to solve include the problem of personal existence, the problem of knowing, the problem of truth, and the problem of values.

Man is conscious of *present existence*. To doubt this fact borders on insanity. The use of the term "I" denotes the fact of present personal existence. The Christian does not desire to argue this point.

Next to the problem of personal existence is that of *knowing*. Some philosophies provide a record of man's tendency to doubt the *reality* of knowledge:

Agnosticism — questions man's capacity to know.

Skepticism — definitely denies the possibility of knowledge.

Positivism — knowledge comes *only* through the senses.

Phenomenalism — admits that knowledge is possible, but limits it to the objects of sense experience or phenomena.

Several views assert the possibility of knowing:

(1) Epistemological monism — knowing is immediate and direct.

   Pansubjectivists — idea and object are all one idea.

   This is the position of idealism; in education the consistency theory draws from this position.

   Panobjectivists — idea and object are all one object.

   This is the position of realism; in education the correspondence theory draws from this position.

(2) Epistemological dualism — process of knowledge is twofold.

   There is mind *and* the object.

   This is the position of some realists.

(3) Instrumentalism — thinking consists of problem-solving.

(4) Relativism — all knowledge is relative.

   This is the position of pragmatism.

(5) Authority — knowledge comes through indoctrination.

(6) Intuition — knowledge comes through insight.

(7) Revelation — knowledge is revealed by God.

While the Christian may recognize some truth in certain of the views above, he must rely primarily on the revelation of God.

Closely allied to the problems of personal existence and knowing is the *problem of truth*. This problem is concerned with determining truth and distinguishing between truth and error. At the heart of this problem is the matter of an adequate *test for truth*. A wide variety of proposed solutions have been offered.

(1) Custom — past practice is the criterion of truth.
(2) Instinct — man inherently has the gift of discovering truth.
(3) Feeling — man is persuaded by inward impressions.
(4) Intuition — truth comes by direct cognition.
(5) Consensus gentium—universal agreement determines truth.
(6) Tradition — truth is perpetuated by the cultural heritage.
(7) Sense perception — five senses are the criteria of truth.
(8) Correspondence — truth is correspondence to reality.
(9) Pragmatism — truth is determined by practical efficiency.
(10) Coherence or systematic consistency — a judgment is true when it sticks together with all the facts of our experience.

The last view seems most acceptable to the Christian as a test for truth. It demands that all the facts fall together in a logical, intelligent, purposive and rational relationship. Thus the law of contradiction is not violated, and a systematic account of reality is attained by a devotion to all the facts of experience which make up the content of our knowledge.

The *problem of values* concerns that which matters most. It is also known as axiology. This problem is particularly pertinent to education because values help to directly determine educational aims, motivation, and marks.

    I. Views on the source of values
        A. Hedonism — values are derived from pleasure.
        B. Values are derived from satisfaction of desire and purpose.
        C. Values are derived from right motivation and use of the will.
        D. Idealism — coherence is the source of values.
    II. Classification of values
        A. Consummatory values — satisfy immediate desire.
        B. Instrumental values — those which are good *for* something.
        C. Intrinsic values — those inherently good; objective.
            1. Lower — those with reference to body, recreation, work.
            2. Higher — those with reference to society, character, intellectual, and religious matters.

To the Christian, God is the source of all values. Christians are therefore objective. As a Christian one should be able to appreciate every school subject and see in them a bit of God's self-revelation because all truth is God's truth. It is the teacher's responsibility to guide the pupil to this kind of appreciation.

With reference to this whole problem, three major views are apparent: (1) those who view values subjectively, subject to individual feelings and purposes but without any hierarchy of educational values, and (2) those who view educational values objectively. To these latter adherents, values are intrinsic and derived from their maker. Intrinsic values are considered superior to instrumental ones. (3) The third view is Christian, closely related to (2) but a little different in that the Maker of values is considered to be God and the highest of all intrinsic values is the doing of His will.

4. *Problems of Philosophy in the Past*

Problems of the past include those of cause, origin, purpose, and life. Solutions to these problems provide answers as to what the universe is, where it came from, what its purpose is, and the place of life in its framework. All of these have direct importance for the field of education.

The problem of the external universe is really the problem of *cosmology*, the nature of matter. Several attempts have been made to examine the *cause* behind the universe:

Materialism — the universe is composed exclusively of matter.

Energism — the universe is composed exclusively of energy.

Positivism — the universe is a machine controlled by natural laws.

Pragmatism — matter is a process rather than a system.

Pantheism — all that exists is God who is blind force.

Theism — the universe is the product of the power of an omnipotent personal God who exists apart from and over the universe.

Agnosticism — universe is the product of many separate gods.

Christian theism is the acceptable view to the Christian. His belief in a personal God who created and upholds the universe is at the heart of this view. At the present time a practical dualism is held by many Christians. That is to say, matter was created by God but is separate from Him while at the same time being dependent upon Him.

With regard to the *origin* of the universe, only two views are possible. Either the universe has been eternal or it has been created. Materialists and naturalists deny creation and tell us that matter is infinite, changeless, self-existent, and self-sufficient. Observation, however, reveals that matter *is* changing, that forms of matter are dependent on others, and that matter is composed and compounded of elements or parts. Furthermore, recent discoveries in the structure of the atom, radio-activity, and astro-physics are leading away from a purely materialistic viewpoint.

The problem of *purpose* is the problem of teleology or theory of ends. It endeavors to show that the universe is motivated and dominated by purposes or goals. Mechanism denies this possibility and maintains that the universe is a vast machine composed of atoms in motion. Emergence seems to be the chief explanation of this process. The Christian position is teleological. To the Christian there is an existent personal God who has disclosed His purposes in his Word. God is transcendent but works in the universe both providentially and miraculously. In this way He becomes immanent and guides the universe to certain desired ends.

The problem of the nature and purpose of *life* involves the problem of psychology. The first step in dealing with this problem is to note the *kinds* of life. There is life in plants and animals and life in human beings. Both hold life in common but not the same kind of life. Vegetal life is living but does not possess knowing. Its operations include nutrition, growth, and reproduction. Sentient life has all these plus the power of knowing and of acting on knowledge. In addition, sentient bodies or animals are capable of appetite and movement. These are classified into species. Man is also a sentient being but is to be distinguished from animals because of his rational powers. He possesses understanding, will, and reasoning. Essentially, man is a spiritual personality.

There are two possible answers to the problem of the origin of life: (1) evolution, or (2) creation. Adherents of evolution include:

Casual evolution — eternal origination.

Modal evolution — God used evolution as His method of creation; also called theistic evolution.

Cosmic evolution — theory that matter has existed always but in primitive form, yet by laws.

Emergent evolution — all things have emerged from Space-Time.

Organic evolution — all life has evolved from a primordial cell or cells.

The Christian position is that of creation. The Christian theistic world view accounts adequately and satisfactorily for the origin of matter, force, motion, law, order, design, and life.

5. *Problems of Philosophy in the Future*

Future problems include those of death and destiny. The Christian theistic world view is the only adequate answer for these problems. Other positions either ignore them or consider them irrelevant. Jesus Christ solved these problems and left us with the promise, "I am the resurrection and the life: he that believeth in me, though he were dead, yet shall he live" (John 11:25).

6. A World View and Education

The discussion up to this point has dealt with the possibility of man finding the solution to basic problems. In the solutions to such problems reside the content of a rational world view. The relevance of such a view to education in general is seen in the fact that it supplies a sense of direction, an objective to strive for, and the content for subject matter. An analysis will reveal a sense of frustration in the ranks of modern education — there seems to be no chief end in view. The unifying factor is absent — a world view.

The practical value of a world view will be seen also upon examination of its substance recorded in Chapter II.

SUGGESTED ACTIVITIES FOR CHAPTER IX

1. Give your definition of the Bible, Christian Theology and Philosophy.
2. Discuss the values of these subjects for education and personal living.
3. Draw your own chart to show how the subjects comprising the Biblical Studies area can be integrated and organized.
4. Discuss the use of the inductive method in Bible study and teaching.
5. Trace the development of the Biblical idea of education. Cover such matters as education in the Bible, the Bible and educational principles, and the place of the Bible in education.
6. What have been the contributions made by Jesus Christ to education? This may be approached by considering the influence of Jesus in general on the world at large and then His specific influence in the field of education.
7. What were some of the contributions made by the early church and by Paul?
8. Discuss the relation of teaching and preaching in the early church.
9. What methods were used in proclaiming the Gospel?
10. Make a particular study of the influence and teaching methods of the Apostle Paul. Consult *The Pedagogy of St. Paul* by Howard Kuist.
11. Discuss the influence and place of the Bible in education.
12. Discuss the definition, purpose, and function of theology.
13. Discuss each of the doctrines of theology and show their implications for education.
14. Do you think that secular education has a theology?
15. What are the implications of the attributes of God for teaching and learning?
16. Discuss the effects of sin on Adam and Eve, on the human race, on the social order, on the material world, on God, and on education.
17. Discuss the place of philosophy in education.
18. Discuss the relevance of the various problems of philosophy to education.

THE CHRISTIAN PHILOSOPHY OF
SOCIAL SCIENCES

OUTLINE FOR CHAPTER 10

A. NATURE AND PURPOSE
   1. Definition
   2. Purpose
   3. Scope
   4. Historical Developments
   5. Values
   6. Integration
   7. Interpretation
   8. General Objectives

B. THE CHRISTIAN VIEW OF MAN, SOCIETY, AND HISTORY
   1. The Christian View of Man
   2. The Christian View of Society
   3. The Christian View of History

C. THE SOCIAL SCIENCES
   1. Psychology
   2. Sociology
   3. Political Science
   4. Anthropology
   5. Economics
   6. History
   7. Geography
   8. Law
   9. Education

10 | THE CHRISTIAN PHILOSOPHY OF SOCIAL SCIENCES

A. NATURE AND PURPOSE

1. Definition

The Social Sciences are those disciplines which are primarily concerned with social institutions and with individual and group interaction. This definition involves two basic assumptions. First, the individual is a person who operates in a social structure. Second, the individual cannot be divorced from his fellowmen, nor from the factors in his environment affecting him. The social sciences, therefore, are concerned to a large extent with man's efforts to understand himself and influence his human environment. For man to influence his environment he will have to understand the interacting forces of the past, show their relationship to the present, and then apply his findings in determining the factors which influence human environment and determine future progress.

2. Purpose

From the definition above one can observe that the purpose of the social sciences is to focus attention on man himself and organizations of men. Men and organizations, however, cannot be studied out of relation to their environment, their problems, their beliefs, their aspirations, their products. The historian and anthropologist determine what is to be studied from the recorded and observed testimony of men themselves. Other scientists in this group study problems arising out of the relationships of men and groups of men. They study the behavior which results from all of this interaction. Behavior, however, is not thought of as automatic but results from the combination of many causes and factors in the total situation. Each separate discipline within the area of social sciences concentrates on one facet of the whole, but most social scientists recognize the importance of seeing society as a whole.

The wholeness that each scientist sees in his domain is the wholeness of a system. The system is composed of interacting subparts, and the interaction is regulated by the system as a whole. The social scientist is thus concerned with society, with institutions, with groups, and individual persons as systems in action. Some of the disciplines in this area are concerned primarily with the *structure* of such a system, as for example anthropology and psychology, where society and persons are approached as social units whose integrative parts in culture and personality are the objects of study. Other disciplines are concerned primarily with the *function* of these systems, as, for example, political science. Although this concept of systems is a theoretical one, it has the practical purpose of permitting us to interpret and order data from many other sources within unifying broad conceptions such as "culture" or "institution."

3. Scope

Traditionally, the scope of studies embraced in this area of subject-matter has included the fields of anthropology, history, sociology, psychology, political science, geography, economics, and law. While it is recognized that the field of economics is classified as a natural science in some circles, we choose to classify it also within this area because of its direct implications for individual and social welfare. Because of the social purpose and power of education and its development of leaders, this field, too, is included. Penology is embraced by sociology. Ethics is classified with philosophy. Art is listed among the humanities.

Traditionally, it has been customary to differentiate between social sciences and social studies, the latter being used for public school courses.

We do not mean to imply in the above definition that the scope of considering man in his relation to other men is limited to the social sciences. We recognize that philosophy, religion, literature, even biological science and geography in some aspects, are also concerned with factors in social relationships. Neither is the content of social sciences unique in this respect, for they draw on other fields of learning, such as literature, philosophy, religion, and art.

4. Historical Developments

Politics, economics, history, and law represent the oldest disciplines in the social science group. The Greeks developed the first three and the Romans were prominent in law. In more recent times the other disciplines in this group were developed, such as anthropology, penology, and sociology. In addition to these relatively pure social sciences, a second group of disciplines closely related to these and classified as semi-social sciences, has included ethics, education, and psychology. A third group related to the social sciences because of their social implications has included biology, geography, medicine, linguistics, and art. The history of these disciplines has revealed how closely the social sciences are related. Modern developments have added a particular thrust to each separate discipline. We may conclude that we not only see this group of sciences correlated by common concerns but also see each with its distinctive contributions.

R. S. Lund pointed out that the basic assumptions of any science of society are consonant with the total culture of which it is a part.[1] This means, therefore, that the development of ideas in the social sciences closely paralleled the ideas of men held in the periods when they lived. Samuel Kamm traced this principle in the development of the social sciences.[2]

In Western culture Greek views of society prevailed up until the time of Jesus who injected new thoughts and motives into society. From that time the Christian philosophy of society as viewed from the Christian theistic presuppositions dominated throughout much of the medieval period. Augustinian thought largely prevailed during this period. However, during the Medieval period a conflict arose which resulted in a division of thought life between those who followed along in the Christian framework of ideas and those who began to adopt a scientific framework. Thomas Aquinas attempted to synthesize both positions but Luther and Calvin tried to swing back to thoroughly Christian presuppositions.

Thomas Hobbes motivated a complete breakaway from the Christian tradition and renounced all revelational elements, placing social sciences completely in the framework of the natural sciences as viewed by the Greeks. Nature and the philosophy of naturalism became the dominating factors in the social thought of the West. Nature replaced God in the thinking of social scientists. The universe was presumed to be mechanistic in operation, mathematical in composition, and geometric in design. God could be understood only as a part of Nature. Therefore, society was the creation of man in harmony with the laws of nature. Thus, social scientists began to develop a science of society based upon a study of the "natural laws" of society. The fruitage of these efforts is now quite evident in the writings of such men as Comte, Marx, and Spencer in the Nineteenth Century, as well as in that of their followers in this century.

Today new developments have caused some shifts in thinking. The idea of law derived through empirical observation is now admitted to be at best a statistical average. Scientific prediction

[1]R. S. Lund, *Knowledge for What? The Place of Social Science in American Culture* (Princeton University Press, Princeton, N. J., 1939), quoted in *Asbury Seminarian*, Fall, 1949, Vol. 4, No. 3, p. 116.
[2]Samuel R. Kamm, "Social Science Seeks Enlightenment," *Asbury Seminarian*, Fall, 1949, Vol. 4, No. 3, p. 116 ff.

has moved from the realm of the absolute to that of the relative or probable. This means that scientific truth in the social realm is verified primarily through historical experience.

The present scene among social scientists is one which pictures a desire for and efforts to attain a reorientation of inquiry in the social fields. Recent research is calling for *a priori* assumptions in one's work, for the necessity of defining terms and concepts used in research, and for the considerations of the opinions of men in studying human behavior. The cultural order embracing the realm of ideas in traditions, faith, and philosophies is just as important as technical considerations. The empirical method is now being considered as only one of the methods of obtaining information. Furthermore, outstanding social scientists, such as Sorokin of Harvard and Toynbee of England, are rejecting the limited universals of the natural science approach by recognizing within the existing culture various orders of truth including that of religious faith. This break with naturalistic presuppositions should encourage every Christian. It opens the way for a reconsideration of the problems of our time in the light of Christian revelation. The Christian doctrines of sin and redemption have real meaning for social sciences as we attempt to apply the Gospel to the amelioration of human problems in our time.

5. *Values*

Certain benefits for both teacher and students are derived from the study of the social sciences. The general purpose of the social sciences, however, is not so much to establish fully the chief values of life as it is to deepen appreciation for such values, clarify them, and point out ways and means whereby they can be achieved in the social structure. In carrying out this function these sciences strongly augment the disciplines in the area of Biblical Studies where life's chief values are clearly denoted. Other values which may be derived include:

1. Personal Values
   a. Survival
   b. Self-understanding
   c. Home-life
   d. Courtship and marriage
   e. Student relationships
   f. Satisfactory personal adjustments
   g. Responsibility
   h. Acceptance of authority

2. Social values
   a. Understanding other people
   b. Cooperation
   c. Respect for rights of others
   d. Understand and appreciate group situations
      (1) Religious
      (2) Economic
      (3) Political
      (4) Civic
      (5) Recreational
      (6) Educational

3. General Values
   a. Benefits are derived from the experience of wrestling with the *problems* of the Social Sciences, identifying such prob-

lems and proffering some solutions for them. Some of these problems arise from the search for values. Others arise from our concern for understanding and knowledge.

b. Benefits are derived from experiences with the *concepts* of the social sciences — concepts which help students to analyze and examine complex social phenomena.

c. Benefits are derived from experiences in arriving at *defensible generalizations* about social phenomena and social problems. This does not mean the accumulation of a great volume of specific facts but rather the ability to draw conclusions and act intelligently on the basis of such conclusions.

d. Benefits are derived from the *methods* of social science — raising and answering questions, observing, classifying, analyzing, and recording data, etc.

6. *Integration*

The term, "social sciences," conveys the notion of a variety of interests bearing a kinship to one another. All of these sciences are concerned with the study of society and are united by a similarity of interest and a community of methods in treating their common subject matter. There has been common acceptance of this notion of unity in higher educational circles. Other evidences of this include the traditional customs of organizing these sciences into departments and divisions, the formation of a variety of social science professional organizations and research commissions, the work of foundations and the publication of a wide variety of materials along this line, not the least of which is the *Encyclopedia of Social Sciences.*

Recent developments reveal how unhesitatingly one science borrows from another. The present attitude is not to consider each discipline as completely autonomous in possessing an exclusive range of material but rather as a social science which deals with one phase of human activity related to the others. Thus, each discipline has a "slant" or "thrust" of its own.

The short historical survey of these sciences was sufficient to point out their close kinship. In fact, the relationships are so close at times that one virtually grew out of another. These close relations and interrelations point heavily toward the use of the pattern approach in the organization of these sciences.

The Christian, however, must be careful to avoid artificiality in integration and, above all, forcing the disciplines into a semblance of order which results in integration. This we can do by encompassing the whole area with the Christian philosophy of man, society and history (see chart below).

It is quite evident that the disciplines included in the social sciences are concerned with man as an individual and with man in groups and the interactions resulting from the associations involved. We believe that the Biblical Studies, including the Bible,

Christian Philosophy and Christian Theology, provide the clues and directions sufficient to provide adequate coherence, integration, and interpretation. This they accomplish through providing a Biblical philosophy of life which in turn provides the integrating factor. Furthermore, a curriculum process is made evident when the scholar moves from the consideration of man as an individual, pictured particularly by psychology, to an examination of social processes, pointed up specifically by economics, geography and sociology on the periphery of life movements.

The chart below pictures the Christian approach to integrating the social sciences. It provides for unity by showing how the Christian view of man, society and history, as supplied by abstractions from the Biblical Studies area, unites the entire area into one unified whole. It also shows how each separate discipline maintains some individual distinctiveness while at the same time being closely correlated with the others.

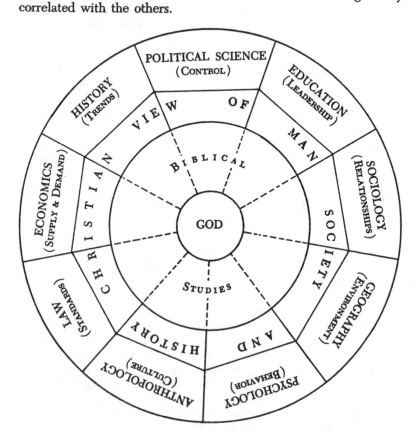

7. *Interpretation*

The Christian teacher does not have to depend entirely on his own skill or on past achievements to interpret his subject matter. Clues are provided in Biblical Studies, as pointed out earlier. Therefore, he should expect to see God revealed in the subject matter of social science. By bringing the Christian philosophy of life in general and the Christian view of man, society, and history, in particular, to the truths in this area and throwing them as a frame of reference around the facts provided by social sciences, the Christian teacher will find the specific truths involved in the various disciplines illumined with a vast array and depth of knowledge and wisdom. The procedure by which this is done was outlined in Chapter III. Wherever possible direct parallels of truth in the subject matter of the Biblical Studies area must be compared with those found in the social science area. The attributes of God, such as love, power, goodness, and justice, can also be used as clues by which truths can be evaluated, illustrated, and applied. Of course, there will be many opportunities for practical application of social science truths to meet human need and increase human efficiency. The Christian teacher is not only interested in interpreting social science truth for the intellectual benefits to be derived therefrom but should point out how practical and useful such truths are in the development of personality, a better world and a greater church. Above all, he will be interested in glorifying God through the ministry of truth in this area of knowledge.

With this general pattern of interpretation in mind it is now possible to look at this area very practically from the standpoint of each separate discipline. Space prohibits a detailed analysis of each of these disciplines but at least some broad outlines of interpretation may be pointed out.

According to the chart above it is evident that each separate discipline has a "thrust" of its own by which it makes a distinctive contribution to the totality of truth. Some of these major thrusts are indicated below along with the relationships involved.

SUBJECT	MAJOR THRUST	APPLICATION
Psychology	Behavior	
Sociology	Relationships	
Political Science	Control	
History	Trends	
Economics	Supply and Demand	The Christian
Anthropology	Culture	Point of
Education	Leadership	View
Geography	Environment	
Law	Standards	

Certain generalizations abstracted from the Christian philosophy of life are also helpful to the teacher. God moves in the midst of men. He does this through *divine providence* and *divine presence*. The person and work of God are evident among men. The social sciences deal with *experience* and are revelatory of God and man in a twofold way: (1) they provide evidences that man is a sinner and in need of redemption both personally and socially, (2) they reveal evidences of God's justice, goodness, and redeeming love. Both the perfect man in Christ and the perfect society in the Kingdom of God form the ideal. In motivating men toward these ideals God uses His goodness, the call to repentance, and judgments to lead men to repentance (Romans 2:4).

8. *General Objectives*

The foregoing discussion makes evident certain general objectives for social sciences, as follows:

1. To acquaint students with the Christian philosophy of man, society, and history and to explore some of their implications.
2. To impress the student with the importance of recognizing the destructive effects of sin in the social structure.
3. To point out the need for spiritual regeneration of both individuals and the social order in order to accomplish God's will for mankind.
4. To acquaint the student with the Christian philosophy of history (providence).
5. To impress students with the importance of the church in society.
6. To show the importance of the individual and institutional life in the social structure.
7. To cultivate an interest in and understanding of the culture of nationality groups other than American.
8. To acquaint students with the sources of American culture.
9. To acquaint students with modern social problems — origin, character, and possible solutions.
10. To cultivate an objective attitude toward social issues.
11. To cultivate habits basic to intelligent and informed citizenship.
12. To acquaint the student with the techniques employed for investigating problems in the various social sciences.

B. The Christian View of Man, Society, and History

1. *The Christian View of Man*

The Scriptures present man as created in the image of God, a free moral agent, possessing the powers of personality represented by intellect, emotions, and will power. Man's purpose in living is to enjoy life and glorify and exemplify God. His ultimate destiny is to live with God. Man is an educable being through creation.

As originally created, there was unity in man's personality. God planned for self to be the person in the totality of his being. Heart is the Bible term for self — it is the sum-total of spirit, soul and body. Personality, therefore, becomes the sum-total of all expressions of the self. Thus, personality is more than the adjustment of the individual to the universe. Instead, the self provides a *cause* which shapes such adjustment to personal and ultimate ends.

The entrance of sin into man and the world brought disharmony to the world and destroyed man's inner peace and purity. The human spirit became disturbed and selfish and man rebelled against God. Sinful personality is now subject to disruption and corruption. Tension within and without is now man's daily experience. Guilt feelings are common experience. Finding that he does not have the power to cope with these problems man now requires the help of God. God set in motion the plan of redemption whereby He did something *for* man and *in* man to bring about the work of rehabilitation and reconstruction. This He did through redemption provided by the Lord Jesus Christ. In this solution man finds not only personal assistance but the highest type of educational experience — regeneration and education for the whole man.

2. The Christian View of Society

Believing as he does that mankind originated in God, the Christian also believes that God planned for social relationships to be expressed in human fellowship. Actually, the human race is one mighty organism. The human body is the channel of personal expression by which the individual can contact other persons.

The purpose of the human race is to complete man and glorify God and to have a racial brotherhood of moral and responsible persons.

The entrance of sin brought corruption to the individual and disruption to the social structure. These conditions have been handed down from one generation to another and have become universal in scope. The racial brotherhood was broken and man was banished from fellowship with God. These facts made necessary the creation of two great forces to help redeem man: indirectly the government, and directly the plan of redemption. In these ways man could be forgiven and restored as an individual, also reorganized, harmonized and reunited in a Christian brotherhood.

Government is a divine institution the purpose of which is to restrict the operations and activities of evil men and to promote cooperation among men of good will (Romans 13:1-7). Public officials, therefore, are servants of God and the public. All government authority should reflect the power of God in the universe.

Since God's original purpose through creation was the establishment of a holy fellowship, the plan of redemption had to include the entire race. Jesus Christ stands at the center of God's plan. Through Him the process of redemption became twofold: (1) provisional and (2) actual. The atonement on the cross made redemption possible for the entire race. The method to be and now employed is the salvation of mankind one by one through the atonement and the work of the Holy Spirit in the hearts and lives of saved men. Thus, the plan involves the actual building of a new race toward the social goal of the perfect kingdom state. This kingdom is called the Kingdom of God and represents the great ideal toward which men as individuals and society, both redeemed, are heading.

The Church represents the present form of the Kingdom of Christ. Ultimately, this kingdom will be objectively expressed to the entire universe as the glorified church without spot or blemish. Presently, the church is holy and universal, not that each individual is holy, but it is an organism which is holy and available to all men.

As an organism the church is also a brotherhood of moral persons which is dominated by the Lord Jesus Christ. The church is personal because it provides the opportunity for personal witness to the Gospel of Jesus Christ. It is social because it gives the opportunity of group cooperation in worship, service, and fellowship. The heart of this whole process is Jesus Christ. There must be worship, fellowship, and service for the Lord Jesus Christ in the power of the Holy Spirit.

The triumph of the church will be the triumph of the new race. This will be accomplished at the Second Coming of the Lord Jesus Christ. At that time, either through previous resurrection or present translation, the saints will be welded into that perfect social relationship centered in the Lord Jesus Christ. Here each person will not only be a perfect man but also a perfect brother, capable of perfect fellowship and service. "This vast community of perfect brothers, all saved by Jesus Christ, all completed by Jesus Christ, all organized by Jesus Christ, all living in union with Jesus Christ, is the make-up of the perfect race."

Today, the church is the basis for a redemptive society. Composed of regenerated individuals, the church is the only hope for a sinful world. Its great responsibility is to move out into society to be the "living witness" originally called for by Jesus Christ, the Head and Founder of the Church. This is the function of the church now. Man cannot hope to realize the ultimate kingdom now for a number of reasons listed in the Scriptures. (1) Jesus prophesied of chaotic and warlike social conditions which would prevail until His return (Matthew 24:4-8). (2) Paul tells us that wickedness will increase steadily until the reign of the antichrist (II Timothy 3:1-13; II Thessalonians 2:3-12). This is echoed by other New Testament writers (II Peter 3:3; Jude 18). (3) Apostasy will affect even the church (II Thessalonians 2:3; Acts 20:29, 30; I John 2:18, 19, 22). Actually, the church member who is spiritual is a member of two societies: physical and spiritual. As a witness, he must learn to operate in both, keeping the spiritual paramount.

3. The Christian View of History

The Christian philosophy of history begins with the existence and acts of a personal God. The origin, purpose, and destiny of the universe and mankind are adequately explained only upon this basis. The universe and mankind came into existence by the creative act of an all-wise and all-powerful personal God. There was purpose involved in this creation in harmony with the nature and wisdom of God. God is at work in history directing all things to His honor and glory. History, therefore, is a revelation of God in His dealings with man and the universe.

The race of mankind with all its diversity is a wonderful unity (Acts 17:26-28). All races have sprung from one common genetive head, Adam. According to Acts 17, God also made the nations and determined their times and habitations in order that they might seek Him.

The entrance of sin into the human family has had a widely disturbing effect upon both the individual and the race. Human nature is now warped and social conditions are corrupt, making coercive civil government necessary. Furthermore, sin has become a disruptive force among human events and in the hearts and lives of individuals. Man is now divided into two general camps — sinners and the children of God. It has now become necessary for God to invade history with His redemptive plan to make it possible for sinful men to become the children of God.

Men become the children of God through the grace of God and regeneration of the heart on the basis of the work of His Son on Calvary's cross. Thus, the Incarnation, Crucifixion, and Resurrection of Jesus Christ are unique and important events around which all history turns. He will bring history to its glorious culmination.

The Christian interpretation of history is God-centered. The teacher must operate upon this premise — God is not only Creator but Administrator of the universe. Historical events, therefore, should be studied for their theocentric significance. Teachers and students must learn to read God's providence and presence in history. They should look for God's direction, control and purpose. These are seen, not only in unique events, but also in the course of ordinary events. Both God's goodness and justice are revealed by His acts in history. God's goodness and justice should lead men to repentance (Romans 2:4).

This kind of interpretation shows that there are no isolated facts in history. All facts and their relationships are related to God. It is impossible, therefore, for a true Christian to divorce life or any part of it from a divine relationship. The Christian teacher, consequently, will find many opportunities to point this out. This should be done naturally without forcing the Christian interpretation on the facts. In doing this the teacher will not have to preach or moralize. Instead, a word here and there or an implication alluded to may be all that is required. When the meaning of specific events is hidden, the Christian teacher and students may exercise "faith" in the Living God who overrules all.

C. THE SOCIAL SCIENCES

1. *Psychology*

Psychology has been defined as the systematic study of the experiences and behavior of organisms, and of the interaction between the organism and its environment. To this the Christian would add that this subject is concerned with the study of human nature. It includes the study of the inner states of consciousness (including the soul) with their outward expression in human behavior. In a very real sense psychology is the study of the whole-man-in-his-environment.

The fields of psychology indicate its scope. Many areas within its scope show its extent: it deals with physiological psychology, vision, memory, audition, learning, thinking, imagination, intelligence, personality, social psychology, aesthetics, developmental psychology, language, clinical psychology, selection and placement, labor-management relations, etc. Within these areas some psychologists are concerned with functions, such as seeing, thinking, etc. Others are concerned with differences. The common theme which underlies these diverse studies is an interest in the organism — what it does, how it does it, and what it can do. The purpose of these studies is to throw light on human behavior. Thus, the long-range goal of psychology is explanation of the behavior of each individual person.

It is this interest in the individual which most distinguishes psychology from other social sciences. Herein is found the major thrust of the subject. Other social sciences tend to be interested in people in general rather than a particular individual. Their questions seek out that which is common to all people, or to all people in fairly broad categories.

As a subject psychology draws upon other social sciences heavily at times. Among these are biology, sociology, and anthropology. It is also closely related to theology and philosophy. It depends upon theology to interpret many of its findings because the true nature of man cannot be discovered alone by psychology. The place where greatest assistance is given is the revelation of the nature of man with regard to his origin and purpose in living. Spiritual realities are necessary to complete the picture. Psychology provides assistance to theology by supporting, corroborating, and illuminating theological data, particularly in the area of human behavior, the mind, and the educative process.

Philosophy also works closely with theology in examining the basis for the findings of psychology. Many psychological concepts are intertwined with philosophical thought. Some topics, such as the details of sensory experience with its physical conditions, can be treated empirically but beyond them psychology is constantly on the brink of metaphysical issues. The nature of the mind is a good example.

Educational psychology is the field most closely related to education. Although it has much in common with general psychology, it has developed its own areas of specialization which include instructional methods in school subjects, teacher-pupil relationships, vocational guidance, learning difficulties, handicapped children, superior pupils, counseling, and group dynamics. At the present time, most authorities agree that the purpose of a course in this field is to provide the prospective teacher with skills and insights which are required to successfully guide the growth, learning, and adjustments of the pupil. Textbooks vary greatly in the nature of content but most of them deal in the main with growth and development, learning, personality adjustment and evaluation.

A study of the field of psychology reveals certain areas of the subject which have primary significance for the educational process:

1. Human equipment and behavior which focus attention on the nature of the pupil as the focus of the process.
2. The learning process which determines the way of approach to the pupil.
3. The teaching process which focuses attention on methodology.
4. Tests and measurements which provide a basis for evaluation and analysis.
5. The psychology of school subjects with psychological adaptations in subject matter.

We are now able at this point to summarize some of the further implications of psychology for education:

1. The pupil is the focus of the educative process.
2. The teacher's task is to create a favorable environment for learning, to motivate the pupil, and to guide the learning process.
3. Motivation demands that the teacher know and study the learner, because motivation depends on the interests, activities, needs, and maturity of the learner.
4. Because of the presence, nature and work of sin, Christian education requires a definite system of indoctrination for the pupil. Instead of being subject to his environment and making adjustments to it, indoctrination of divine truth imparts power to subjugate environment and control conduct.
5. The true interpretation of reality is spiritual, therefore, both pupil and teacher must depend directly upon the Spirit of God for both truth and interpretation.
6. Christian service should arise out of a Christlike nature, not simply from the selfish motivation provided by expressional activity *per se*.
7. Man should reveal God in his total personality and conduct.
8. The soul of man is an expression of Pure Ego, the spirit which provides for the unity and continuity of consciousness.
9. Redemption is at the heart of the educative process.
10. Instruction should be geared to the maturation level of the pupil.

In concluding this section on psychology it is now possible to enumerate some generalizations whereby the Christian teacher can relate psychology to the Christian faith in the interpretation of his subject matter. These are merely illustrative.

1. Man was created in God's image — Psalm 8:3-8.
2. The Holy Spirit works in supernatural and natural ways. He works also through the laws and principles of the mind; He gains and holds attention, He activates the will through thoughts and emotions; He transforms ideas into conduct and character.
3. The natural mind needs the supernatural influence of the Holy Spirit — I Corinthians 2.
4. The human mind is the product of God's creative power and is meant to glorify Him.
5. Man is to use his mental operations in God's service.
6. The soul surmounts the mind and brain to be self-directive.
7. Natural stimuli are present but the supernatural agency of the Holy Spirit is necessary for illumination and guidance.

8. Man should be a co-worker with God in his intellectual life.
9. Psychology, in general, provides the student with the opportunities of studying at close hand man as the "image of God."

2. *Sociology*

There are many definitions of sociology. Generally, it is the study of the nature, development, and relations of human society. It is the study of man in his social relations. Primary emphasis here is laid upon the interaction of man with other men. Simply stated, sociology is the study of society as the word itself implies. Here the word society is used to describe the social experiences wherever people associate and live together.

Sociology, like any other field of study, has developed its subspecialties, such as population studies, institutional studies, comparisons between societies, etc. However, sociologists, in spite of divergencies of interest, position and method, are commonly concerned with how groups function as social units regardless of varying size, composition and kind. They are interested in the complex web of social relationships that exist among the members of any group. They are also interested in the consequences of the existence and function of groups upon other groups and society as a whole. Herein lies the major thrust of this particular discipline.

Christian sociology presents the Scriptural teachings as to the nature, development and relations of human society. It is the *Christian* teaching about men in their group relationships. It is descriptive of that kind of society which is controlled by Christian principles. Christian sociology has been defined as "the study of the Christian ideal for human associations."[3]

One of the primary aims of sociology is to assist people to understand themselves and others more adequately and objectively as they associate and live together. Only in this way will it be possible to reach desirable goals for group life. To the Christian, this aim is inadequate and fragmentary. He must have an aim much more comprehensive than social adjustment.

The purpose of sociology which is Christian is twofold. First, social problems and theories should be evaluated in the light of the Christian world view. *Christian* standards are used as criteria. The norm by which this is done is the Christian ethical ideal as recorded in the Holy Scriptures.

The second and most important purpose, however, is positive. Christian sociology should show what a Christian society is and

[3]A. D. Mattson, *Christian Social Consciousness* (Rock Island, Ill., Augustana Book Concern, 1953), pp. 207-08.

how it is accomplished. Furthermore, it will stress the importance of all other disciplines in filling their places in such a way as to contribute to the social well-being. Still further, it will stress the purpose of human institutions in conserving human and spiritual values.

The major problems of our day are problems of group relationships — class with class, creed with creed, race with race, nation with nation. Rapid communication and transportation have made these problems greater and more evident. Some of the purposes of sociology, therefore, should include the following:

1. To study men in groups, why they live in groups, how they are organized, put together and operated.
2. To note biological differences between people in different groups and what these differences mean.
3. To note differences of customs and ideas of right and wrong and what such differences mean.

Man is a social being. As such he has a relationship to a number of social units; the family, school, church, occupation, community, citizenship, and world community. All of these relationships should be governed and controlled by basic principles. There are social, economic, and civil laws by which society ought to function. Ignorance of these principles and laws results in maladjustment, injustices and conflicts. Education should lead to an understanding of these areas so that men may live together in peace, happiness, and prosperity. It follows naturally, therefore, that the school has an important function to fulfill if this is to be accomplished. This function is seen from two angles: that of the content to be studied and the role of the school in society at large.

There are four factors in the social life of man which provide a stock of sociological things to learn: (1) natural environment, (2) heredity, (3) culture, and (4) the group. Culture is here defined as "learned ways of doing things."

Group life assumes institutional form in organized society. Most sociologists divide society into the following groups: (1) the family, (2) the nation, (3) the church, (4) the race, and (5) for the Christian, the Kingdom of God.

In general there are three positions regarding the role of the school in society: conservative, progressive, and neutral. Conservatives say that the school should preserve the existing social culture. This is perhaps the most prevalent view. Because of the vast complexity of the social structure and culture, the school must be selective in realizing its conservative purpose.

Progressives react against the conservative view and maintain that the school should function as a vehicle by which society can forge ahead through the initiation of changes as well as preserving that which is valuable. In this view the school becomes creative in the realization of progress. In spite of this stand, the advocates of this view, largely "progressive educators," have failed to provide a definite plan for social reconstruction. Consequently, aims and purposes are hazy. Where the school's purposes are constantly changing in a changing society, there is no stability.

The third view is neutrality which demands that the school be neutral on controversial social views. Instead, eternal values and universal truths should dominate.

The Christian point of view might be said to include the best in the above views. Admittedly biased in its stand on a world view, this view nevertheless maintains that there is room for both conservatism and progress. Christians believe in preserving the best of the cultural heritage, but at the same time they believe that the school can initiate many salutary changes in the light of its ideal social objective. The Kingdom of God is that objective.

Generally speaking, the school reflects the culture of society. It can also be a force for constructive social change. It can reflect this in its choice of content and emphasis on selected values; its policies and procedures can shape attitudes with regard to human relations. By providing the fundamental background of knowledge along with resourcefulness and initiative, the school can lead out toward constructive social change.

In bringing the Christian philosophy to the subject matter content of this field of knowledge the Christian teacher is supplied with a goodly number of generalizations to use in the teaching process illustrated as follows:

1. The social sciences are instruments for achieving intelligence among human affairs and the application of Christian truths to human needs.
2. They supply remarkable evidences of the sin of man on the one hand and the love of God in redemption on the other.
3. They deal with an area of human relationship in which one finds unusual opportunities for the demonstration of practical Christianity.
4. The worth and dignity of the individual is the basic premise of democracy — Matthew 16:26.
5. There is a divine element in human relationships which provides both an ideal and a dynamic for accomplishing it — the ideal standards for social relationships in the Decalogue and Sermon on the Mount; the dynamic supplied through perfect love, love for the individual and the group, "love thy neighbor as thyself."
6. Social service should be motivated by Christian principles and motives.

7. We are our brothers' keeper.
8. The Golden Rule applied will achieve fairness and justice in social, economic, and civic relationships.
9. There is great value in "come let us reason together" in employer-employee relationships.
10. All men are precious in God's sight, therefore, there must be brotherhood and cooperation.

All of this points out clearly what some of the implications of sociology for education and the church are. Some of these are noted below.

Educational sociology is the study of the interaction of the individual and his cultural environment. This includes other people, social groups, and patterns of behavior. Emphasis is here placed on interaction. The process of social interaction provides the subject matter of educational sociology. This subject utilizes what has been learned in both the fields of education and sociology and joins this knowledge into a science of educational sociology. Thus, the subject of educational sociology actually becomes the application of social principles to the educative process.

Further implications indicate that the church, and particularly evangelicalism, needs to be more aggressive in the field of sociology. There should be the development of competent Christian literature in the field. Christians need to be heard and read. The claims of the Christian philosophy should be pressed. Christians must be active in community affairs and develop a sharp social sensitivity.

From the standpoint of the curriculum there are direct implications of sociology for education. Today, modern education emphasizes the important place which studies related to the general field of sociology have. In public schools subject matter is organized into what is called social studies. In higher education it is called social science. Such sciences are concerned exclusively with the nature of society, the art of living in society, and the means of improving social relations and conditions. Outside Christian circles, such studies are largely dominated by empiricism. It is the Christian contention, however, that philosophical and theological data also have their place in the development and instruction of the social sciences.

More specifically, there are further implications for the curriculum:

1. The social structure is so complex that it must be simplified for curriculum purposes, particularly for children.
2. The principles of psychology must be utilized and integrated with the presentation of sociological data to the pupil. This demands a recognition of maturation.

3. Subject matter should be definitely integrated with life-situations as the pupil actually lives in them.
4. The religious and spiritual implications of the Christian world view must be constantly applied to curriculum areas.
5. Methods of teaching are effective insofar as the skills and knowledge acquired there are used in social situations by the pupil.

3. Political Science

Political science is one of the oldest disciplines in this group. It has been defined as the science of the state, or as a branch of the social sciences dealing with the theory, organization, government, and practice of the state. The state in this view is considered the nation or the country.

Political science covers such subjects as the origin and development of states; political and governmental processes; systems of law; economic regulations; processes of law enactment; organization and activities of political parties; public opinion and propaganda; local, national, and international relationships; and research procedures and findings in the field. In this work it shares many areas of inquiry with related disciplines, such as history, economics, sociology, psychology, statistics, law, anthropology, geography, philosophy, and others.

The purpose of political science philosophically is to make the effort to identify the ends, organization, function, and structure of the state and government. Here it is related to both psychology and sociology. Some of the goals include the following:

1. The primary goal is education for citizenship; career preparation is secondary.
2. To gather and impart knowledge and understanding of the complexities of modern government.
3. To impart an appreciation for and understanding of democracy as the American way of life.

Some of the implications of political science for Christian education makes it possible for the Christian teacher to relate this field to the Christian faith by emphasizing some of the following observations:

1. God's providence is given evidence in the world by the power of control vested in government.
2. God's power is manifested through this control.
3. Government is a divine institution the purpose of which is to restrict the operations and activities of evil men and to promote cooperation among men of good will (Romans 13:1-7).
4. The practice of Christian ethics in civic concerns.

5. The necessity for Christian citizenship and statesmanship.
6. The values of participation by Christians in all democratic processes worthy of support.
7. The Church should interpret the will of God to the state.

4. Anthropology

Broadly, anthropology is defined as the comparative study of man. This discipline started with the objective of studying man as a whole — as a biological organism, a social being, and as a creator and carrier of culture — and of seeing these aspects in relation to one another. More specifically, therefore, anthropology is the scientific study of the physical, social, and cultural development and behavior of man.

Today, this discipline is concerned with several general areas of knowledge directly related to man. Physical anthropology looks at man in terms of his physical characteristics, his origin and development, the formation of the races, and the biological basis of behavior. Cultural or social anthropology studies man's culture and social arrangements with their interpretation. Archaeology examines the artifacts and other records of man's past to reconstruct a picture of earlier man. Scientific linguistics is concerned with the sounds, vocabulary, and grammatical structure of language, how languages compare, and the changes involved.

Other fields of knowledge related to this discipline include biology, genetics, geography, economics, religion, history, theology, and particularly sociology. Some of the values to be derived from and purposes involved in the study of anthropology include the following:

1. To see and appreciate the cultures and characteristics of other peoples.
2. Through a study of racial differences and distinctives to become more closely aware of our own distinctives and why we have them.
3. To point out the importance of culture in formulating lives and concepts.
4. To understand how behavior habits are often cultural in nature rather than biological.
5. By comparing institutions the student can come to appreciate any one of them better.
6. After evaluation, to draw upon the past for ideas and practices which have been fruitful.
7. To counteract cultural provincialism.
8. To see how man has utilized culture in overcoming physical handicaps and achieving satisfactory living.
9. Christian evangelism in other lands depends directly on understanding other people and their culture.

In the interpretation of the subject matter of this particular discipline, clearly it has a "major thrust" by which the Christian can be guided. Anthropology obviously is concerned not with particular men as such, as in the case of psychology, for example, but with men in groups, with races and peoples and their happenings and doings. Outstanding in such study is what is called culture. Culture is the peculiar product of human endeavor and consists of the vast mass of learned and transmitted motor reactions, habits, techniques, ideas, and values along with the behavior they produce. Anthropology of all the social sciences is most culture-conscious. While sociology tends to be concerned with society in general along with the social problems involved, anthropology is concerned with man and his human product — culture. It is considered with how culture originates, how it operates, and how human behavior is affected thereby.

Some of the broad generalizations by which the Christian teacher can integrate his faith with the subject matter in this area include:

1. Man was created by God in the image of God.
2. Sin has had a destructive effect on man, the races of men and their culture.
3. Man received a mandate from God to control his physical environment (Genesis 1:28).
4. The "cultural lag" shows that it is impossible to transform the moral and spiritual nature of man simply by putting more knowledge and technical skill at his disposal.
5. God has appointed the boundaries for the nations (Acts 17).
6. Language is used as a vehicle for communication and proclamation of the Gospel.
7. Stewardship demands a recognition of God's ownership and His control over the cultural products of mankind.
8. Perfect love is the standard for social relationships.

5. *Economics*

Economics is concerned primarily with a variety of phenomena relating to production, distribution, and consumption of goods and the services and the organizations of society to carry out these functions. It also focuses on what has been called "scarce resources." This means anything that does not exist in sufficient quantity to enable us to use as much of it as we would like without being concerned about the amount that is left. Generally, therefore, economics deals with man's cooperative efforts to make a living.

Economic theory has moved from a theory dominated by natural law to one which pictures the economic system as a human mechanism, an instrument to be judged by its results, and one to be guided by personal and group choices toward preconceived ends, including both rewards and penalties.

Two present-day types of analysis of economical problems dominate. One is the approach of Lord Keynes who advocates an analysis of factors which determine the total flow of income, production, and employment. The second type of analysis is an exploration of the ways an economic system serves or disserves the people's welfare. Both approaches claim to be objective and scientific in making their analyses.

The purpose of economics is to help bridge the gap between the market "value" and ethical values of what is right and wrong in the economic system. Other purposes include (1) an explanation of how economic systems operate, and (2) an analysis of how *well* these systems operate. Some of the values to be derived from a study of this discipline include:

1. Economists continuously emphasize the necessity of considering alternatives, which is the appropriate one to choose to reach an objective.
2. To see which choice decided upon is the least costly for a given result, or that results in the greatest gain product or satisfaction for a given cost.
3. A greater understanding of the world and men who live in it will be supplied by studying the problems of production, exchange, distribution, and consumption.
4. Individual welfare is greatly dependent on one's knowledge of economic problems and skills and on the performance of the economic system as a whole.

Although the Gospel does not endorse any one economic system, and in spite of the fact that there are few if any economic techniques to be derived from the Gospel, the Christian teacher can relate his faith to his subject matter in this area by emphasizing the following factors and others related to them:

1. He can point out the failures of such economic theories as Communism and Fascism.
2. He can show the dignity of labor and the corruption of idleness.
3. He can stress the quality of one's labor.
4. He can show the Christian roots of capitalism.
5. He can point out the Christian use of money.
6. He can reveal the importance of law, order, justice and freedom in any economic system.
7. He can show the possibility of being in business for God.
8. He can point out that industry was made for man and not vice versa.

9. He can reveal that the dominant virtue in the economic realm is to minister to our fellowmen and supply their economic needs.
10. He can show that profits are not more important than people.
11. He can point to the destructive effects of sin on the economy.
12. He can insist that property rights be made secondary and subservient to human rights.

6. History

History has been defined as that discipline which examines the records of the past and seeks to provide public verification for its generalizations. It is concerned with past human affairs. It is the study of men enmeshed in time. In the past this definition referred to political history primarily but now the modern historian has broadened his horizon until any and every aspect of life is comprehended within this term. This range runs from a general study of civilization to local history. All that they have in common is their concern with past human affairs.

The purpose of history is to assist the student in his efforts to understand each age, to "get inside" the life of the people and present them in the light of their day.

The place of history in the curriculum is a matter of conjecture to some. Some authorities would include it among the humanities; others would classify it with the social sciences. A study by the American Council on Education entitled *Cooperative Study of Evaluation in General Education* recommended that this discipline be included in the social science area. Focus in the area, however, should be on social processes and institutions and not on history *per se.*

There are a number of values to be derived by the student from the study of history, among which are:
1. It provides the student with a sense of perspective.
2. It gives him the long view, enabling him to relate effects to causes.
3. It cultivates a balanced judgment, freeing one from narrow provincialism and blighting prejudices.
4. It gives the student a discriminating touch.
5. It provides him with the ability to disentangle motives.
6. It gives him practice in the ability to sift the truth from propaganda.
7. It broadens one's sympathies.
8. It creates understanding of people, events, and things.
9. It guides future planning and conduct, by calling attention to principles.

There are various ways of interpreting history. One theory is called the climatological theory which explains the development of civilization in terms of climate and changes in climate. The racial theory explains the stream of events in terms of inherent qualities of ethnic groups. However, inherited racial characteristics do not give the full picture and deny the place of the human will and intelligence in human events. There are the cyclical theories of Spengler and Toynbee. Spengler draws an analogy between history as the biological cycle of birth, growth, decline, and death. Toynbee uses a Christian concept of man in his theory that history repeats itself but this does not reveal the meaning of history.

The Christian view of history, theologically oriented and developed, may not be acceptable to the non-believer but it is to the believer. Actually, the Christian does not have to please the non-believer anyway.

The theological approach to history provides it with a sense of direction although it does not give the details in evaluating and arranging the concrete data of historical knowledge.

The Christian message is concerned not only with the church history and Scripture but with the entire sweep of human experience. History is the circle of which Jesus Christ is the Center. Although many specific facts of history may not reveal the hand of God, or appear to reveal it, the Christian is right in believing that the "strategy of God" is at work. This he has to do by bringing his faith to the facts of history. This cannot be revealed by the facts of history themselves.

The Christian believes that the reins of history are in the hands of God. Our failure to see and hear does not eliminate the reality of God's providences. Human wickedness may momentarily frustrate God's purposes but God overrules in the end. Men may defy God and His sovereignty only at their peril.

The Christian message is concerned with history, with what the Germans call *Heilsgeschichte:* history as the vehicle of faith, as the operative field of a plan of salvation which coheres and finds its climax in Jesus of Nazareth. It is an interpretation and evaluation of the human story based on the judgments of faith.

7. Geography

The word "geography" is a derivative of two Greek words, *ge* (the earth) and *graphein* (to write). The literal meaning, therefore, is to write about the earth. Today, geography is considered to be the study of the earth in its relation to life, particularly that of man. It is concerned with the relationship between physical things and circumstances and human affairs. The geographer will take facts from many fields of study and rationally relate them. This means also that geography is the study of how man adapts the earth's resources and conditions to his own purpose.

Geography, though in part within the province of the physical sciences, deals with man's physical environment. A recent tendency, however is to include this subject in the social science area because man's physical environment directly and deeply affects his conduct and his relationships with his fellows. Aspects of geography, including commercial, social, economic, industrial, human, regional, and political elements, have been used in the social category. Physical geography probably lies more specifically in the natural science category.

Because geography is concerned with many kinds of physical phenomena, such as climate, water, earth, animals, plants, and birds, it has direct relations with many other subjects, including astronomy, geology, botany, chemistry, zoology, history, economics, physical, and political science. In fact, the subject matter of geography is derived from at least three general sources: (1) the social data of human affairs, (2) the physical data of nature, and (3) the data from abstract correlation, integration, and relationship between the first two sources.

Some of the values to be derived from a study of this subject by the student will include:

1. Knowledge of important world regions and differences which occur on the earth's surface are becoming increasingly important.
2. Nations can no longer live in isolation.
3. More knowledge about world affairs is needed to help meet life situations.
4. Because the life of man is so dependent on his physical environment and his social development has been so greatly influenced by his geographical location, it is important for the student to study geography.
5. Geography helps to tie other studies together.
6. A study of geography develops the spirit of tolerance.

Geography is based on the premise that life can be understood best in the place where it occurs. Events, situations, and problems in human society have meaning only in the light of their relation to the characteristics of that part of the earth which stands in the background. It is clear, therefore, that environment in this subject supplies the student with the "major thrust" of the discipline. It is important to see the place and impact of environment on human nature and conduct. In integrating this discipline with the Christian faith the Christian teacher can show the relation of environment in its impact on both the individual and the groups of mankind.

8. Law

The term law is used in two main ways: (1) as a rule prescribed by authority for human action, and (2) in science and philosophy to describe a uniform order of sequences. The general principles of law in the legal sense are considered under what is termed jurisprudence. In this latter sense the jurist considers law to be the sum of the influences that determine decisions in courts of justice.

The field of jurisprudence covers considerations involving man's liberty, property, relations to fellowmen, rights, and crime, to mention only a few. It generally deals with these factors in terms of individual relationships and the public interest. Public jurisprudence concerns the relations between the individual and the state. Generally speaking, therefore, the creation and protection of legal rights are the primary objects of law.

That law is directly related to social science and has been amply illustrated in the cases involving racial discrimination. In fact, law is having to draw heavily on non-legal sources to make decisions.

Law is widely related to education. It compels every child to get a minimum of education. It protects every man's right in securing an education. It guarantees basic neutrality on the part of the state in religious education. It protects the teacher's academic freedom. It lays out rules, regulations, and policies governing the administration of education.

Ordinarily one does not think of law as particularly related to the Christian faith except from the standpoint of the moral law, but following are some broad generalizations that a Christian teacher might possibly use:

1. The Christian life is not created nor ruled by external laws and rules but by the indwelling of the Holy Spirit who creates a disposition to please God (Romans 8:9, 14, 15; II Corinthians 3:6; 5:14).
2. This life, however, has definite ethical principles, moral laws, and rules of right conduct.
3. They serve as ideals, standards, and guides (Romans 8:3; Matthew 5:3-9; Romans 6:1-14).
4. The three fundamental laws of the Kingdom essential to the Christian life are:
   (1) The law of love — Matthew 7:21-23; 10:34-40; Romans 13:8-10; 14:10; I Corinthians 13:1-3; I John 4:20.
   (2) The law of service — John 13:1 ff; Matthew 20:28; Luke 22:27; Matthew 25:40, 45.

(3) The law of sacrifice — John 3:16; Romans 5:6, 8; Luke 9:23.

(4) Summarized in the Golden Rule — Matthew 7:12.

9. *Education*

This discipline has been classified previously as a semi-social science. Because of its primary importance in leadership training, it finds an important place in the social science area. Herein one finds its major thrust. The contributions which this field of learning has made to the academic world is without question. Its emphasis on citizenship and vocational training without question, mark it as a social science. A great deal has already been said about the nature and purpose of both education and Christian education so it will not be necessary to enlarge on those aspects at this point. Previous chapters have covered the subject relatively well.

SUGGESTED ACTIVITIES FOR CHAPTER X

1. What is your definition of the Social Sciences?
2. Draw your own chart on how these sciences can be integrated and organized.
3. What are the implications of Biblical Studies for interpretation of the subject matter supplied through the social sciences?
4. Explore the implications of the Christian view of man, society, and history for education.
5. Develop further some of the generalizations whereby the Christion teacher can relate the various social sciences to the Christian faith. Show how God may be revealed and how these sciences can help individual Christians to be more like God.
6. List and define the methods of psychology.
7. Make a comparative chart on the schools of psychology, showing date, place of origin, main premises, subject matter, methods, and theory of learning.
8. List the fields of psychology.
9. Compare the views of naturalism, realism, pragmatism, and idealism with Christianity on the nature of man.
10. Make a chart which compares the various theories of learning.
11. Compare various sociological theories with the Christian view on (1) the nature of society, (2) politics and education, and (3) church and state.
12. Discuss the Christian philosophy of history.
13. Discuss the relation of the Gospel and sociology.

THE CHRISTIAN PHILOSOPHY OF
NATURAL SCIENCES

OUTLINE FOR CHAPTER 11

A. NATURE AND PURPOSE
   1. Definition, Scope, and Purpose
   2. History of Science
   3. Values of Science to Students
   4. Limitations of Science
   5. Integration
   6. Interpretation
   7. General Objectives

B. THE CHRISTIAN PHILOSOPHY OF NATURE
   1. The Bible and Nature
   2. The Christian Philosophy of Nature in Education

C. SCIENCE AND EDUCATION
   1. Science in Education
   2. Christianity and Science
   3. The Place of the Empirical Sciences in Christian Education
   4. The Place of the Christian School in a World of Science
   5. Basic Ideas in the Natural Sciences

D. THE NATURAL SCIENCES
   1. Anatomy
   2. Astronomy
   3. Botany
   4. Chemistry
   5. Geology
   6. Physics
   7. Physiology
   8. Zoology
   9. Mathematics

11 | THE CHRISTIAN PHILOSOPHY OF NATURAL SCIENCES

A. NATURE AND PURPOSE

1. *Definition, Scope, and Purpose*

The natural sciences are "those systematically organized bodies of accumulated knowledge concerning the physical and biological universe which have been derived exclusively through techniques of direct, objective observation." Traditionally, it has been customary to make a distinction between "pure sciences" and "applied sciences." Pure sciences are concerned with descriptions and explanations of scientific data. In these processes interpretation and understandings are primary. In the applied sciences, such as medicine and engineering, emphasis is placed on the use and application of scientific data pursuant to the solution of practical problems.

The subjects commonly embraced in the area of natural sciences are anatomy, astronomy, botany, chemistry, geology, physics, physiology, and zoology. Psychology and sociology are also included in this classification by some but they also fall in the social science category. Engineering and medicine and clinical psychology are considered technologies rather than sciences. It is generally recognized that there is a great deal of overlap between these sciences.

Mathematics is an essential tool of science. The facts and laws of the physical sciences are expressed in terms of mathematical symbols. Communication in these sciences is therefore dependent upon some understanding and manipulation of mathematical symbols. An understanding of all sciences to some extent requires some understanding of mathematics. This is illustrated in the use of statistics.

The word, "science," is a derivative of the Latin word, *scientia,* meaning knowledge or possession of the truth. Commonly conceived, it is thought of as a systematized body of knowledge, logically arranged, and derived from a set of principles. Scientific knowledge is that kind which is gained and verified by exact observation, repeated experimentation and correct thinking.

Like science, philosophy also seeks knowledge which is exact, well-organized and certain. Philosophy, however, seeks *compre-*

hensive knowledge. It is not only concerned with causes and effects, as in science, but it reaches out for *ultimate* explanations, first causes, purposes, meanings, and values. Its function is not only explanation but interpretation. Thus, philosophy includes the knowledge supplied by science and adds to it the knowledge supplied by religion and ethics. It then reflects on the *whole* situation, seeking meaning, purpose, and value. Furthermore, it also examines critically the concepts made use of by science and in daily experience. These two functions of philosophy are called speculative philosophy and critical philosophy.

Because philosophy and theology supply fundamental principles and ultimate norms, the *Christian* believes that they should take precedence over science. Philosophy and theology are the ultimate guides for all sciences. Thus, in education where one is faced with the formulation of objectives, the selection of subject matter and methods, as well as the procedures of administration, philosophy, and theology only can supply the right norms. On the other hand, the scientific aspects of education must be used for the general advancement of the cause. Research must proceed but not as an end in itself.

The general purpose of science is to provide a system of knowledge which is universal and systematic, seeking the explanation of phenomena, their causes, and the laws which govern their operation. The scientist should collect his facts, analyze and clarify them, study their causes, determine their laws, and set all of this down in systematized form. This is the limit of his work. Actually, then, the scientist should not attempt to make *ultimate* explanations. This function is pictured as follows:

    I. The acquisition of facts
    II. The description of facts
       A. Definition and general description
       B. Analysis
       C. Classification
    III. Explanation of facts
       A. Causes
       B. Laws

To the *Christian*, the functions of science as above described seem fragmentary. Factual knowledge is limited to phenomena. The Christian must insist that theological and philosophical knowledge of science be added to facts in order to arrive at a comprehensive world view which includes *interpretation*, meanings, purposes, and values.

Ultimately, the Christian believes that the primary function of science is to glorify God. Believing as he does in the Creation, the

Christian asserts that science must be a revelation of God and His glory. "The heavens declare the glory of God and the firmament showeth His handiwork" (Psalm 19:1).

Science provides a tool in the hands of man to increase his own efficiency. As an image of God, man should glorify God through a manifestation of the attributes of God. Through science man comes to know more about God and is thus put into a better position for manifesting godliness.

Besides the general values mentioned above, science provides specific values by other functions. Through systematization of knowledge, the vast universe of truth is made more intelligible and simple to the pupil. Furthermore, the powers of observation, discrimination, and insight are developed. The powers of correct thinking are certainly needed in our day of widespread unbelief and sin.

2. History of Science[1]

Modern science represents man's latest and most fruitful method for studying nature. It, possibly, represents the most significant contribution of western civilization to the unending search for knowledge and understanding of the cosmos. Like many other great contributions it is not an entirely new thing, but rather the bringing together into new relationships of some very old ideas. The antecedents of modern science have their roots in ancient classical times and in the more recent period called the Renaissance.

Some rather rudimentary forms of science are traceable in Egypt and Chaldea but it is in the great classical period of Greece (600-300 B.C.) that the first definite steps were taken. The ancient Greeks were concerned with trying to discover the intelligible essence underlying the world of change. They pursued natural science more for understanding than for its practical application. Unfortunately, Greek science suffered seriously from bifurcation. There existed the rationalistic schools of thought that attempted to interpret the universe, for instance, in mathematical terms. A less prominent movement emphasized the empirical approach. During the Hellenistic period these two movements were usually antagonists, but a discernible drift toward union was present.

With the rise of Christianity a new idea was added to Greek rationalism. Nature was thought of as sacramental, symbolic of spiritual truths. Both attitudes are found in St. Augustine. During the Dark Ages men were more concerned with preserving the facts which had been collected in classical times than to attempt original interpretations themselves. What they valued most was

[1]Statement by Ralph Gallagher, Professor of Science, Fort Wayne Bible College.

a mystical immersion in nature, the union with that which already existed. It was pre-eminently an age of contemplation. Sometime during the period there was added from the social situation an activist attitude which initiated a period of technical invention. This had an important effect upon the development of scientific apparatus.

During the Renaissance the union of rationalism and empiricism became an accomplished fact. The recovery of the full tradition of Greek and Arabic science in the Thirteenth and Fourteenth Centuries greatly stimulated men's minds. Aristotle and Euclid were particularly important. Leonardo da Vinci gave to science what it needed most, the artist's sense that the detail of nature was significant. Until science had this sense, no one could care or think that it mattered how fast two unequal masses fall. New and improved apparatus facilitated the detailed study of nature. From the marriage of the empiricism of techniques with the rationalism of philosophy and mathematics was born a new conscious empirical science seeking to discover the rational structure of nature.

At first the church reacted negatively to the startling pronouncements of the scientist, many of whom were sons of the church. But it was gradually realized that the new science did not conflict with the idea of Divine Providence, though it led to a variety of attitudes toward the relation between reason and faith. Scientist churchmen played a major role in developing modern science. Galileo and Newton demonstrated the fertility of the union between mathematics and empiricism. Francis Bacon and Christian Huygens set down the intellectual bases of induction. Many others could be cited who found no conflict between science and their Christian faith.

By the late Seventeenth Century the great scientists, whatever their philosophical differences, had found a place within scientific method for careful and systematic observation, mathematical theory, and experimental practice. Since that time no fundamental change in the conception of scientific method has taken place.

3. Values of Science to Students

Living in a world in which science plays such a dynamic and vital role, a knowledge of science has great practical value for the Christian student. The following list is suggestive:

1. Through a study of science students find opportunities to sharpen their powers of observation, discrimination, and insight.
2. Science will help the individual to deal with himself and his environment.

3. Biological sciences help students to understand the animal and plant worlds.
4. Physical sciences give the student an understanding of the nature of the physical world in which he lives.
5. Science can supply corroborative evidence for the validity of conclusions from testimony. Radioactive carbon is a good example.
6. Science validates testimony and history as vehicles for the attainment of truth.
7. Science with its descriptions and explanations of reality deepens the Christian's appreciation of God's handiwork.
8. A better understanding of God comes to the student through a better understanding of God's handiwork.
9. A larger trust in God results from a study and appreciation of His wisdom and power.
10. Study of science should give each student an awareness of the unity of all knowledge and of Jesus Christ as the integrating center of truth.

4. *Limitations of Science*

While the salutary effects of science should be recognized, it also should be pointed out that history reveals that the effectiveness and influence of science in society has been very definitely limited. It is no substitute for faith, hope, and charity which move the world, and great as it is, it provides no happiness for man in life nor hope for him in death. Neither does it have the power to make men good.

Science is limited in methodology. When science claims inclusiveness for its methodology, it becomes scientism. Thus it claims far more for this method than it is possible to realize. When he becomes blinded by his own presuppositions and assumptions, the scientist is disqualified from recognizing objective truth. Again, scientists quite often forget that they are dealing with sensory data subject to the *mind*. It is not possible, therefore, to completely separate sensory data from non-sensory data. Still further, there is the existence of other kinds of knowledge besides that of the empirical, also subject to scientific analysis and use. It is quite possible that the scientist can overlook the fact of God's existence as one of the most evident and necessary sources of data.

It should be noted that the scientific method is only *one* method of discovering truth. While we recognize the validity of the scientific method for dealing with natural phenomena, it is not equally useful in the realm of moral and spiritual data. This feeling is shared as well by some atomic scientists who warn us that moral and spiritual truths are outside the realm of the scientific method.

No more is it the primary question as to *what* we can control, but now it is primarily important as to *who* controls things and *why*. The scientific method is definitely limited in this sphere. Finally, there are always present the dangers involved in placing too much trust in science and limiting one's appreciation for the contribution of other disciplines. The Christian must look to the power of God for his own welfare and for the salvation of his fellowmen.

In the final analysis, science is limited in its scope of knowledge. The truth of the matter is that in spite of its claims to the contrary, science itself is based on axioms, articles of faith, and assumptions which can neither be proved, comprehended, nor be the complete explanation of the facts. Even the exact science of mathematics requires that one should believe without further proof in order to deduce from this belief other conclusive facts. Some knowledge is simply beyond the power of science. Some of these unknown areas include the following: what is the real essence of matter? What is the essence of force? How does gravity work? What is the ether of outer space? What is life? There are many other unsolved problems.

At best, scientific knowledge is only proximate truth, not ultimate truth. This has been illustrated over and over again by the necessity of revising theories which have been thought to be unchanging. New discoveries bringing knowledge to hitherto undiscovered truths have forced a change in conclusions. Taylor has commented on this as follows:

> The more we pursue scientific investigation the more we discover that it does not lead to knowledge of the *intrinsic nature* of things. The knowledge it attains is *symbolic* knowledge rather than *intimate* knowledge; behind the symbolism there is a reality which escapes the measuring techniques.[2]

Although science has made outstanding contributions to analyzing the past and establishing the present, it knows little of the future, particularly of the ends and goals involved. Again, Taylor has pointed this out clearly.

> Science, knowing little of ultimate causes, cannot determine ends, nor can it direct society to ends which are external to its discipline. That is why in matters concerning ends, peace, justice, liberty, or any other heart's desire, the scientist cannot be and is in fact not conspicuously superior to other educated men. We do not go to the scientists to seek out the saints or the sanest in modern society. Indeed, it may justly be said that, to the extent that the scientist is ignorant of the social sciences, of history, of philosophy, of art, and of the humanities, he may well be a danger to society precisely because of that ignorance. The success which attends his methods of abstraction in the solution of a scientific problem may

[2]Hugh S. Taylor, "Physical Science" in Hoxie N. Fairchild, *Religious Perspectives in College Teaching* (New York, Ronald Press, 1952), p. 226.

make him susceptible to solutions of human conduct or national welfare in which important elements in the problem, personal, social, political, have been ignored by him as scientist.[3]

5. *Integration*

No scientist can escape his own assumptions. All scientists subscribe, at least implicitly, to a code of basic assumptions or primary postulates, a group of fundamental axioms. This is illustrated by Lachman, who describes the *secular* position, by saying that the secular scientist subscribes to

> a philosophy or code of axioms which attests to the existence of a temporo-spatial universe which contains matter. The scientist is interested only in the finite aspects of this universe. This he calls nature or the natural world. He assumes that what exists can be measured. Science maintains that the universe is stable and orderly, and there is consistency and uniformity in the universe; that all events which occur in the universe are determined and in turn serve as determiners; that man can comprehend the universe in which he lives. The scientist cannot prove these propositions; these are *a priori* assumptions to which he attests.[4]

The *Christian* likewise begins his philosophy of science with some basic assumptions. Some of these stated in outline form include:

1. God is the Source of all truth; the Creator of the universe.
2. God has made His truth known to man through revelation.
3. All truth is a unity because of the Unity in the Godhead.
4. General revelation is comprised of God's handiwork in the universe.
5. The Christian philosophy of nature provides the educator with the integrating factor in the field of natural sciences.

The direct implication of the assumptions listed above is that truth in the field of natural sciences hangs together because God provides for it. Nature itself is a product of God's creative power and therefore is a manifestation of the person of God. The Christian educator, therefore, should expect to find unity and correlation present in the relationships of the various courses of study which make up the field of natural sciences. The pattern resulting will look something like the chart on page 302.

The chart above shows how the various subject matter areas in the field of natural science are related and inter-related. The Christian philosophy of nature is determined by drawing heavily upon Special Revelation as recorded in the Bible. Where possible, the Christian educator will use the principles derived from the Scriptures to guide him in teaching and learning. Although the Bible is not a book of science, many general principles provide

[3]*Ibid.*, p. 229.
[4]Sheldon J. Lachman, *The Foundations of Science* (Detroit, Hamilton Press, 1956), pp. 108-09.

practical assistance to the instructor in the use and evaluation of scientific data and subject matter. The arrows running vertically show how scientific data supplied in the specific subject matter areas supplement the theological data in the building of the Christian philosophy of natural sciences. The arrows running laterally show how each of the specific subjects is directly related to the other subjects. The unity of truth, therefore, makes both correlation and integration possible and clear.

It should be noted also that each subject makes a distinctive contribution of its own to the totality of truth in the entire field. In doing this it is evident that each subject has a "thrust" of its own without which the total picture would not and could not be complete.

SUBJECT	CONTRIBUTION
Anatomy	Shows the structure of organisms
Astronomy	Shows order and movement of the celestial bodies

Botany	Study of plant life
Chemistry	Shows the composition of matter
Geology	Shows the structure of the earth
Physics	Study of energy and its transformation
Physiology	Shows the internal activities of organisms, their functions
Zoology	Study of animals
Mathematics	Communication through numbers and symbols

By constantly relating the "thrust" and factual data of each specific discipline to the Christian philosophy of nature, the teacher will find many clues for interpretation. Each separate discipline shows us something of the reality which is God. No one view shows us everything. By supplementing and complementing one another these disciplines provide us with a full picture of the knowledge of God.

6. *Interpretation*

The Christian philosophy demands that the Christian educator follow the pattern of interpretation laid out in the Special Revelation of God, the Bible. This means that scientific data will be interpreted supernaturally as well as naturally. The natural sciences comprise the content of God's General Revelation in curriculum form. The Bible testifies that this content is a self-revelation of God, that creation is God-revealing (Psalm 19:1; Isaiah 6:3; Psalm 103:22; Romans 11:36).

This position precludes for the Christian any possibility of subscribing to the view that a scientific study of nature should be exclusively descriptive in character, that each scientific fact is completely independent in and of itself. Instead, the Christian claims that all facts stand in relation to the Author of those facts and that such a relationship is revelatory of His character.

While it is recognized that General Revelation is definitely limited in its revelation of God, Romans 1:20 shows at least two primary attributes of the Almighty manifested in nature: His eternal power and Godhead. Each Christian teacher, therefore, should be alert to these revelations in the handling of study content.

The clues to the interpretation of subject matter in this area of knowledge are supplied in general by the principles and content of Biblical Studies and in particular by the Christian philosophy of nature. The pattern so demanded involves a process somewhat as follows:

Facts ——⟶ Principles ——⟶ The Christian Point of View

The Bible clearly shows what part nature plays in the use of the apperceptive method of teaching. Spiritual meanings are revealed through the use of material objects. "That was not first which is spiritual, but that which is natural: and afterward that which is spiritual" (I Corinthians 15:46). Beginning with that which is known, the teacher can move into the spiritual realm of the unknown. Beginning with that which is concrete he can move into the abstract. Jesus illustrated this principle over and over again by using nature in His teachings. "Without a parable spake he not unto them" (Matthew 13:34). By pointing out objects in nature Jesus led His disciples into the deeper truths of the Spirit. Wiley has pointed out this process as follows:

Consider the lilies — His primary observation
Solomon was not arrayed like
        one of these — secondary and historical knowledge
How much more shall your heavenly
        Father clothe you — Spiritual value and ultimate teaching goal[5]

Thus, nature and the Bible are the two textbooks for Christian teaching.

7. General Objectives

From the foregoing discussion we are able to outline some general objectives for use by teachers and students in the teaching-learning process as follows:

1. An appreciation of a scientific attitude and of scientific methods. This will include an appreciation for completely honest and unswerving logic.

2. An understanding of the language and basic principles of science.

3. To show the relationship between science and society, that science is a part of our culture and that technological advances have made outstanding contributions to the development of civilization.

4. The cultivation of intellectual curiosity and creativity.

5. The cultivation of critical thinking.

6. To show the student that science attempts to describe and explain phenomena which occur in the universe and the relationships involved.

7. To point out that the discoveries of science are primarily discoveries concerning the nature, purpose and activities of God.

8. An appreciation for the personalities who have made scientific contributions, their mistakes, and their successes.

9. To show the need for an ethic to control science based upon the dynamic which Christianity can supply.

[5]H. Orton Wiley, *Christian Theology* (Kansas City, Mo., Beacon Hill Press, 1949), p. 140.

10. To point out that the disturbances in the order and regularity of nature are often caused by sin.

11. In general education, to point out some of the universal laws of nature and some general methods of discovering such laws.

B. THE CHRISTIAN PHILOSOPHY OF NATURE

1. *The Bible and Nature*

The Bible is full of nature. From the opening moments of the creation in Genesis 1:1 to the New Creation in Revelation 21 and 22, there is constant reference to the significance of nature, to men's relation to it, and to God's providence in it and ultimate purpose for it. All creation exists for, through, and unto God. The scope of the Scriptural revelations of nature may be seen in the following list which is by no means exhaustive:

1. The Creation by God was to reveal God, His glory, power and goodness.
2. Man was created to rule nature.
3. The fall of man into sin brought the curse of God upon nature.
4. Oriental nature was the setting for the great Patriarchs.
5. Moses, the great prophet, was prepared by God in nature's setting.
6. The Hebrews were educated for life in Canaan's nature atmosphere.
7. The Ten Commandments and laws of Sinai rest upon nature as a foundation.
8. Israel was a nation of nature with God's blessing on their laws, festivals, ritual, and sabbaths.
9. Job drew great wisdom from nature and saw God's hand of providence in it.
10. The Psalms record the admiration of David for nature and his exaltation of the Creator.
11. Solomon lectured on nature.
12. The Prophets looked ahead to the perfection of nature.
13. Jesus lived amid nature and used its truth.
14. Paul used also the wisdom derived from nature.
15. In Revelation nature is brought to restoration and perfection.

2. *The Christian Philosophy of Nature in Education*

The Christian Theistic World View determines the Christian philosophy of nature. This in turn provides the clues to the application of science in the process of Christian education. As a derivative of the Christian world view we are able to determine some of the major emphases for the Christian philosophy of nature as follows:

I. God is the Creator and Administrator of nature.
  A. All things are from God, through Him, and unto Him (Genesis 1:1; Romans 11:36).
  B. He is world-ground for nature — He is Reality behind it, supporting and explaining it (Hebrews 1:3).
  C. The Spirit of God works by Divine Providence in this administration.

II. All nature is revelatory of God (Psalm 19:1; 97:6).
  A. All creational and providential forms of reality are the embodiment of divine ideas.
  B. All forms of reality reveal God's thoughts to men.
  C. There is unity back of these forms of reality.
  D. Some attributes of God are revealed by nature (Psalm 104:24; Romans 1:20).

III. Sin has had a destructive effect on nature.
  A. Man's ability to read God's revelation in nature has been impaired.
  B. The forms of revelation in nature have been corrupted.

IV. Man was given a mandate from God to have dominion over nature (Genesis 1:26; Psalm 8:6).
  A. He is expected to control nature to reveal God's glory and realize human efficiency.
  B. The cultural heritage would therefore become a part of the subject matter curriculum.
  C. Redemption of nature is demanded in dealing with nature in order to abstract from it the revelation of God for the educative process.

V. The New Creation will culminate the plan of God.
  A. The curse of sin will be removed.
  B. There will be a new heaven and a new earth.

C. SCIENCE AND EDUCATION

1. *Science in Education*

With the development of statistical methods, a means of measuring educational achievement was made available. Since Thorndike developed means of objective measurement, standardized tests have been used. To date, progress has been limited to the measurement of information and skills. Much needs to be done in the areas of ideals, attitudes, emotions, methods, etc. The results of research have been widespread but much remains to be done.

The greatest advances have been made in child study and educational psychology. The school survey movement and classroom experimentation and statistical methods constitute the areas where greatest progress has been noted. All of these developments have been sufficient to make it possible to speak now of a science of education.

2. *Christianity and Science*

In the past the attitude of some Christians toward science has been characterized by narrow mistrust and timid evasion. This has resulted in shortsightedness and divorcement from the cultural situation. The Bible teaches the validity of searching for truth and of using nature as a part of this search. To withdraw from culture and society is contrary to the spirit of Jesus who said, "Go ye into all the world." Some Christians have gone so far as to become obscurantists. This is contrary to the Christian spirit of love.

Since nature is a part of the general revelation of God, the true Christian will be anxious to become acquainted with it because nature will afford him a greater knowledge of God. Furthermore, he will appreciate all sincere efforts to discover the truth in nature in spite of the secular framework in which such truth is expressed at times. The Christian is exhorted to "prove all things," but it is also commendable to maintain openmindedness.

Science needs the light of revelation to give it purpose and causation without which it becomes virtually meaningless. While it is the primary function of science to gather data, it is the function of theology to give these data their purpose and teleological ordering.

Without theology, science has "weakened the hold of moral principles upon mankind." This it has accomplished by insisting on the priority of science over religion and metaphysics, the relativity of all knowledge, and the ateleological character of the universe. On the other hand the tremendous destructive power of the atom has caused more scientists to realize the need for moral safeguards provided through theology.

Theology also needs science. Here theology reveals the origin, purpose, and destiny of the universe; science reveals the "clues, analogies, and reinforcements of the existence and nature of the invisible universe."

Many scientists have long claimed that the superstitious theology of the Middle Ages deterred the rapid advance of science. John Baillie has submitted another explanation by saying that medieval science was swayed by Aristotle and a pagan conception of theology. The limitations of science were not explained by the corrupt influence of Christian theology. In fact, he says that "modern science could not have come into being until the ancient pagan conception of the natural world had given place to the Christian."[6]

Modern science began with the determination to banish purpose and explanation from scientific procedure. The early scientists, however, including Bacon and Descartes, did not mean that there *are* no final causes but rather that they are not within the province of science. Science cannot discover purpose by way of empiricism. They did believe that there was a providential ordering of nature. The *real* reason, therefore, why Bacon and Descartes broke with Aristotle was a reason of faith rather than one of science. They worked with a different conception of God. They believed that God created nature and impregnated it with the explanation of its Creator. Aristotle, they believed, substituted nature for God, and consequently his science was deductive in method. Bacon and Descartes believed that God created nature but that the pattern is hidden from us. The method of science, consequently, needs to be inductive. Bacon and Descartes learned from Christian revelation and creation that the pattern of nature was hidden to man.

We thus conclude that Christianity has been a motivating factor in the rise of modern science. This, however, has not been fully appreciated even in the ranks of some Christians.

Science renders a service to the Christian by being useful in glorifying God as Creator. Science reveals the marvelous design and handiwork of God in His creation. His power and His glory are unveiled. Science can be used to bolster the assurance of Christians in the certainty of the truth of God's Word. Great evidence to corroborate Bible facts can be marshalled through the discoveries of science.

Christianity provides purposes and objectives for science. Science should be used to glorify God and improve man's welfare. Christianity has promoted the interests of science through its revitalization of cultural life and emphasis on the freedom of political life. It also emphasizes that careers in science provide opportunities for Christians to serve God at His call. In serving Jesus Christ, men not only serve a Saviour but the Creator and coming King of the universe.

3. *The Place of the Empirical Sciences in Christian Education*

The place of the empirical sciences in the curriculum of Christian education is determined directly by the place ascribed to them in the overall Christian world view. Dr. Jaarsma has summarized this position succinctly in the propositions that follow:

1. The object of scientific exploration is the handiwork of God in which His thought is manifest and disclosed.
2. The world has being independent of our knowing, but knowing

6 John Baillie, *Natural Science and the Spiritual Life* (New York, Charles Scribner's Sons, 1952), p. 25.

is the conditioning factor of all being and the true interpretation thereof.

3. Man was charged originally with dominion over God's creation. This charge has not been relinquished and remains man's responsibility and his opportunity. This charge should be the scientist's motivating factor in research.

4. Man's dominion is to be subordinate to God and in harmony with His purpose for the world.

5. Scientific truth is part of the great unity of truth, the many and the one. There can be no conflict among the various manifestations of the great unity of truth.[7]

We must conclude, therefore, that these sciences enable the Christian to come to a greater understanding of God while at the same time raising the level of personal and social efficiency. They must not, however, be allowed to usurp the supreme place of spiritual truth in the curriculum. The application of theological and philosophical truths to the field of the empirical sciences will help to keep them in a proper perspective and use. Science thus becomes a means to an end.

4. The Place of the Christian School in a World of Science

The Christian school must be realistic in accepting the fact that we are living in an age of science. The achievements of present-day science are beyond question. The graduates of our schools are going out into this world. The Christian school must feel, therefore, that it has a divine mission to perform in *this* world.

The first obligation to be faced is that the Christian school is bound to provide elements in its curriculum to afford the student orientation to his scientific environment and in some cases direct preparation for a life vocation in some area of science.

The atomic age, however, has its sad features also, as evidenced by increased anxiety, nervous tensions, and social pressure, not to speak of its sin. Men are now beginning to wonder if science has the answers. Fear has gripped many hearts. The Christian school must not hesitate to reveal this situation realistically, but at the same time it should optimistically point to a solution of our individual and social ills in Jesus Christ. An atomic age cannot afford to be divorced from Life and its source of power. As never before the Christian school needs to bring the witness of the Gospel to a sinful and scientific age. The Gospel is applicable to any age. It cannot be arbitrarily imposed on this age but its inherent transforming power can work from within through dedicated and Christlike individuals, both teachers and scholars, to lead this age to humble obedience to God.

[7]Cornelius Jaarsma, "Christian Theism and the Empirical Sciences," *Journal of the American Scientific Affiliation,* June, 1955, Vol. 7, No. 2, p. 7.

5. Basic Ideas in the Natural Sciences

Before moving on to a consideration in more detail of the separate natural sciences, it is well that we provide an outline summary of that which has been stated thus far in this field to provide a setting for the material set forth in the pages to follow:

Scientific Method

I. The scientific method, although valid within limits as a means to knowledge, is not adequate to lead us to all truth. To it must be added revelation and faith.

Physical Sciences

II. The physical universe reveals the power, wisdom, greatness, and glory of God:

A. In the structure, organization, and vastness of the solar and galactic systems.

B. In the structure and composition of matter.

C. In the availability and inexhaustibility of energy.

D. In the discoverable laws that obtain in the physical world.

E. In the practical adaptability of matter and energy to man's use and welfare.

III. The world of life reveals the power, wisdom, greatness, and glory of God:

A. In the ability of plants to utilize moisture, sunlight and simple chemicals in order to grow, reproduce and store edible foods.

B. In the ability of animal life to grow and reproduce, and in its adaptation, by the Creator, to its environment.

C. In the marvelous structure of the human organism, that makes possible growth and repair, reproduction, and rational thinking and self-consciousness.

D. In the "balance" that is in nature (a balance that has been temporarily disturbed by sin).

E. In the laws of heredity, expressed in the Biblical phrase, "after its kind," which stabilize and perpetuate life, and maintain an organic distinction between the several species.

Man and His Natural Home

IV. Man was created in God's image, and the earth was designed to be a home in which he could live, grow, and fellowship with God. Sin has marred both man and nature, but redemption in Christ is provided to restore them.

Science and Morality

V. To be of the highest use, man's possession and application of scientific knowledge must be governed by the spiritual and moral principles set forth in the Bible.

D. THE NATURAL SCIENCES

1. Anatomy

The word, "anatomy," means literally "to cut up." It denotes the study of the structure of living things both plant and animal. A study of structure, therefore, provides the student with the major "thrust" or purpose of this subject. Animal anatomy covers the study of the structure of man and all animals. Comparative anatomy involves the study of the relationship between the various forms of animal anatomy. Other branches include histology, which covers a study of the minutia of microscopical anatomy, and embryology, a developmental anatomy devoted to the study of the gradual growth of the animal. In the plant world there are also the correlated branches of plant morphology, comparative anatomy, histology, and embryology. The study of the microscopic structure of the single cell is called cytology and of organs, organology. The study of the bone system is termed osteology, the circulation system, angiology, of nerve structures, neurology, of muscles, myology, and of the viscera, splanchnology.

Descriptive anatomy deals with general anatomy while systematic anatomy deals with the anatomy of related organs in related animals. Practical or applied anatomy is given to the diagnosis and treatment of diseases and is often called medical or surgical anatomy. Regional or topographical anatomy deals with the study of special parts or the relation of surrounding parts.

The major "thrust" of this subject is to show the structure of organisms. Here the Christian teacher and student are able to observe in close detail the handiwork of the Creator in the animal and plant worlds. The intricate structure of these organisms reveals the marvelous wisdom, skill, and power of God.

2. Astronomy

As a subject, astronomy is that branch of science given to the study of heavenly bodies, their positions, motions, distances, constitution, relations, history, and destiny. Branches of this science include descriptive or general astronomy, embracing astronometry and astrophysics, practical astronomy and theoretical or celestial mechanics.

General astronomy provides us with our general knowledge of the heavenly bodies, their motions, aspects, and physical constitution. Practical astronomy teaches the methods of observing the heavenly bodies, including the instruments of measurement with the principles and computations involved in their use. Theoretical astronomy treats the mathematical aspects of the orbits and motions of the heavenly bodies, using particularly the laws of motion and gravitation.

The practical use of astronomy is demonstrated by the necessity for knowing the seasons and the tides, the time of day, the skills of navigation, and the boundaries of large tracts of land. Astronomy provides knowledge of great benefit to the physicist, particularly in the study of the atom, not to speak of present-day ventures into space exploration.

The Christian teacher is supplied with much material in this discipline which leads to integrating the Christian faith with this subject — the astronomical evidences of the Being of God, witnesses to the great attributes of God, the Creation, and many other evidences. Truly the "heavens declare the glory of God and the firmament showeth His handiwork."

3. Botany

The word "botany" is a derivative of the Greek word for plant. This science is concerned with the structure, organization, growth, function, development, physiology, inheritance, classification, distribution, and uses of plant life.

The main subdivisions of this science include: (1) taxonomy or systematic botany which deals with plant classification, (2) morphology which is concerned with the form and structure of plants, (3) physiology which deals with the function of plant life, (4) genetics, concerned with the laws of heredity, and (5) ecology which is concerned with the relationships of plants to their environment. Other subdivisions deal with diseases, fossils, and specialized forms of plant life.

Botanical research has contributed largely to a knowledge of food for plants, food from plants, breeding and inheritance among plants, vitamins, hormones, and antibiotics.

The delicacies and beauties of the plant world surely reveal something of the skill and beauty of the Holy One of the Ages. Trees, for example, remind us of God and the Christian (Psalm 1:3; 92:12-15).

4. Chemistry

This science deals with the composition, properties, and changes of substances. It is primarily concerned with the transformations of substances into other substances. Inorganic chemistry is concerned with the preparation and properties of elements and non-carbon compounds and was developed primarily from the study of minerals. Organic chemistry treats of the chemistry of all carbon compounds. It was developed largely from the study of plant and animal products.

Inorganic chemistry treats of all other compounds and of the elements. Analytical chemistry is concerned with the resolution of a compound or mixture into its constituent parts or elements by methods which are qualitative when the nature only of these constituents is determined, or quantitative when their actual quantity or proportion is ascertained. Theoretical chemistry deals with the laws of chemical phenomena and with the theories involved. Biochemistry deals with the chemical compounds and processes occurring in organisms.

Where the sciences of botany, astronomy, and anatomy show the infinite variety of God's creation and power, chemistry, by dealing with the composition of matter, shows the intricately designed processes of the mixture of substances. This science, therefore, turns one's observation inward where we see that God is just as thorough there as anywhere else.

5. Geology

Broadly conceived, geology comprises all branches of science which are devoted to the study of the inorganic solid earth crust and the earth as a whole. More narrowly, this science is concerned with the systematic study of the rocks and rock structure. As such it is concerned with the history of the changes in the structure and shape of the earth's crust.

Some practical contributions to the store of knowledge have been made by this science. It has provided information on the nature of life in past history, the approximate age of the earth, not to mention the nature of the earth itself.

Five distinct subdivisions of geology include (1) cosmogony which deals with the relation of the earth to the solar system and the universe, (2) physical geology which is a study of the various forms of the earth's crust, (3) petrology which describes rock composition, (4) palaeontology which is concerned with fossils, and (5) stratigraphical geology which traces the history of the earth as revealed in rocks and fossils.

Geology provides the Christian with an understanding and appreciation of the home which God has provided for mankind. Here all around him man is able to see the goodness and power of God in making provision for his every need (Philippians 4:19).

6. Physics

Physics has been defined as the science of energy, of the transformations of energy, and of its relation to matter. Actually, the development of other natural sciences has forced this limited conception of this particular discipline, for at first it was broad enough to comprehend almost all science.

While it is recognized that the content of this discipline is changing constantly and undergoing new developments in the light of new discoveries, there are some generally accepted subdivisions to this subject. At present it is divided into mechanics and mechanical properties of matter, sound, heat, light, magnetism, and electricity. Recently, electromagnetic radiation, the electron theory, and the structure of matter have been prominent.

That God is a Person becomes quite evident from a study of the evidence of Special Revelation. However, the empirical evidences of the "force" of His personality are not quite so evident. Physics, therefore, gives the Christian a deep appreciation for the moving power of God as a Person in the world and universe. All energy is a result of His energy, for He "upholdeth all things by the word of His power." The laws of energy and force provide empirical evidence of the very laws of God's nature.

7. Physiology

This science concerns the study of the functions of living things in contrast to their structure, a study of the activities involved. Traditionally, the primary interest in this field has been the structure and function of the human body, but actually all living structures are included in its scope. Naturally, this discipline has been of great practical value to medicine. Plant physiology, however, has been of great value to agriculture as well.

This science now deals with fundamental matters including the composition of living substance, molecular structure, physical and chemical actions and reactions involved in motion, secretion, circulation, etc.

The chief divisions of this discipline include: (1) physical physiology or biophysics which concerns the study of apparent electrical phenomena of living substances, nerve impulses, muscles, growth, blood, etc., (2) chemical physiology or biochemistry, covering the chemical composition of living matter, chemistry of food and growth, metabolism, digestion, etc., (3) general physiology, (4) applied physiology, (5) comparative physiology, and (6) special subjects such as endocrinology and reproduction.

Where anatomy provides the Christian with an appreciation of the structure of organisms and through that of God's skill in design, physiology places emphasis on the "function" of that structure. Here one is able to see the purpose in God's designs and the results therefrom.

8. Zoology

The science of zoology is concerned with the study of animals. Its aim is to understand the lives of animals. Broadly conceived, zoology includes animal morphology (together with anatomy, histology, and cytology), physiology, embryology, genetics, taxonomy, paleontology, and ecology. There are also other divisions named according to the particular groups of animals being dealt with, such as ornithology, treating of birds, etc.

Zoology provides further evidences of the infinite variety involved in God's creation of life forms. Through the various "family groups" or "family forms" of animal life, one is able to get an insight into the fellowship and family life of the Heavenly Father.

9. Mathematics

This term is said to be derived from the Greek word for art. A definition of this discipline is still debatable but originally it was described as "the science of discrete and continuous magnitude." Recently, however, it has been defined as the "science concerned with the logical deduction of consequences from the general premises of all reasoning."

Usually this discipline is classified into at least three categories: (1) pure mathematics which is a statement of mathematical doctrine without regard to its application, (2) abstract mathematics, dealing with pure order, form or extent, regardless of any material or other content, and with their necessary implications, and (3) applied mathematics, dealing with the content of abstract mathematics and with problems and conclusions connected with human life and experience.

Mathematics is concerned with the general and universal. It is perhaps by assisting the scientist in his attempt to understand the structure of the physical world that mathematics can make its greatest contribution.

The study of mathematics seems to point to the changelessness of God. It reveals the wisdom of God and that He is a God of order and system.

Revelation of God in nature involves ideas of number, form, symmetry, system, and laws governing the existence and harmonious working of all things. Everywhere there are evidences of mathematical relationships.

A proper understanding and appreciation of the works of God demands of man a knowledge of the underlying principles of mathematics. To this end God has led man to develop an efficient system of number, computation, and expression of natural laws.

Mathematics is a revelation of the thought life of God. It shows Him to be a God of system, order, accuracy; He can be depended upon; His logic is certain. By thinking in mathematical terms, therefore, we are actually thinking God's thoughts after Him.

SUGGESTED ACTIVITIES FOR CHAPTER XI

1. Discuss fully the definition of science and what its implications are for the Christian educator.
2. What does the history of science reveal regarding the relationship of Christian truth to scientific truth?
3. Add to the list of values which come to the student from the study of science.
4. What other limitations of science can you think of?
5. Draw your own chart to show how the various subjects in this area can be integrated.
6. Discuss fully and give illustrations of how God is revealed in nature in general and in particular phases of nature specifically.
7. Add to the general objectives for natural sciences listed in this chapter.
8. Look up Bible references to nature.
9. What part does a philosophy of nature play in education?
10. Do you think that education can be a science?
11. Explain why Christianity in many instances has been prejudiced in its attitude toward science in the past.
12. What place does natural science play in Christian education?
13. Give illustrations from the various disciplines to show how subject matter should be handled from the Christian point of view.

A CHRISTIAN PHILOSOPHY OF THE HUMANITIES

OUTLINE FOR CHAPTER 12

A. Definition and Scope
   1. Definition
   2. Scope

B. History and Values
   1. Historical Survey
   2. Values

C. Philosophy of the Humanities
   1. Christian Philosophy of Art and Music
   2. Integration
   3. Interpretation
   4. Purposes and Objectives

D. The Humanities
   1. The Visual Arts
   2. The Dynamic Arts
   3. Literature
   4. Philosophy

12 | A CHRISTIAN PHILOSOPHY OF THE HUMANITIES

A. Definition and Scope

1. Definition

Traditionally, the subjects in the humanities' area have been concerned with human purposes and human values. Thus, they are embodiments of the learning, experience, and expression of humanity. As such they are manifestations of man's inner self or spirit.

The ideas and feelings of men are made known articulately through language, symbolically through the arts, and philosophically through the expressed values and meanings of human experience. The humanities, therefore, constitute a record of what men have done with, and thought about their lives. Life and living contribute the subject matter of the humanities. One may well define the humanities, therefore, as "studies concerned with the creative expression of the human spirit."

2. Scope

There are a number of ways of organizing the subject matter in this area of truth. It is purely arbitrary, therefore, how one chooses to embrace what he considers to be the truth comprehended by the various disciplines in this area. For our purposes here we shall use the following organization to depict the scope of subjects under consideration:

I. The Visual Arts
  A. Architecture
  B. Sculpture
  C. Painting
II. The Dynamic Arts
  A. Music
  B. Poetry
  C. Drama
III. Literature
IV. Philosophy

In some circles history is included in this area but it was classified with the social sciences for purposes of this study. It should be noted, however, that there is great overlap when it comes to history.

In the secular world the classification of dynamic arts would have to include the dance. While it is recognized that there are some forms of the dance mentioned in the Scriptures (i.e., II Samuel 6:12 ff), this particular art is excluded from our considerations for practical reasons.

B. HISTORY AND VALUES

1. *Historical Survey*[1]

In spite of great cultural accomplishments of ancient cultures of the Near and Far East, the first focal point of general interest is Greece in her Golden Age, culminating in the Fifth and Fourth Centuries B.C. In Greek philosophy, idealism gained the ascendancy over materialism. Hellas was the cradle of Western drama, epic poetry, and rhetoric. The relics of her architecture and sculpture still influence us. Less is preserved of her painting and music, but we know that the former united with the Byzantine trend, the latter with the Hebrew heritage, to shape medieval practices in those arts.

Greece, from the Fifth to the First Centuries B.C., demonstrated a process, often to be repeated, of a peak of transcendent achievement being followed by a period of imitation and sensationalism, a decline still capable of producing works of great beauty. Some speak of the alternation of classicism and romanticism.

Rome's greatness lies more in military, political, and legal achievements. In the arts she relied on Greek models, yet she did produce architecture and literature of importance.

To the secular mind, the Middle Ages are a time of dark superstition, relieved only by the daybreak of the Renaissance. The Christian must admit, however, that all phases of medieval life were permeated by a fear of God common to all. Christian symbolism is found in every work of art; medieval cathedrals are heaven-directed; philosophical thought is dominated by the authoritarian Church of Rome (Scholasticism); the vast majority of poetic and musical expressions are religious.

One of the great achievements of the human mind, the progression from monophonic to polyphonic music, took place within the confines of monasteries and cathedral chapels from the Ninth to the Fifteenth Centuries. What drama there was, mainly popular mystery plays, served the educational purposes of the Church. France was the cultural center until the Fourteenth Century.

A liberation from ecclesiastical domination was brought about

[1]Statement supplied by Dr. Rene Frank, professor and director of Division of Music at Fort Wayne Bible College.

by the "Renaissance" of ancient Greek and Roman art and literature, but this was not achieved without a decline of morals. Humanism, rationalism, and empiricism were the main philosophical
trends. In art, a great development toward idealistic realism took
place in Italy, under the patronage of wealthy city states and
ambitious families. The Elizabethan age brought to England a
flowering of dramatic and lyric poetry, as well as polyphonic music.
Spain, enriched by overseas acquisitions, became a center of cultural productivity.

The splendor of Renaissance culture was accompanied, however, by ever-increasing abuses within the powerful Roman Church.
This led to the Protestant Reformation, but wherever it was vic-
torious, it also did away with much of artistic value. It did create,
however, a body of church music and sacred poetry that has sur-
vived to this day.

The Seventeenth and early Eighteenth Centuries are often
called the "Baroque" period in art and architecture characterized
by a "Romantic" reaction against the simplicity and clarity of the
Renaissance, in music by the rise of opera — meant to revive Greek
drama, oratorio, and instrumental music. Absolutist France produced highly stylized drama that became the model for the rest of
Europe.

During the Eighteenth Century, a new quest for freedom of
thought swept through educated European minds, claiming the
right to question established powers and values. Rousseau's "return to nature" influenced education, literature, art, and music.
England developed the novel, Germany had her Golden Age of
Literature, Vienna became the musical center, cultivating a direct
and transparent style. The French Revolution and Napoleon's
conquests did not thwart these gains.

Among the political unrest of the Nineteenth Century there
flowered an individualistic literary and artistic movement called
"Romanticism," a movement of escape into the past, the faraway,
the supernatural. Its great achievements took place in French
painting, German music, and English poetry. It also fostered a
rather narrow nationalism that brought Eastern and Northern European nations to the world's attention.

While our time seems dominated by scientific and political
movements, the arts are active, though restive. Realism struggles
against abstract expressionism; functional simplicity has made contemporary architecture widely accepted; the probings of psychology into the abysses of the human mind have influenced drama
and the novel, and even painting (sur-realism). Pragmatism has
not only permeated philosophy but also pedagogy. Russia and
America are taking a place of equal weight in cultural activity.

While in the field of Western literature one can observe a gradual shift from the liberal and humanistic philosophies of the past several centuries, it must be stated that the voice of the Christian has become a dim one among the clamor of godless forces.

2. *Values*

We should be able to profit by the considered experience of other men. Our insight should be enlarged. The Humanities remind us that we are all men and give us a mirror of our common experience which in turn reminds us that each man's experience is uniquely his own.

The Humanities should cultivate in each student a genuine desire to know the cultural heritage. Therefore, the justification for the presence of these courses in the curriculum lies largely at this point. These subjects provide students with an understanding and appreciation of man, an appreciation for the expression of the human spirit and creativity.

From a Christian viewpoint other values are evident and include the following:

1. The humanities reveal truths which add to the glory of God.
2. They can lead to greater sensitivity in worship and to satisfaction derived from much fuller worship.
3. Christians in some cases can learn the nature of the Holy Spirit through some of the characteristics of the arts.
4. The arts can be a means of recreation.
5. Contacts with the unsaved are often found through mutual association in the study and appreciation of the arts, particularly among the upper classes of society.
6. The arts can often be used in making the gospel message more vivid.

C. PHILOSOPHY OF THE HUMANITIES

1. *Christian Philosophy of Art and Music*

God is the source of beauty. He intended that beauty be a reflection of His own nature. Since man was created in the image of God, it is to be expected that he would be created and endowed with the ability to produce beauty and the capacity to appreciate beauty. Man's creativeness is a reflection of God as the original Creator. In this light the ultimate purpose of art is to honor and glorify God. True art reflects divine excellence.

Sin has affected both man's sense of beauty and his capacity to produce it and appreciate it. Art is now used for selfish and corrupt purposes. This is why redemption is so necessary, to restore all phases of man's life to their God-honoring purposes. Thus, the Holy Spirit through regeneration of the hearts of men is restoring the desire, capacity and ability to produce and use art for its original purpose and intent. He makes it possible for real development of artistic sensibilities and abilities in regenerated man.

God's Word plays its part in the Christian view of art. It reveals the God-revealing aspects of beauty and the purpose of beauty to glorify the Creator. It should be the purpose, therefore, of the school, not only to teach this particular philosophy of art, but also to teach students to recognize beauty wherever it is found as a gift from God to be used for His glory.

Music, likewise, is a gift of God to man. It is used to praise God. Music deeply affects the inner life of man, it moves on the heart, ennobling tendencies and morals, motivating men to love and serve God. It provides a means of enjoyment and recreation. It looks beyond the horizon to that future day when all the universe will praise the Creator at the restoration of all things.

Like art, music has been perverted and corrupted by the forces of sin. Both man's ability to produce and his desire to use music have been perverted and impaired. It is used to arouse unholy emotions and to motivate sinful practices.

Christians need to recapture the gift of music and use it for God's glory and holy purposes. In this the Christian school can play a large part.

2. Integration

In secular education three main patterns of organization for effecting integration in the Humanities have been suggested. One is a survey of history, using World Literature as the particular integrating factor. The second pattern is the Great Books approach. Here selections are made from many outstanding sources but in a rather arbitrary manner. The third alternative is to use Literature in relation to all other arts. All of these lack the factor which provides at once unity and correlation.

A fourth suggestion is supplied by this study, namely, the use of the discipline of philosophy. Philosophy has long been concerned with the great issues of living and the great ideas of men. The enduring ideas of the past have been preserved in Great Books, in great works of literature, in the arts and philosophy. Literature and the arts are expressions of philosophical insights.

The practical value of philosophy in supplying the integrating factor lies first in laying the foundation whereby the Humanities can be seen in relation to all other subject matter areas. This was made evident in an earlier chapter devoted to a philosophy of Biblical Studies. There the unity of total truth was made clear.

In addition to seeing the relationship of the Humanities to Biblical Studies and other areas of study, it is important also to note the internal and close relationship of each separate discipline within this area to the other disciplines. It was suggested earlier that the "pattern approach" to integration seems best suited to show these relationships. This approach demands some internal unity and internal relationships between the subjects comprising the area of humanities. According to our definition of the humanities, these disciplines are concerned with the creative expression of the human spirit. Creative expression demands a personal point of view, a way of looking at life, purposes, values, and ultimate concerns. Actually, this is philosophy. The Humanities, therefore, are tangible evidences of the philosophy of the author or artist. Thus, philosophy seems basic to all the other disciplines in this area of truth. The secret of integrating the various disciplines consequently rests upon this particular subject. In chart form the organization of the disciplines would take the following form as revealed below:

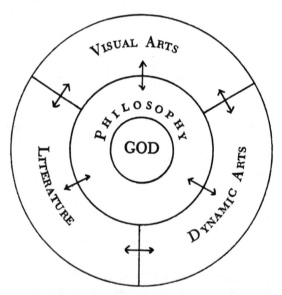

Above it is seen that philosophy serves as the integrating factor by being the means whereby the personal expression of the author is linked with the Ultimate on the one hand and the views of the individual author on the other while at the same time being related to one another. The visual arts, the dynamic arts and literature, as well as the discipline of philosophy itself, are seen to be the results of the life-view of the authors and artists involved. Through the arts, whether visual, audible or written, the readers and observers are able to feel, to see and experience those things purposed and planned by the authors and artists.

While it is admitted that artists and authors have been affected by political, social, economic, and religious environments, still the arts, literature, and philosophy are records of personal reactions, the expression of feelings and thoughts in relation to these things. Therefore, philosophy seems to be a better means of integration than any other.

While it is recognized that humanities provide the Christian with channels of personal expression thereby revealing his philosophy or point of view, at the same time each Christian artist or musician or thinker must be guided in his expression by his personal relation to God through the Lord Jesus Christ. In this way his art is dynamically related to his source of life and truth — God.

The Christian also must be careful to keep his philosophy in its proper perspective in dealing with the philosophies of men. This provides us with a clue to interpretation. Since Christ is the *Logos* (John 1:1) and the Wisdom of God (I Corinthians 1:24), all philosophy, and through it all humanistic study, should have Him as center or as providing a standard of values. This leads us to the question of interpretation.

3. *Interpretation*

The process involved in interpreting the Humanities is the same as for the other areas already considered. The reader must gather the facts, interpret them, and then subject them to the scrutiny of the Christian philosophy of life as recorded in the Biblical Studies. This means that each reader must do his best to discover the "message" of the particular art under consideration. He must do his best to put himself in the place of the author or artist under consideration. He must make an effort to get the point of view of the creative artist.

The Christian, however, must not stop at this point. He must ask himself in what ways God is related to the particular matter under observation. This involves the application of the Christian philosophy to the matter being considered.

Like other areas already considered, there is a Christian point of view in the Humanities. God never abrogated His covenant with Adam to have dominion over the earth. In spite of the presence and corruption of sin, God has given mankind all things to enjoy. "Charge them that are rich in this world that they be not highminded, nor trust in uncertain riches, but in the living God, who giveth us richly all things to enjoy" (I Timothy 6:17). The

Christian, therefore, in engaging in these things must be sure to "do all to the glory of God" (I Corinthians 10:31). He must do his best "to possess the land." A point of caution is to be noted, however. Each Christian should be constantly alert in this area particularly to discover the battle between the "flesh and the spirit." He must be constantly aware of the distinctive difference between natural beauty and artistic beauty (formed through the efforts of man). These difficulties, however, should not deter the Christian from getting the greatest possible enjoyment out of the arts and using them to further the interests of His kingdom.

In relating this field of inquiry as a whole to the Christian World View as recorded in Chapter II, the following observations are made:

Regarding God and Cosmos

God has created the universe in beauty and harmony. The humanities are attempts to express or reflect such beauty and harmony. The standards of excellence in the humanities are derived from the design found in creation.

Regarding God and Man

The aesthetic sense in man is part of the divine image. Ideally, man would be guided by his aesthetic sense to create works of art which glorify God and edify his fellow men. Actually, as a consequence of sin, man has put self in place of God, and his artistic creations reflect in varying degrees his alienation from God. Redemption redirects his creative efforts Godward.

Regarding God and Truth

The Humanities provide a medium to convey truth so as to make it more vivid and penetrating, and more easily apprehended.

Regarding God and Values

Artistic expression provides a potential for influencing men aesthetically, intellectually, emotionally, and morally; as far as God is allowed to direct such expression, its influence will further His purposes.[2]

4. Purposes and Objectives

Traditionally, the humanities have been distinctive in providing worthy goals for students to achieve. Some of the most prominent among these include the following:

1. To provide for the student a broader understanding of his cultural heritage and an enlarged cultural perspective in his own view of life

[2]Statement of Committee on Humanities, Fort Wayne Bible College.

2. To bring each student face to face with the great issues of living

3. To develop in each student intellectual maturity and a sustained interest in life's major problems

4. To encourage the student to apply himself to the solution of present-day problems by using principles of successful people of the past

5. To assist the students in building a coherent set of ideals for themselves by which they can face the present

6. To make it possible for each student to understand and appreciate great works of art and thereby to acquire deeper insight into himself and his fellowmen

7. To provide the student with a concrete awareness of the role of literature and the arts in the development of our civilization

8. To show the significance of artistic expression in our lives today

9. To enable each student to discern true quality and value; develop the ability to discriminate and to evaluate critically

10. To encourage each student to use his leisure time for worthy purposes

11. To discover, develop and use creative abilities

12. To show the importance of developing a Christian philosophy of life

13. To encourage capable students to choose some area of humanities for a ministry

14. To show the student the importance of being alert to the battle between the flesh and the spirit

15. To help each student to enlarge his sympathies for the feelings and aspirations of man

16. To assist the student in building a Christian philosophy of the Humanities to embrace God's place as Creator, of the Humanities as gifts from God, showing the destructive effects of sin, and man's need of revelation and redemption, of restoring the arts to a God-glorifying position in life

D. The Humanities

1. *The Visual Arts*

In the past the term, *art*, had a rather wide scope of meaning embracing skill and ability as well as aesthetics. Today the term is used to describe human activities involved in the fine arts and in an aesthetic sense.

The area of fine arts has generally included at least two categories in the list of subjects comprising the area. The static or visual arts include architecture, sculpture, and painting. The dynamic arts include music, poetry, and drama (rhetoric).

The function of *art* is also difficult to define. Some believe that the purpose of art is to give pleasure but others maintain that its purpose lies deeper than this. Art is actually the reflection of civilization. History is made to live through art which preserves the relics of civilization. Art exalts the individual above the sordid realities of everyday life. It feeds the hungry imaginations of men. It satisfies the emotional urge to create.

Art, then, is really an expression of man's inner feelings, beliefs, hopes, and ambitions. It is a result of reflection, meditation, and experience. It is more than imitation. It includes beauty, communication of ideas, some entertainment, but above all, expression. "A work of art is the record in comprehensible form of the essential truth which the artist has perceived in analyzing his experience."

Painting is a layman's term for art, at least for two-dimensional art. Generally, the word signifies the act of laying on, or adorning with, paints or colors. In the fine arts it is considered the work of a painter, a representation of objects or scenes in color on a surface by means of paints, colors or pigments.

While the architect deals with space and the sculptor with three-dimensional form, the painter is limited to two dimensions. Other qualities have to be *suggested* in a painting. In the Western world painters have sought to represent three-dimensional form in space through the use of two principles of visual representation — perspective and modeling. Perspective is a device by which pictorial depth is suggested. Modeling is used to produce an effect of plastic form.

In the past the predominating style of painting for long periods of time was to represent nature. Today, however, the abstraction of contemporary art shows that artists are using a particular style for expressing their own views and feelings.

One cannot escape the centrality of spiritual values when he studies the visual arts of the past, particularly of the Middle Ages and Renaissance. Sculpture, painting and architecture are filled with explicit and implicit expressions of Christian thought-life and devotion.

Without a full acquaintance with Christian patterns of thought and life it would be impossible to understand and appreciate Gothic architecture. There is certainly no doubt as to the preponderant importance of Christian values in English literary art.

The *values* of art and art study are many. Some of the more general values for the Christian may be stated as follows:

1. Art translates beauty.
2. Art conveys meaning.
3. It develops creative imagination.
4. It develops a deep appreciation for the beautiful.
5. It contributes to spiritual values and idealism.
6. It shows that beauty reveals God — Psalm 19:1; 104:1-3.
7. The arts carry meaning and value and thus reveal the fateful and intangible factors which operate in the hearts of men.
8. The arts reveal to the church the way the layman feels about the chief concerns of life.

For education Wickiser has noted some values by showing that the function of art in education is threefold:

1. Art aids child growth and development:
   a. By promoting physical, mental and aesthetic growth
   b. By contributing to self-realization
   c. By developing creative imagination
   d. By contributing to problem-solving
   e. By emphasizing original thinking, doing and evaluating
   f. By contributing to personality development
   g. By contributing to emotional development
2. Art fosters aesthetic development:
   a. By educating the eye
   b. By developing appreciation and judgment
   c. By encouraging expression
   d. By developing creative ability
3. Art aids us to live fully:
   a. By enriching the creative side of life
   b. By contributing to social growth
   c. By developing economic efficiency
   d. By maturing talent[3]

Architecture is that visual art given to the art or science of building. A number of factors enter into a proper concept of good architecture. The purpose for which a building is to be used is one factor which determines its form. Another factor is the method and means of construction. These factors provide the elements by which the building is brought into being.

Great architecture, however, is not the result of use and construction alone. It is in the quality of design where one notes the difference between good and bad architecture. In fact, it is to the degree that the elements of design, function and construction combine to provide distinctive appeal to the observer that one finds the greatest architecture. Creative design, in other words, integrates function and construction into significant art.

Sculpture, the third visual art, has been defined as the act or art of carving, cutting, or hewing wood, stone, metal or other

[3]Ralph L. Wickiser, *An Introduction to Art Education* (Yonkers-on-Hudson, New York, World Book Co., 1957), Ch. 2.

similar materials into statues, ornaments, figures, and groups of figures according to the purpose and design of the sculptor.

There are two general types of sculpture: (1) figures in relief, and (2) free-standing figures. The first type refers to figures attached to some kind of background whereas free-standing figures can be viewed from all sides.

Sculpture is primarily an art of form and mass through which the artist seeks to express the things he feels or thinks about his subject. Such order and arrangement are given to it as will express also the spirit of the age in which the artist lives.

2. The Dynamic Arts

In these arts we have classified music, poetry, and drama.

To the layman *music* is simply conceived as sound. It is not like a picture or statue which occupies space. The real meaning of music, however, appears to be deeper than sound. Professionally, music is defined as the science or art of pleasing, expressive or intelligible combination of tones; the art of making such combinations into compositions of definite structure according to the laws of melody, harmony, and rhythm. Philosophically, music is a "symbolic, immediate, and untranslatable presentation to our comprehension and response." In this it strikes directly and deeply beyond portrayal or depiction to the mind and heart by symbolic articulation.

When words are combined with the music, then the meaning involved is fully expressed in an intelligible way. Wordless music may express extra-musical thoughts or depict feelings and situations. We call this program music. The composer's plans are then made known by titles or written explanations. Most instrumental music, however, is "absolute music" and does not intend to convey anything beyond what feelings or thoughts the sounds alone evoke.

While intrinsically there is nothing sacred or secular in a piece of music *per se*, its classification into sacred or secular is determined by the nature of its technical substance and the practical use to which a particular work is devoted. This means that the characteristics of music used for sacred purposes are markedly different from those of music used for secular purposes. Davison has described the characteristics of worship music as

> that music from which rhythmic activity, chromaticism, tunefulness, and extensive dissonance were absent demonstrated how the eloquent manipulation of technical resource could result in a type of music so remote from any suggestion of the secular as to make it the normal conveyance of the ideas contained in sacred poetry and the ideal agent for setting up the detached, unworldly atmosphere appropriate to divine worship.[4]

[4]Archibald T. Davison, *Church Music* (Cambridge, Harvard University Press, 1952), p. 120.

He goes on to point out that the purpose and function of music in the church service of worship was not to call attention to itself, but rather to God and contributing to the atmosphere and spirit of worship.

This attitude, we believe, is the true one for the Christian. The arts have been widely used to give greater glory to God and to edify those who participate in worship. The church has closely practiced the art of music. This has been true from the very beginning. The Bible is full of music and references to it. Wiley found 460 such references in the Old Testament and 50 in the New Testament.[5]

In a day when secularism has had strong influence in the music world, Christians need to be on guard constantly so that the music which is used may be used purely for the worship of God. We must make sure that our music is dedicated to His service, not to please men, nor serve self, nor display selfish interests. In addition to this, the true Christian will avoid the concert-hall attitude where the tendency is to display mastery and skill. The service-attitude must replace the concert-attitude. Anyway, the role of the hymn in the history of the church has shown us that songs were never sung for the purpose of creating beauty but in order to express the emotions of the soul. By dedicating ourselves and our music to God we are actually engaging in a form of prayer and praise. Music thus may become a pathway by which we open a way to God for our church congregations.

Music originated with God. He has given both the ability and capacity for producing and appreciating music. The student, therefore, should expect to derive some real genuine values from this great art. Some of them are as follows:

1. Music provides relaxation and enjoyment.
2. Music contributes to worship and meditation.
3. It is used to praise God — Psalm 90:1-3; 150.
4. It lifts men to higher levels of thinking and living.
5. The industry and skill of great musicians provide real incentive and inspiration.
6. Opportunities for a Christian ministry are provided through the medium of music.

Poetry has many definitions. Generally, it concerns emotional and imaginative discourse in metrical form. It represents experiences or ideas in an emotional context, in language characterized by imagery or rhythmical sound. It differs from painting and sculpture in that it is better adapted to represent continuity and movement as well as in the use of purely abstract ideas and

[5]Lulu R. Wiley, *Bible Music* (New York, The Paebar Co., 1945), p. x.

images. It is also related to music but differs from it in its capacity for representing both concrete and abstract ideas with some exactness. This kind of literature is commonly classified as narrative, lyrical or dramatic. In narrative poetry the principle subject is action; in lyrical poetry feeling is prominent; in dramatic poetry both action and feeling are emphasized.

The Bible has deeply influenced English poetry. In fact, poetry has been considered "the most Christian part of our English literature." Work has pointed out two obvious reasons for this: (1) the Bible is itself comprised of a great amount of poetry and much of its prose is imbued with the spirit of poetry; (2) the Scriptures have deeply appealed to the poets because of the peculiar character of the poetry in the Book.[6]

We not only find records of Biblical reference and allusion in these poets but we also note that they turned to the Bible for their themes. Outstanding among these are Browning, Tennyson, Longfellow and Whittier, the latter two being American. Some of these are noted for their references also to Christ. It is not so much the historic Christ that they love to picture as it is the living, present Christ of today.

Drama is commonly thought of in terms of an art concerned with the writing or performance of plays. It is classified as a branch of the literary world embracing compositions in prose or verse.

Drama has been distinguished from other forms of art in at least four ways: (1) the drama is temporal in nature; (2) it is mimetic, that is, it recreates speech and action; (3) it is interpretative of an original creation, and (4) it is a synthesis of several elements in final form.[7] Elements of drama are listed generally as script or composition, acting, directing, and design.

A religious drama is "one which has a religious effect upon an audience; that is, it sends the audience away exalted in spirit and with a deeper sense of fellowship with God and man." Such dramas have been classified as Biblical and non-Biblical. The last group can be religious or non-religious. According to Eastman there are five types of religious drama: (1) the prepared play, (2) the dramatized Bible story, (3) the pageant, (4) the visualization, and (5) the liturgical drama.[8]

The Bible is full of drama. The life of Jesus and that of the early church are packed with it. In keeping with the true spirit

[6]Edgar W. Work, *The Bible in English Literature* (New York, Fleming H. Revell, 1917), ch. 17.

[7]H. D. Albright, et al, *Principles of Theatre Art* (Cambridge, Houghton Mifflin Co., 1955), p. 3 f.

[8]Fred Eastman and Louis Wilson, *Drama in the Church*, rev. ed. (New York, Samuel French, 1942), p. 27.

of the Scriptures, the purpose of drama, therefore, is not enter-tainment but rather a means of ministry to the souls of men through a great art. If people are drawn close to God and inspired to live more Christlike lives, then a play is a religious play. True religious drama should be a demonstration of sincerity with the least amount of show. It should have the elements of a sermon, "a demonstration of decision and consequence, a spur to and a foretaste of perfection, and an incitement to action."

Some of the values to be derived from religious drama include the following:

1. Religious drama can teach religion.
2. It can reveal life, beauty and striving for truth.
3. Drama develops strength, beauty and power in the imagination and creative life of the players and audience.
4. It ministers to the aesthetic and emotional life of the people.
5. It reveals the ideals and goals of living that are essentially religious.
6. It makes vivid the glorious adventures of purposeful and meaningful life.
7. It stimulates the fancy and imagination of men, giving them the pattern as well as the incentive to larger and more distinguished experience.
8. The church can use drama to interpret life to the people outside through religion.

3. Literature

Literature as a term is hard to define. In some circles it is thought of as that which stands for the best expression of the best thought reduced to writing. Sometimes the term is applied to all printed matter that is intended to be preserved for permanent use. More specifically, the term is reserved for those forms that are intended to serve artistic rather than utilitarian purposes, and which are developed chiefly by the processes of imagination rather than those of reason. This latter view is generally the preferred one, for it denotes the more polished or artistic class of such products, together with the critical knowledge and appreciation of them. Thus, the term is applied in this sense almost exclusively to writing which has claim to consideration on the ground of beauty of form or emotional effect.

Literary forms are classified inclusively under the main divisions of prose literature and poetry. Drama may be classified in both divisions. The essay, fiction, and drama are the chief forms of prose literature. Poetry and drama were classified in this study under the dynamic arts above.

Some of the most obvious values which come to the students through the study of literature include:

1. Literature is a means of relaxation and enjoyment.
2. It is a source of information.
3. It is a means of getting acquainted with people, places and things.
4. It leads to an understanding of one's fellowmen.
5. It is a storehouse of great values of life.
6. It gives evidence of man's response to his environment.
7. It develops the ability to evaluate and criticize literary art.
8. Free discussion of ideas in literature will help the student to clarify his own philosophy of life.
9. Literature can produce a state of mind favorable to Christianity.

The last recorded above suggests the close relation literature has had and does have to Christianity. English literature particularly is saturated in the language and thought of the Bible, theological ideas and ecclesiastical history. Students need to know much about Christianity to understand English literature because the Christian church has been profoundly influential in shaping Western Civilization.

Luccock has noted that the study of literature reveals three real relationships to religion. (1) It discloses much of "implicit religion" by revealing attitudes and spirit which are an outgrowth of the Christian conception of life, (2) it shows the symptoms of the times, and (3) it presents a challenge to religion.[9]

Amos Wilder pointed out that it is hardly possible to adequately criticize many literary works without some knowledge of theology.

The time is past when literary appreciation could slight the theological aspects of the work of art, as though all such elements were external. . . . It is important to note that theological aspects of literature and art bear on the very substance of the work, on the literary form and style.[10]

When it comes to American literature, without a doubt the Bible has been the greatest single influence. American writers have been steeped in Biblical imagery, phrasing and rhythms. Even unsympathetic writers have felt this influence indirectly. The first and perhaps the greatest evidence of Biblical influence was the persistence of Puritan theology in early American life and times. Although the last two centuries marked a trend away from

[9]Halford E. Luccock, *Contemporary American Literature and Religion* (New York, Willett, Clark and Co., 1934), p. 14 f.
[10]Amos N. Wilder, *Theology and Modern Literature* (Cambridge, Harvard University Press, 1958), p. 29.

orthodox Biblical faith in literature, the present century has already witnessed a definite trend marking a return somewhat to the original emphases of early America.

Stewart has pointed out that Christian writers in this country have reacted against some prevailing views of their time.[11] Against the rationalism of Jefferson, the deism of Emerson and Whitman, and the naturalism of Zola, Crane, and Norris was arrayed the Nineteenth Century creations of Hawthorne, Melville, and James. In our own century writers like Cather, Eliot, Faulkner, and Warren have fought the implications of naturalism. It is encouraging to find publications like that of Stewart's reaching the market.

Secular literature may not equal Holy Writ but it may illustrate, reinforce, verify, and illumine it. The Christian teacher can point out in secular literature what is missing with regard to highest values. He can make a comparison with the Christian position and awaken a sense of highest values. With Calvin the Christian today can believe that beauty serves not only necessity but our pleasure and delight.

Early writers conveyed to a pagan culture through their recording of values inherent in the Christian tradition a witness to that tradition. If these writers are to be understood, then interpreters must know the Christian position. Even in interpreting those periods where there has been open revolt against Christianity and religious doubt was rampant, the Christian teacher can show where confusion and error prevailed. One of the great objectives in teaching and studying literature is to develop powers of discrimination in the search for permanent values.

4. Philosophy

The term "philosophy" is commonly defined as the love of wisdom. To some, however, the term is hard to define because philosophy is considered "a human and cultural enterprise to be enquired into, rather than a mere term to be defined." Traditionally, philosophy has been concerned with intellectual attempts "to establish human life in some satisfying and meaningful relation to the universe in which man finds himself, and to afford some wisdom in the conduct of human affairs." In doing this, philosophy is more than a mere set of beliefs; it involves also critical and reflective thinking. Concepts and abstractions are used in an effort to formulate principles and laws. Such concepts are not concerned with so-called practical pursuits but primarily with the meaning of human experience and the significance of the world in which man lives.

[11]Randall Stewart, American Literature and Christian Doctrine (Baton Rouge, Louisiana State University Press, 1958), p. 147 ff.

Philosophy is concerned with the organization of the materials of human experience into coherent arrangement. This involves what is called reflective evaluation. On the one hand it is concerned with a world view and on the other hand with an analysis of what it all means. Thus, philosophy has a double function to perform, one synthetic or speculative and the other analytic. In performing its analytic function, philosophy is concerned with the task of clarifying and criticizing the fundamental methods, rules, procedures, and norms of all theoretical enterprises, including scientific inquiry itself. This is important because meaning is often dependent on the method of gathering data for examination. It is just as important at times to know *how* to get the right kind of knowledge as it is to use knowledge already accepted as truth.

We may conclude, therefore, that there are two main types of philosophy. Analytical philosophy is the examination of the nature, methods, procedures, and foundations of all human reflection culminating in criticism, clarification, and definition. Speculative philosophy is the formulation of a universal perspective based on a synthesis and interpretation of the results of all human reflection. In this its concern is to unify all the phases of human experience into a comprehensive and meaningful whole commonly called a world view.

In carrying out the two functions mentioned above, the Christian is concerned that both analysis and synthesis deal with the broadest possible understanding and interpretation of experience. This demands the inclusion of data derived from emotional, volitional, valuational, and religious experiences. This will guarantee reflection on the total range of human experience.

From definition and function we move to content of philosophy. The reader can refer to Chapter IX, Section E, for a complete discussion of content, making it unnecessary to repeat at this point. Suffice it to say that the most satisfactory resting place for the mind is in a positive and authoritative statement of content supplied by the Christian philosophy of life or world view.

Philosophy holds an important place in the Humanities for some good reasons. It supplies the integrative core by which the disciplines in this area can be correlated and used. It provides the Christian with a survey of great ideas and of the thought, life and world views of mankind. It provides a basis for coordinating the various spheres of life as a whole. It relates knowledge systematically. It examines the pre-suppositions, methods and basic concepts of each discipline and group of disciplines. It strives for coherence, the formulation of a world view. Its method is to consult data from total experience.

SUGGESTED CLASS ACTIVITIES FOR CHAPTER XII

1. Give your definition of the Humanities and indicate the scope of subjects to be included in the area.
2. How would you organize the disciplines which comprise this area of study?
3. What general values to be derived from Humanities as a whole would you add?
4. Draw your own chart to show how to integrate the disciplines in the Humanities area.
5. Discuss the pros and cons of using the subject of philosophy to integrate the subject matter in this area. In what two directions does the Christian have to look when using philosophy in this way?
6. How is the general theory of interpretation, as indicated in the Chapter on "Constructing a Christian Philosophy of Education," applied in the Humanities area?
7. What would you add to the general purposes and objectives for the Humanities area?
8. Discuss the pros and cons of teaching the various arts in a Christian school. What place would they have in the life and ministry of a Christian?
9. What are some of the prejudices to overcome in developing a Christian point of view in the Humanities?
10. Write papers or make oral reports to the class on the place of the various arts in Christian education.

A CHRISTIAN PHILOSOPHY OF
COMMUNICATIVE SKILLS

OUTLINE FOR CHAPTER 13

A. Nature and History
   1. Definition and Scope
   2. Historical Statement
   3. Education and Communication
   4. Values

B. The Christian Philosophy of Communication
   1. God and Communication
   2. The Bible and Language
   3. Integration
   4. Interpretation
   5. General Objectives

C. Subject Matter and Communicative Skills
   1. English
   2. Speech
   3. Language
   4. Research Procedures
   5. Audio-Visual Aids

13 | A CHRISTIAN PHILOSOPHY OF COMMUNICATIVE SKILLS

A. NATURE AND HISTORY

1. *Definition and Scope*

As a curriculum area communication has been defined as "the study of the ways in which people try, primarily through language, to get their ideas across to others, and, in turn, try to understand the meaning and significance of what others are trying to say to them whether the avenues used are reading, writing, speaking or listening."

Communication is not an end in itself; it is rather a means or a process. People exist, live, and think. They seek to share their thoughts, feelings, and experiences. This is done in a multitude of situations and conditions but is done primarily through language. Language, however, should be used as a means, not the end, of communication. This all means that the student needs to be clear on what he wants to say, why he wants to say it, and how to say it. Teachers can be of great assistance, therefore, to students if they demand that students weigh evidences carefully, report accurately, examine generalizations, read extensively and intensively, and assume intellectual and moral responsibility for what they say. Thus each student can see how important good communication is in his education.

Traditionally, the skills involved in communication have included reading, writing, speaking, and listening. Others have gone so far as to include demonstration and observation in this list also.

The above skills are developed by such courses as English Composition, Journalism, Speech, languages, Critical Interpretation, Research Methods, Hermeneutics, and Audio-visual Methods with the latter embracing radio and television.

2. *Historical Statement*[1]

The first formal training in communication was undertaken 2500 years before the Greeks began their work in the field. The ancient Egyptians of the Fifth Dynasty were the first ones to begin such training of their youth.

[1]Largely indebted to the Committee on Communicative Skills, Fort Wayne Bible College, for this statement.

It remained for the teachers of ancient Greece, however, to develop fully the teaching of communication as a skill. The founding of special training in rhetoric is generally accorded to Corax of Syracuse. The need for training in this field grew out of the establishment of a democracy in Syracuse and the immediate consequences which followed, viz., a mass of litigation on claims to property. Since this became quite complicated, Corax developed a set of rules to help in the oral presentation of the special cases.

Contemporaneous with and following the work of Corax was that done in the field of communication by the Greek Sophists. Many of these men became known for their ability to teach rhetoric as a means of achieving one's own ends, whether these were worthy or unworthy.

Socrates, Plato, and Aristotle were also important figures in the development of the communication skills, both from a grammatical viewpoint and a rhetorical one. Socrates' end in all of his intercourse with men was the moral improvement of mankind, and this he felt he could best achieve by the "dialectical process," a process in which he led along the one with whom he was conversing by asking leading questions. The first notable observations on grammar were made by Plato. Aristotle went so far in his grammatical analysis as to distinguish nouns, verbs, and connectives. In addition to this, he developed what is known today as Aristotelian logic. With reference to rhetoric, he firmly believed and taught that the aim of rhetoric is not to move the emotions so much as it is to prove your point or appear to prove your point logically.

About 110 B.C. Hermagoras of Aeolis founded what has come to be known as "Scholastic Rhetoric." This was an attempt to counteract the view that oratory is a mere knack founded on practice and recalled attention to the study of it as an art. This type of rhetoric was a combination of the practical rhetoric of pre-Aristotelian times and the philosophical rhetoric of Aristotle, who had emphasized rhetoric as an art.

Cicero and Quintilian also gave great impetus to this particular art of communication. Cicero became famous for his statement of his belief that the perfect orator was the perfect man. Quintilian gave a very complete expression of "scholastic rhetoric."

During the time of the Empire, again there came into being a group known as the Sophists, whose aim was to impress the multitude and whose entire emphasis was upon style rather than content. "Academic oratory" is the name that has been given to their particular emphasis.

During the Middle Ages and Renaissance, the art of communication became highly important and was therefore strongly emphasized. Grammar, logic, and rhetoric were the subjects of the trivium, i.e., the course which a student took following his four years of undergraduateship. With the revival of learning during the Renaissance, as was true in other areas, there was a revival of the best teaching of the ancients. The writings of Aristotle, Cicero, Quintilian, and others came back into vogue.

During the Eighteenth Century, however, a decay in the teaching of rhetoric as a formal study set in and the function of the rhetoric lecturer became the correcting of written themes. However, in more recent years, American educators, if not those of other countries, have had an increasing awareness of the importance of educating all citizens in the arts of communication. Great strides have been made in the elimination of illiteracy and in the cultivation of habits of abstract thinking. As part of this movement, the colleges of the country have been examining their instruction in the day-by-day life of the average person. Some institutions have already made basic changes in conventional courses in English Composition and Rhetoric by making them less a formal study of the rules of grammar and rhetoric, and by using the actual experiences of students as vehicles of instruction.

In recent years there have even been radical departures from tradition by the integration of various subject matters that up to this time have been more or less separate. Subjects like English, speech, psychology, and writing are today commonly grouped in departments called Communications or Communication Skills. These courses are based on a recognition of the fact that all the processes of communication such as reading, writing, listening, and speaking are intellectual operations having much in common.[2]

3. Education and Communication

We live in a complex civilization these days. Our culture is a dynamic and expanding one. Rapid communication has brought about many advantages but it has also created many problems. To keep up with world happenings and to understand the problems has made it necessary for everyone to communicate — to receive by seeing, listening, and reading; to contribute and communicate by writing and talking.

Skill in communication is necessary for successful and intelligent living. It is incumbent upon each individual to develop the skills necessary to communicate, particularly in the field of education. Thus, the skills of reading, listening, talking, writing, and thinking become extremely important. In fact our very destiny both as individuals and as a nation depend upon our skill in communication.

[2]Earl J. McGrath, ed., *Communication in General Education* (Dubuque, Iowa, Wm. C. Brown Co., Publishers, 1949), p. vi.

Educators are becoming increasingly aware of the importance of educating our citizens in the arts of communication. Many institutions are making particular studies on how to make these arts functional for everyday use.

From the standpoint of Christian education, however, one thing needs to be stressed at the outset. No medium of communication must be allowed to hide either the message or the person who is to receive it and actively make it his own.

4. Values

There are practical values to be derived from a mastery of communicative skills by the student. Not only is this true of the subjects in the area itself but these skills enable the student to master all other areas, thus cutting across all curriculum areas. Some of the most obvious values to be derived include:

1. The ability to communicate thoughts, words, feelings, and messages to one's fellowmen
2. The development of a sense of responsibility for honest communication
3. The ability to do critical thinking
4. The ability to discover, organize and report information
5. Acquaintance with the linguistic and cultural heritage of the English-speaking peoples
6. The development of an appreciation for the literature and language of other peoples
7. The development of a Christian philosophy of communication

B. THE CHRISTIAN PHILOSOPHY OF COMMUNICATION

1. God and Communication

In the Christian view, communication, like everything else, finds its origin in God the Creator. God is a God of communication. His nature is to communicate. Many Biblical passages point to this: "God said," "the word of the Lord came unto me," "thus saith the Lord" (used hundreds of times), "and God said, Let there be light," and many others.

God has chosen to speak and make known both His existence and nature. "The word of the Lord came to man." This is communication and it implies the relationship that God has with men. Fellowship, therefore, depends directly on communication.

We have already seen in the Christian Philosophy of Revelation how God has used two primary agencies to affect His communication with man: (1) through nature or general revelation, and (2) through the Scriptures and His Son or special revelation. In fact the writer of Hebrews shows that God has maintained a continuous discourse with man through these two methods.

God, who at sundry times and in divers manners spake in times past unto the fathers by the prophets, hath in these last days spoken unto us by his Son, whom he hath appointed heir of all things, by whom also he made the worlds; who being the brightness of his glory, and the express image of his person, and upholding all things by the word of his power, when he had by himself purged our sins, sat down on the right hand of the Majesty on High (Hebrews 1:1-3).

While it is recognized that the clearest and best channel of communication God has had with man is through His Son, the Bible itself is religious communication. The prophets dramatized their message. To them, the message of God was important and they sought many ways to communicate it. In the New Testament Paul's letters were widely used to communicate the gospel message. Many New Testament references, as well, reveal this. The coming of Jesus was heralded by the song of the angels and a glorious star. "Let your light so shine," and many others. Jesus said, "He that hath seen me hath seen the Father" (John 14:9). The Holy Spirit is the Revealer and Communicator of truth (John 14:16, 17).

God created man for communication with Himself and with his fellowmen. Man is to live in communion and communication with Him and other men. Thus, at creation man was endowed by God to express thoughts as well as to receive thoughts from others. In fact, the power to communicate in the use of language marks man as an image of God distinct from animal species. Since God spoke and received and understood the expressed thought of His creatures, man, in exercising these same qualities, is thus able to be like God.

Adam and Eve were able to read the book of Nature. They were capable of reading the ideas of God as they were given objective form in nature.

The presence of sin has interfered with the communication between God and man. Now, defective communication is a sign of sin's presence and effects. It accounts for the discord and disharmony between men. When man sinned and fled from the presence of God, all other aspects of his life were affected. Language, for example, the means of communication, became the source of curse as well as blessing, a curse by being the source of misunderstanding, disruption and deceit.

God saw that it would take redemption to restore proper communication. It would take redemption to restore the close personal relationship that He desired and planned to have with men. In this, God took the initiative. After Adam sinned it was God who came down to seek him. His covenant with Israel was an expression of communication. It remained, however, for the cross to demonstrate the great lengths to which God went to restore fellowship and harmony among men. In fact, communication comes to its climax when the individual experiences the provisions of the cross, allowing direct access to his heart by the Spirit of God.

Communication is to be maintained by a closeness of communion and fellowship characterized by love. Love is the means whereby true communication comes to its greatest fruition.

> Hear, O Israel: the Lord our God is one Lord: and thou shalt love the Lord thy God with all thine heart, and with all thy soul, and with all thy might. . . . Thou shalt love thy neighbor as thyself (Deuteronomy 6:4, 5; Leviticus 19:18).

Communication, therefore, is an expression of the will and nature of God, imparted also to man and used to maintain direct and close relationship between them in time and eternity. It follows naturally that Christian educators should give serious attention to the nature of and practices involved in the demands of this great concept.

Jesus demonstrated that the nature of communication is twofold: communication of and communication between — "That they all may be one; as Thou, Father, art in me, and I in thee, that they also may be one in us; that the world may believe that thou hast sent me" (John 17:21).

Today, the whole program of the church is one of communication. Witnessing, preaching, teaching, singing, praying, writing are some of the many channels for communicating the Gospel to mankind. Thus, the Christian school must be alert to affecting the greatest possible communication with God and the world of men.

2. The Bible and Language

The concept of language in the Bible is wrapped up in the concept of the Word. The Word of God is central in the Christian view of language.

First, God created by His Word. "And God said" (Genesis 1:3); "By the Word of the Lord the heavens were made; and all the hosts of them by the breath of his mouth. . . . For he spake and it was done; he commanded, and it stood fast" (Psalm 33:6, 9); "Through faith we understood that the worlds were framed by the Word of God, so that things which are seen were not made of things which do appear" (Hebrews 11:3). We are also told that He "upholds all things by the word of his power" (Hebrews 1:3). The Apostle John tells us that it was the Word of God (the Son of God) through whom all things were made (John 1:1-4).

We may conclude from the above that God planned for language to be the means of communication between Himself and man. The closeness of fellowship between God and man originally was illustrated when God came down in the cool of the day to talk to Adam and Eve. The tragedy of broken fellowship is also illustrated in God's refusal to communicate directly with man after man had sinned, using intermediaries instead. The classic example of that broken fellowship and also of the misuse of language is in the experience of mankind at the Tower of Babel (Genesis 11). The entrance of sin broke communication between God and man and everything else felt its impact.

Redemption is required to restore the right use and significance of language as well as to release language from the curse of sin. This is fully demonstrated in Acts 2 where we see the full power of the Holy Spirit poured out on the disciples on the day of Pentecost and where the Spirit released language from its bondage in restoring communication to its rightful place. Here is seen that, once redeemed, language is made universally intelligible once more as it was in the beginning when "the whole earth was of one language and of one speech" (Genesis 11:1).

Since the Tower of Babel man has struggled for universal understanding and a world-wide language. This cannot take place again until the problem of sin is solved, the heart of men regenerated, and the channels of communication to God are restored. Pentecost is the secret of it all.

The role of language is illustrated in Genesis 2 where it is recorded that Adam named the beasts. This implies not simply communication used as a source of information but it also shows how man conquers reality through the use of language. It becomes, therefore, a great source of individual power and usefulness.

Language also has a social function, for there is "communication between" as well as "communication of." In the beginning language was actually a dialogue between God and man. Since the entrance of sin, it can and has been used to combat ideas and persons as well as to bless. Christians, therefore, need to be alert to the misuse of language as well as to its use. Furthermore, it is necessary to note carefully what words mean, for communication and the use of language depend directly on an understanding of ideas and presuppositions which give meaning to the words.

Today, the church has the obligation to communicate the Word. "The Lord hath spoken." All the activities of the church — evangelizing, preaching, teaching, and witnessing — are bent to this purpose. The proclamation of the Gospel is the great purpose of the church. Teaching should embrace this proclamation.

The church has the Gospel and in a very real sense the Gospel has the church. In the New Testament the Gospel was not only proclaimed as a message, but also as a faith and experience (I John 1:1-3). So it must be today.

The Bible says that the message must be communicated but this is not confined to "verbalism," it is not dependent on human ability, it must be proclaimed in the power of the Holy Spirit.

Because of sin the purpose of this proclamation, of necessity, cannot be persuasion. It must be conversion and sanctification. The hard hearts of men must hear the Gospel, be softened thereby and made open to God and His truth "who will have all men to be saved and to come to a knowledge of the truth" (I Timothy 2:4).

Science cannot open man's eyes, for men are blinded, bound, and enslaved by sin. Men must be liberated from this bondage through dynamic communication of the language and life of the Gospel.

In summarizing this discussion on the Scriptures and language, we note that the Bible contains for us basic principles for the proper use of language. Some of these are:

1. Language must be logical and consistent with reality.
   Philippians 4:8 — Finally, brethren, whatsoever things are *true*, whatsoever things are *honest*, whatsoever things are lovely, whatsoever things are of good report; if there be any virtue and if there be any praise, think on these things.
2. Language must be with grace, i.e. gracious, fitting, manifesting the fact that grace dwells with us.
   Colossians 4:6 — Let your speech be always with grace, seasoned with salt.
   Ecclesiastes 10:12 — The words of a wise man's mouth are gracious.
3. Language must be seasoned with salt, i.e. wholesome.
   Colossians 4:6 — Let your speech be always with grace, seasoned with salt.
4. Language must be edifying, instructive, choice.
   Ephesians 4:29 — Let no corrupt speech proceed out of thy mouth, but such as is good for edifying, as the need may be, that it may give grace to them that hear.
5. Language must be pure, free from filth and smut.
   Ephesians 4:29 — Let no corrupt speech proceed out of thy mouth.[3]

4. Research Procedures

The Christian philosophy of communication discussed above reveals the clues by which the skills and subject matter areas concerned can be related to the Christian faith and to one another. Since God is the Author of both communication and the means through which communication is accomplished, it is possible to chart the pattern by which integration in this field of study is achieved. This is done in the chart form on page 349.

From the chart we note that the skills and subject matter areas comprising the curriculum division of communicative skills

[3]National Union of Christian Schools, *Course of Study for Christian Schools* 2nd ed., revised (Grand Rapids, Mich., Wm. B. Eerdmans Pub. Co., 1953), p. 137.

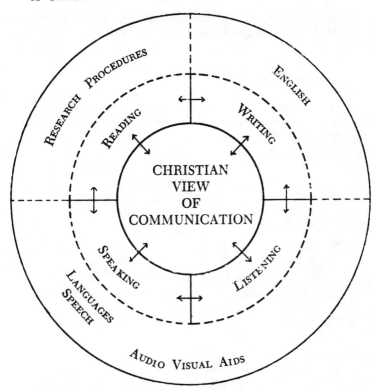

are related by means of the integrative power inherent in the Christian view of communication. This view begins with God who has chosen to communicate Himself to man and who has created man with the powers of communication with God and other men. This we know because the Christian view of communication is developed from sources abstracted from the truths supplied by Biblical Studies. These studies supply the principles of truth by which integration is made possible. They provide us with the record of what God had to say about communication. Reading, writing, speaking, and listening are skills exercised by man in the providence of God. They are the divinely supplied channels through which communication is achieved and are definitely, particularly, and closely related. In fact the relation is often so close that there is remarkable overlap involved. The fact of the matter is the processes of communication being considered here have much in common intellectually. Actually, they are really facets of the single process of communication. Meaning is conveyed in the form of symbols.

The disciplines in the subject matter fields represent the curriculum approach to communication. The separate disciplines become channels through which the content and skills involved in the processes of communication are presented to the student. Some form of reading, or writing, or listening, or speaking is particularly dealt with in each discipline. Sometimes a discipline will deal with two or more of these skills.

While each particular discipline has a distinctive "thrust" of its own, it is sufficiently related to the others so that one discipline can draw heavily on the others to complete the picture of truth in the total area. Thus, God is revealed specifically through these subjects as individual disciplines and generally through the area as a whole. With the development of his skills in reading, writing, listening, and speaking, the student is able to be a "living witness" of God in the world of communication. Skills reveal somewhat the nature and actions of God and should issue in Christian service. This is illustrated as follows:

SUBJECT	SKILLS	APPLICATION
1. English	Writing, Reading, and Speaking	
2. Speech	Oral Communication	Christian Living
3. Languages	Speaking and Reading	and
4. Research Procedures	Reading and Writing and Thinking	Christian Service
5. Audio-visual Aids	Reading, Seeing and Hearing	

4. Interpretation

The principles of interpretation involved here are the same as those involved in the areas previously considered. We should expect to see God in the revelation of the subject matter content in this curriculum area.

Whereas in some of the other areas of truth the *being* of God is revealed, in the communications area the *actions* of God in communication and communicating are disclosed. God acts to communicate and He does this efficiently and effectively. The pattern He has shown us sets the standard for our emulation. In learning to communicate effectively man comes closer to a manifestation of the character and conduct of God.

The Christian teacher should handle the truth in this area as in the others previously considered, using the inductive principles of thinking, research, and presentation. Thus, he will move from facts to principles to the application of truth in Christian living and Christian service.

5. General Objectives

From the discussion above it is now possible to lay out some general objectives for communicative skills as follows:

1. Students should understand sentence structure and how it reflects relationships of ideas.
2. Students should be able to listen with concentration and judgment.
3. Students should understand the role language plays in influencing social behavior.
4. Students should develop skill in logical thinking.
5. Students should be able to read with critical apprehension.
6. Students should be able to utilize the basic fundamentals of speech making.
7. Students should be able to develop a Christian philosophy of communication skills embracing the place of subject matter in the revelation of God.
8. Students should note the destructive effects of sin on the various skills of communication and the work of the Spirit of God in overcoming these effects.

C. SUBJECT MATTER AND COMMMUNICATIVE SKILLS

1. English

The term, "English," used in a curricular sense, means a course of study or a class in the English language or literature. Emphasis here is placed on the skills involved in handling the language. Literature has already been classified with the Humanities, but where one is particularly concerned with the skills and techniques involved in the *production* of literature, he is talking about English.

The first steps in learning to use the language are covered in *English Composition,* which has been defined as "the art by which ideas and mental impressions are conveyed in written language." The student, therefore, is called upon to master grammar which is the art of arranging words properly into statements or sentences either written or spoken. This involves mastering parts of speech, sentence structure, punctuation, pronunciation, and composition.

There are obvious values which come to the student through a study of English. Some of them include:

1. A knowledge of English affects the student's knowledge of all other subjects.
2. It affects one's capabilities in almost every sphere and activity.
3. A knowledge of English and the ability to use it determines to what degree one may succeed or fail to succeed in life.

4. A knowledge of English assists one to think more clearly and work more fruitfully each day.

5. To the Christian, English provides greater skill in Christian living and service.

While English Composition is concerned primarily with the mechanics of writing, the field of English also embraces principles and techniques of advanced writing, for composition is the art of writing. This not only means essays, stories, plays, and poetry, but also a wide field known as journalism.

Journalism is concerned with news and the various forms in which news reaches the public. In the secular world, to some the philosophy is to give the public what it wants; to others it means to give the public the truth which it needs. In performing this task the journalist is expected to be independent, fair, accurate, honest, responsible, and decent.

In general, the purposes in this field embrace the functions of informing the people, interpreting the news, guiding and entertaining the people. Its primary concern, however, is with the news. Life has become so complex today that people need, along with the announcements of facts, the explanation and interpretation of them. Accordingly, journalism is devoted to efforts at helping the individual to achieve a better understanding of the significance of what he reads, sees, and hears.

Journalism is closely related to literature. In fact, it is hard to distinguish between the two at times. However, the basic difference seems to lie in the author's purpose. Whereas the author expresses his personal thoughts and feelings, the journalist expresses those of the community.

Journalism utilizes the chief media of mass communication. These include the spoken word by means of radio and television, the printed word by means of newspapers, magazines, books, pamphlets, etc., and the visual media, including motion pictures and television.

Writing of all kinds is important to the *Christian.* The written symbol was created and revealed by God. The ability of man to manipulate these symbols is a divine endowment. The purpose of writing for the Christian is to glorify God, also to express thought and to meet the vocational and practical requirements of life.

Sin has affected the quality of writing as evidenced by indifference, imperfect letter formations and legibility. The Holy Spirit helps man by restoring the desire to write to serve God and to write well. He gives strength and ability to improve the quality of writing.

The spread of the Gospel depends on communication. The field of English, therefore, provides the Christian with one of his most potent and useful means for disseminating the good news of the Gospel throughout the world. Some of the objectives to be set up include:

1. A realization that the ability to write is a gift of God to be used to His glory
2. A recognition that faulty handwriting is a result of sin
3. Awareness of the fact that indifference to quality of handwriting is a result of sin
4. A realization that the development of a desire to write well and the ability to do so depend upon the grace of God and the work of His Spirit
5. The desire to write well in all situations
6. Knowledge of correct letter and word formation
7. Development and maintenance of skill in handwriting
8. Neatness and good form in all written work, e.g., margins, indentations, paragraphing; and habitually good practice in all written work.
9. Appreciation of good handwriting[4]

Before leaving the field of English entirely, our attention should be turned to another skill closely related to writing — *reading*, a skill so necessary to become proficient in the field of English. Reading is the power to glean thoughts from the written symbolic representations of oral expression. The power to arrange and rearrange these symbolic elements into intelligible combinations is called spelling.

The possibility of communication by means of symbolic representation of thoughts and emotions was created by God who endowed man with these capacities. The ability to read was given to man by God to help man understand and love God and to better equip man for personal efficiency and for living to the glory of God. Other functions of reading for man include recreation, information, and appreciation.

Sin has corrupted man's thought life, confused his understanding, and crippled his ability to master the mechanics of reading. The result is often indifference, inefficiency, and selfishness.

The Holy Spirit helps to restore man's reading ability, both philosophically and mechanically, by quickening the powers of comprehension and dexterity in reading mechanics. He awakens the desire to use reading ability to the glory of God as well as a desire to be more mechanically perfect.

Some of the objectives for reading have been stated as follows:

1. A recognition that the ability to read is a gift of God to be used for His glory
2. A realization that man's ability to read and his desire to use that ability to God's glory have been disrupted as a result of sin
3. A realization that the Spirit of God and Special Revelation are necessary to restore man's ability to read as well as his desire to use that ability to God's glory
4. The desire to read well

[4]*Ibid.*, p. 200.

5. The cultivation of skills and abilities essential to proficiency in oral and silent reading
6. The cultivation of study skills
7. The development of Christian standards of judgment and discrimination in the selection of reading material
8. The development of desirable reading interests
9. The development of increased appreciation of literature[5]

2. Speech

Speech is the communication or expression of thoughts and feelings by spoken words, vocal sounds, and gestures. It embraces both theory and practice of oral expression and communication when organized as a course of study. Speech is an individual's use of language; it is his own expression and he is the producer of it. It is a means of developing distinctiveness of personality. It is essential to mental health and wholesome intellectual development.

Oral expression can take many forms. It may be sentences, thoughts for letters, facts for a record, storytelling, preaching, teaching, or witnessing. Constant use of these forms will lead to greater personality development, vocational competence, and to greater influence on the part of the Christian in building the Kingdom of God.

Other values coming to the student in this field of study include:

1. Through oral communication we transmit, interpret and vitalize our heritage of ideas, ideals and aspirations.
2. Oral communication is a means to social action.
3. Oral communication contributes to the gathering and dissemination of information.
4. Oral communication makes cooperation possible in solving common problems.
5. Oral communication provides a means of contact by which individuals and groups can adjust to times and conditions.
6. Oral communication helps students understand and use the various devices of communication, such as television, radio, etc.
7. The skills provided in oral communication make it possible for the Christian to serve God in the spreading of the Gospel throughout the world.

We need to remember, however, that the primary concern is the use of language and speech as a means of communication. In accomplishing this the function of speech is to cause others to act through instruction, persuasion or commands and to cause others to feel and think.

Generally, in the field of education the purpose of speech is to

[5]*Ibid.*, p. 138.

increase one's effectiveness in dealing with other people. This is particularly true in our working world. It is felt that one functions most precisely in terms of his ability to speak effectively. To this the Christian educator must add that the purpose ultimately is to reveal, glorify, and serve God in the communication of the Gospel to the whole world.

Speech development has marked influence on personality development. The ability to speak makes social contacts easier whereas speech difficulties often lead to self-consciousness, lack of self-confidence, and timidity. Marked improvement in exercising the skills of oral communication, therefore, seems to contribute largely to becoming a better person and, for the Christian, a better servant of God.

Oral language is used in a wide variety of ways, such as

Talking	Reporting	Preaching
Conversing	Explaining	Teaching
Sharing	Evaluating	Praying
Planning	Solving Problems	Witnessing
Discussing	Creative Thinking	

Clarity of speech and language demands accurate articulation of sounds, clear enunciation, pronunciation which can be understood, usage which fits commonly accepted standards, and choice of words which carry the meaning which is intended.

To achieve such worthy aims schools and colleges organize speech departments and offer courses of study to lay the foundations for effective speech skills, to teach students to interpret and share with an audience various types of literature intellectually and emotionally, to practice the principles of parliamentary procedures for conducting business meetings, to analyze speech sounds with emphasis on breathing, tone quality, phonation and articulation, to utilize principles of argumentation and discussion, and many other aspects of speech, including speech science, speech correction, broadcasting, drama, etc.

The objectives for speech are largely the same as those suggested for language in the succeeding section. The Christian teacher can relate this field to his faith also by following the suggestions in the section devoted to a discussion of the Christian philosophy of communication. The Bible itself is full of the various forms of oral expression.

The skill of *listening* is probably used more than any other skill. It is certainly the first to operate in the life of the normal individual. Listening has increased in importance in our day because of greater interest in radio, talking pictures, and television.

Listening, like reading, is a mental process which calls for thought and response. It is deeper, therefore, than hearing.

Listening and speaking are closely related. Listening is receiving what is expressed orally. Like speech, true listening has to be learned. The more a listener attends to the thoughts of others with self-forgetfulness, the more mature is his response.

Continuous development in the art of listening goes hand in hand with progress in speaking. The increasing pressures of our day call for listening, not only with sympathy and understanding, but also with discrimination. Therefore, students need to be taught how to listen purposefully, accurately, critically, and responsibly.

There are degrees of listening ranging from mere marginal attention to absorbed self-forgetful interest and thinking. It is important that teachers do everything possible to set up the proper atmosphere and environment conducive to good hearing and listening.

3. *Language*

Language is a channel of communication through which ideas are transmitted in the form of symbols from a person who speaks to one who listens. Thoughts, feelings, and decisions are transmitted in this manner. However, the heart of language is the ideas or meanings represented, not the symbols used. Thus, language seems to be primarily a cultural product, not inherited, but learned as a part of our culture. Teachers consequently must make sure that students know the meaning of ideas and concepts which are expressed through language.

By means of language ideas become social. In this way a community of understanding is made possible through language. Thus, language enables one to share life with others.

The ability to use language is a distinctive mark of human nature. This is true because God planned it this way. A great deal has already been said about the philosophy of language in a previous section of this chapter, enough to suffice at this point.

The values of language to the student are many. The following list shows this.

1. Language is informative.
2. Language helps to control future behavior.
3. Language is the channel through which the individual can express his own feelings and values.
4. The study of language cultivates exactness, clear thinking, and reading and listening with attention.
5. Language puts the student in touch with other cultures besides his own.
6. Language broadens the student's mental life, deepens his sense of fellowship, and dignifies human relationships.
7. Through studies in language the student learns much about himself and others.

8. To the Christian, language becomes the vehicle for transmitting the Gospel.

9. It should also be the expression of regenerated character.

Not the least of values which can be mentioned are those connected with acquaintance with and use of foreign languages. The basic reason for learning a foreign language is not a mechanical one, but rather the ability to understand truly and inwardly the culture and people represented. Other values embrace the widening of horizons, the deepening of appreciations, and the creation of new perspectives.

Some of the more general objectives for the teaching of language have been stated as follows:

1. To teach a Christian interpretation of the origin and the use of language
2. To create a desire for correct expression
3. To foster the development of an adequate vocabulary
4. To increase the ability to organize thought
5. To develop language skill in the common situations of life
6. To develop an understanding of the principles of the structure of language through a formal study of grammar[6]

The Christian teacher can relate language to the Christian faith in several ways:

1. By showing that God endowed men with the gift of speech
2. By stimulating the use of language for the glory of God and deprecating its use to profane His name and holy things
3. By pointing out that respect is due all languages and people who use them
4. By rejoicing in the use of all languages to extend God's kingdom
5. By revealing, according to the Word, how languages reveal the nature and purposes of God
6. By indicating the importance of language in maintaining communication and fellowship with God through prayer

4. Research Procedures

There is a place for careful, ordered reflection involving processes of thought in the solution of the problems faced by mankind. Good thinking is necessary for good living in all walks of life. This is no less true for the Christian than for others for "out of the heart are the issues of life" and "as man thinketh in his heart, so is he."

Good thinking is necessary for good communication. The skills in communicating are directed by man's thought life. The search for and use of truth, therefore, is dependent both on thinking and communication of thought. Since man is expected to think God's thoughts after Him, the pursuit of truth wherever he may

[6]*Ibid.*, p. 172.

find it should lead man closer to God and the use of it properly should issue in Godlikeness.

Reflective thinking and science have much in common. In fact, the thinking method of reputable scientists is in terms of a complete act of carefully organized reflection. Thus, ordered thinking is the method of true science. The scientific method is the method of reflective thought.

Simply stated, research is the constant search for facts, the true actualities, and their unprejudiced analysis. It involves careful and critical inquiry and examination in seeking facts and principles. It is a diligent investigation to discover truth but a search which is prolonged, intensive, and purposeful.

Educational research concerns the discovery of the solutions to problems arising in the field. The purpose of this kind of research is to discover procedures, rules, and principles relating to the various aspects of education.

Some of the more important research traits and abilities include reasoning power, accuracy, intellectual honesty, open-mindedness, objectivity, originality, discernment, excellent memory, independence, persistence, purposefulness, alertness, application, executive ability, and the like. All of these and more are needed in handling truth. Of all people the true Christian needs to practice these traits and exercise such abilities in handling the sacred truths of Almighty God. In fact, there are some Scriptures which emphasize these things. For example, "Prove all things; hold fast that which is good" (I Thessalonians 5:21). Christians need to be especially careful not only in the discovery of truth but also in handling and reporting it. Here is where these concerns are so relevant to communication.

Some of the skills involved in the field of research include the recognition, selection, definition, and evaluation of problems for research, the evaluation of previous research on the problems, including bibliography work and research reading, acquaintance with procedures, methods and techniques and tools of gathering data and evidence, knowledge of weighing, sifting, classifying, organizing the data, drawing conclusions, and reporting the findings to others. All of this is making it possible to communicate truth to others.

In relating research procedures to the Christian faith, the Christian teacher can show the relation of Revelation to research. He can point out that the inductive method of thinking and research is only *one* way to discover truth, that Revelation is also a way to truth. He can stress the importance of being as objective as possible, of thinking creatively and critically, and of exercising absolute honesty in the handling and reporting of truth. He can emphasize that research is not discovering "original truth" but rather a revealing of truths about God previously known, for all truth in the Christian view is related to God, its Source. He can stress the importance of accurate and intelligent techniques of reporting truths to possible readers.

5. Audio-visual Aids

Generally speaking, audio-visual aids are tools or channels through which things to be taught and learned can be more effectively communicated. To this the Christian would add that the purpose of such communication is to accomplish the goals of Christianity in the creation and development of Christian personality and service.

In education these tools are used to affect better communication. In Christian education the purpose of these tools is not confined to the process of communication but also embraces the function of enabling Christian educators to accomplish the goals of Christian education, primary of which are the creation and development of Christlike personalities (Ephesians 4:13) and revealing a Holy God.

More specifically these tools are means whereby the senses are appealed to and used as channels for the delivery of truths to the person to be learned. Audio aids appeal primarily to hearing; visual aids appeal primarily to seeing. The term audio-visual aids, therefore, is properly used to cover all types of materials which appeal to the eye and ear, used as aids in teaching and learning. The purpose of these aids is to make teaching more concrete and vivid; the objective is to achieve learning which is more accurate, more effective, and more lasting.

Traditionally, visual aids have been classified into two primary types — non-projected and projected. Non-projected aids are those which are viewed directly without the aid of a projector, such as maps, posters, flat pictures, objects, and others. Projected aids are those which are viewed by projecting them on a screen. Motion pictures, slides, and filmstrips are examples. Audio aids are those which use the medium of sound and include records, recorders, phonographs, radio, and the like.

Values which come to teachers and students by using these aids are many. The following list is illustrative:

1. They can create a mood.
2. They can interpret customs.
3. They can suggest a conduct pattern.
4. They supplement other methods.
5. They make learning faster.
6. They make learning more permanent.

7. They make learning more enjoyable.
8. They help bridge the gap of time and space.
9. They help overcome language barriers.
10. They make teaching more interesting, concrete, and vivid.

While we recognize the above values and many others, it should be remembered that audio-visual aids are means to an end, not ends in themselves, and also that they are not cure-alls. In fact, they have some real disadvantages at times among which are the following:

1. They cannot picture things that are purely spiritual.
2. They cannot teach small children through symbolism.
3. The appeal to children to manipulate the tools often over-shadows both teaching and learning.
4. The cost of some of the aids is prohibitive.
5. It often takes too much time for preparation, practice, and handling.
6. Untrained personnel cannot use them adequately.
7. Lack of long-range planning dilutes their value.
8. Coherence of knowledge is often missing.
9. Over-simplification is often experienced.
10. Techniques often overshadow concepts.

Earlier in the chapter it was pointed out that the Bible is a record of God's communication to and with man. It is full of illustrations of the use of audio-visual aids of many kinds. Twenty-five examples are listed as follows to show the versatility of their use in the Scriptures.

1. The great lights in the sky (Genesis 1)
2. Adam named (symbols) the beasts (Genesis 2)
3. Sight was used by Adam and Eve (Genesis 3)
4. Sound was used in communication (Genesis 3)
5. The rainbow was a sign (Genesis 9)
6. The Tower of Babel (Genesis 11)
7. The stars (Genesis 15)
8. Signs and visions given to Abraham (Genesis 15)
9. A pillar of salt (Genesis 19)
10. Visions to Jacob (Genesis 32)
11. The dreams of Joseph (Genesis 37)
12. Moses and the Burning Bush (Exodus 3)
13. Miracles of Moses (Exodus 4)
14. The plagues of Egypt (Exodus 7-11)
15. The Passover Feast (Exodus 12)
16. Presence and power of God (Exodus 13-14)
17. Miracles of the Canaan Journey
    a. Red Sea Crossing (Exodus 14)
    b. Waters of Marah made sweet (Exodus 15)

    c. Bread and meat (Exodus 16)
    d. Water from the Rock (Exodus 17)
    e. Ten Commandments (Exodus 20)
    f. Written laws (Exodus 21-23)
    g. God's presence in glory (Exodus 24)
    h. The Tabernacle (Exodus 25 ff)
    i. The Priest's garments (Exodus 39)
18. Laws, feasts and sacrifices (Book of Leviticus)
19. The prophets dramatized their messages
20. Symbolical acts used by the prophets
21. Object lessons used by the prophets
22. Birth of Jesus announced by songs and a star
23. Jesus used parables and stories
24. Jesus used concrete objects and illustrations
25. Jesus referred constantly to nature

In teaching, audio-visual aids are used in many ways, chief of which are the following:

1. They supplement other teaching methods.
2. They are useful in introducing new ideas and subjects.
3. They are useful in developing new ideas and subjects.
4. They provide background information.
5. They help to clarify and explain difficult meanings.
6. They drive home important points.
7. They are useful in review work, summary and drill.
8. They are useful in covering a great deal of materials quickly.
9. They are useful in correcting false impressions.

In Christian education additional uses include these aids being used as tools in leadership education programs, in worship, in evangelism, in missions, in social work, and in recreation.

SUGGESTED ACTIVITIES FOR CHAPTER XIII

1. What is your definition of communicative skills?
2. What skills do you classify in this curriculum area?
3. What does the history of these skills show about the trends in the use of them?
4. How much importance do you attach to communication in the field of education?
5. What values can you add to the list included in this chapter?
6. Have a discussion on the Christian philosophy of communication. What ways indicate that God is revealed? By communicating how does man reveal God?
7. Trace the use of language in the Scriptures.
8. Draw your own chart to show how you would integrate skills and subject matter in this area.
9. Add to the list of General Objectives.
10. Discuss ways and means of integrating and interpreting subject matter of communicative skills in a way to reveal God and qualify man to be more like God.

SELECTED BIBLIOGRAPHY*

Baillie, John, *Natural Science and the Spiritual Life* (New York, Charles Scribners Sons, 1952)

Bell, Bernard I., *Crisis in Education* (New York, McGraw-Hill Book Co., 1949)

Bent, Rudyard K., and Henry H. Dronenberg, *Principles of Secondary Education*, 3rd Ed. (New York, McGraw-Hill Book Co., Inc., 1955)

Berkhof, L., *Systematic Theology*, 4th Ed. (Grand Rapids, Michigan, Wm. B. Eerdmans Pub. Co., 1949)

Black, Marvin M., *The Pendulum Swings Back* (Nashville, Cokesbury Press, 1938)

Bossing, Nelson L., *Teaching in Secondary Schools* (New York, Houghton Mifflin Co., 1952)3rd Ed.

Bower, William C., *Christ and Christian Education* (New York, Abingdon Cokesbury, 1943)

Bower, William C., *Church and State in Education* (Chicago, University of Chicago Press, 1944)

Bowman, Isaiah, *The Graduate School in American Democracy* (Washington, D. C., U. S. Government Printing Office)

Brackenberry, Robert L., *Getting Down to Cases* (New York, G. D. Putnam's Sons, 1959)

Brameld, Theodore, *Philosophies of Education in Cultural Perspective* (New York, The Dryden Press, 1955)

Branscomb, Harvie, *The Teachings of Jesus* (Nashville, Abingdon-Cokesbury Press, 1931)

Brightman, Edgar S., *A Philosophy of Religion* (New York, Prentice-Hall, Inc., 1940)

Brooks, Phillips, *The Influence of Jesus* (New York, E. P. Dutton and Co., 1879)

Broudy, Harry S., *Building a Philosophy of Education* (Englewood Cliffs, N. J., Prentice-Hall, 1954)

Brown, Charles R., *The Master's Influence* (Nashville, Cokesbury Press, 1936)

Brown, Francis J., *Educational Sociology* (New York, Prentice-Hall Inc., 1947)

Brubacher, John S., *A History of the Problems of Education* (New York, McGraw-Hill Book Co., Inc., 1947)

Brubacher, John S., *Modern Philosophies of Education* (New York, McGraw-Hill Book Co., 1950)

Buswell, J. Oliver, Jr., *The Philosophies of F. R. Tennant and John Dewey* (New York, The Philosophical Library, Inc., 1950)

Butler, J. Donald, *Four Philosophies and Their Practice in Education and Religion* (New York, Harper and Bros., 1951)

See ADDENDA for more recent listings.

Buttrick, George A., *Christ and Man's Dilemma* (Nashville, Abingdon-Cokesbury, 1946)

Butts, R. Freeman, *A Cultural History of Education* (New York, McGraw-Hill Book Co., Inc., 1947)

Byrne, Herbert W., *A Study of Administrative Practices in Selected Bible Institutions* (an unpublished doctoral dissertation in the library of Bradley University, 1952)

Cairns, Earle E., *A Blueprint for Christian Education* (Wheaton, Ill., Faculty Bulletin of Wheaton College, June 1953, Vol. 16, No. 3)

Carnell, Edward J., *A Philosophy of the Christian Religion* (Grand Rapids, Mich., Wm. B. Eerdmans Pub. Co., 1952)

Carnell, Edward J., *Introduction to Christian Apologetics* (Grand Rapids, Mich., Wm. B. Eerdmans Pub. Co., 1948)

Casserley, J. V. L., *The Christian in Philosophy* (New York, Charles Scribner's Sons, 1951)

Caulkins, Raymond, *How Jesus Dealt with Men* (Nashville, Abingdon-Cokesbury Press, 1942)

Chambers, Oswald, *Biblical Psychology* (Cincinnati, God's Revivalist Office, 1914)

Clark, Gordon H., *A Christian Philosophy of Education* (Grand Rapids, Mich., Wm. B. Eerdmans Publishing Co., 1946)

Clark, Gordon H., *A Christian View of Men and Things* (Grand Rapids, Mich., Wm. B. Eerdmans Publishing Co., 1952)

Clark, Henry W., *The Philosophy of Christian Experience* (New York, Fleming H. Revell Co., n.d.)

Collins, Carl A., Jr., *Paul As a Leader* (New York, Exposition Press, 1955)

Colwell, Ernest C., *An Approach to the Teaching of Jesus* (Nashville, Abingdon-Cokesbury Press, 1947)

Cooke, Robert L., *Philosophy, Education, and Certainty* (Grand Rapids, Mich., Zondervan Pub. House, 1940)

Craig, Samuel G., *Christianity Rightly So Called* (Philadelphia, The Presbyterian and Reformed Pub. Co., 1946)

Cranford, Clarence W., *Taught by the Master* (Nashville, Broadman Press, 1956)

Crooker, Joseph H., *The Supremacy of Jesus* (Boston, American Unitarian Association, 1911)

Cross, Hildreth, *An Introduction to Psychology* (Grand Rapids, Mich., Zondervan Pub. House, 1952)

Cully, Iris V., *The Dynamics of Christian Education* (Philadelphia, Westminster Press, 1958)

Curtis, Olin A., *The Christian Faith* (New York, Eaton and Mains, 1905)

Davis, Rupert E., Ed., *An Approach to Christian Education* (New York, The Philosophical Library, Inc., 1956)

DeBlois, Austen K., and Donald R. Gorham, *Christian Religious Education* (New York, Fleming H. Revell Co., 1939)

Delitzsch, Franz, *A System of Biblical Psychology* (Edinburgh, T. and T. Clark, 1890)

DeYoung, Chris A., *Introduction to American Education*, 3rd Ed. (New York, McGraw-Hill Book Co., Inc., 1950)

Dewey, John, *Democracy and Education* (New York, Macmillan Co., 1916)

Donlan, Thomas C., *Theology and Education* (Dubuque, Iowa, Wm. C. Brown Co., Publishers, 1952)

Douglass, Harl R., and Calvin Grieder, *American Public Education* (New York, The Ronald Press Co., 1948)

Douglass, Paul F., *Spiritual Experience in Administration* (Washington, D. C., The American University Press, 1951)

Eavey, C. B., *Principles of Teaching for Christian Teachers* (Grand Rapids, Michigan, Zondervan Publishing House, 1940)

Eavey, C. B., *The Art of Effective Teaching* (Grand Rapids, Michigan, Zondervan Publishing House, 1953)

Eberhardt, Charles R., *The Bible in the Making of Ministers* (New York, Association Press, 1949)

Edge, Findley B., *Teaching for Results* (Nashville, Broadman Press, 1956)

Educational Policies Commission, *The Purposes of Education in American Democracy* (Washington, D. C., National Education Association, 1938)

Emerson, Wallace, *Outline of Psychology* (Van Kampen Press, Incorporated, Wheaton, Ill., 1953)

Fairchild, Hoxie N., et al, *Religious Perspective in College Teaching* (New York, The Ronald Press Co., 1952)

Fakkema, Mark, *Christian Philosophy: Its Educational Implications* (Chicago, National Union of Christian Schools, 1952)

Fakkema, Mark, *How to Educate Children Mentally* (Chicago, National Association of Christian Schools, 1948)

Ferm V., Ed., *A History of Philosophical Systems* (New York, The Philosophical Library, 1950)

Ferre, Nels F. S., *Christianity and Society* (New York, Harper and Bros., 1950)

Fitzpatrick, Edward A., *Philosophy of Education* (Milwaukee, Bruce Pub. Co., 1950)

Frost, S. E., *The Basic Teachings of the Great Philosophers* (Garden City, N. Y., The Standard Bookshelf, 1942)

Gaebelein, Frank E., *Christian Education in a Democracy* (New York, Oxford University Press, 1951)

Gaebelein, Frank E., *The Pattern of God's Truth* (New York, Oxford University Press, 1954)

Glenn, Paul J., *The History of Philosophy* (St. Louis, B. Herder Book Co., 1950)

Glenn, Paul J., *Introduction to Philosophy* (St. Louis, B. Herder Book Co., 1947)

Good, H. C., *A History of Western Education* (New York, Macmillan Co., 1947)

Hamilton, Edith, *Witness to the Truth* (New York, W. W. Norton and Co., 1948)

Hamilton, Floyd E., *The Basis of Christian Faith*, 3rd Ed., rev. (New York, Harper and Bros., 1946)

Hardie, Charles D., *Truth and Fallacy in Education Theory* (London, Cambridge University Press, 1941)

Hay, Clyde I., *The Blind Spot in American Public Education* (New York, The Macmillan Co., 1950)

Hegland, Martin, *Christianity in Education* (Minneapolis, Augsburg Pub. House, 1954)

Henderson, Stella V. P., *Introduction to Philosophy of Education* (Chicago, University of Chicago Press, 1947)

Henry, Carl F. H., *The Drift of Western Thought* (Grand Rapids, Michigan, Wm. B. Eerdmans Pub. Co., 1951)

Henry, Carl F. H., *Fifty Years of Protestant Theology* (Boston, W. A. Wilde Co., 1950)

Henry, Carl F. H., *The Protestant Dilemma* (Grand Rapids, Mich., Wm. B. Eerdmans Pub. Co., 1949)

Henry, Carl F. H., *Remaking the Modern Mind* (Grand Rapids, Mich., Wm. B. Eerdmans Pub. Co., 1946)

Henry, Carl F. H., *The Uneasy Conscience of Modern Fundamentalism* (Grand Rapids, Mich., Wm. B. Eerdmans Pub. Co., 1947)

Herberg, Will, "Toward a Biblical Theology of Education," *The Christian Scholar* (December, 1953, Vol. 36, No. 4)

Hinsdale, B. A., *Jesus As a Teacher* (St. Louis, Christian Pub. Co., 1895)

Horne, Henry H., *The Democratic Philosophy of Education* (New York, The Macmillan Co., 1932)

Horne, Herman H., *Jesus As a Philosopher* (New York, The Abingdon Press, 1927)

Horne, Herman H., *The Master Teacher* (New York, The Association Press, 1942)

Horne, Herman H., *The Philosophy of Christian Education* (New York, Fleming H. Revell Co., 1937)

Horne, Herman H., *The Philosophy of Education* (New York, Macmillan Co., 1915)

Horne, Herman H., *The Psychological Principles of Education* (New York, Charles Scribner's Sons, 1913)

Hutchins, Robert M., *The Conflict in Education in a Democratic Society* (New York, Harper and Bros., 1953)

"Is Evangelical Theology Changing?", *Christian Life* (March, 1956)

"Is Liberal Theology Changing?," *Christian Life* (April, 1956)

Kepler, Thomas S., Ed., *Contemporary Religious Thought* (New York, Abingdon-Cokesbury Press, 1941)

Kepler, Thomas S., Ed., *Contemporary Thinking About Jesus* (New York, Abingdon-Cokesbury Press, 1944)

Kepler, Thomas S., Ed., *Contemporary Thinking About Paul* (New York, Abingdon-Cokesbury Press, 1950)

Jaarsma, Cornelius, "Christian Theism and the Empirical Sciences," *Journal of the American Scientific Affiliation* (June, 1955, Vol. 7, No. 2)

Jaarsma, Cornelius, *Fundamentals in Christian Education* (Grand Rapids, Mich., Wm. B. Eerdmans Pub. Co., 1953)

Keyser, Leander S., *The Philosophy of Christianity* (Burlington, Iowa, The Lutheran Literary Board, 1928)

Koehler, Edward W., *A Christian Pedagogy* (St. Louis, Concordia Publishing House, 1930)

Kuist, Howard T., *The Pedagogy of St. Paul* (New York, George H. Doran Co., 1925)

Learning and Instruction, 49th Yearbook (National Society for the Study of Education, 1950)

Leber, Lois, *Education That Is Christian* (Westwood, N. J., Fleming H. Revell Co., 1958)

Limbert, Paul M., Ed., *College Teaching and Christian Values* (New York, Association Press, 1951)

Lotz, Philip H., *Orientation in Religious Education* (Nashville, Abingdon-Cokesbury Press, 1940)

Lueck, William R., *An Introduction to Teaching* (New York, Henry Holt and Co., 1953)

Marshall, Max S., *Two Sides to a Teacher's Desk* (New York, The Macmillan Co., 1951)

Marston, Leslie R., *From Chaos to Character* (Winona Lake, Indiana, Light and Life Press, 1948)

Mascall, E. L., *Christian Theology and Natural Science* (New York, The Ronald Press Co., 1956)

Mason, Harold C., *Abiding Values in Christian Education* (Westwood, N. J., Fleming H. Revell Co., 1955)

Mattson, A. D., *Christian Social Consciousness* (Rock Island, Ill., Augustana Book Concern, 1953)

Miller, Randolph C., *Biblical Theology and Christian Education* (New York, Charles Scribner's Sons, 1956)

Miller, Randolph C., *Education for Christian Living* (Englewood Cliffs, N. J., Prentice-Hall, Inc., 1956)

Monroe, Walter S., Editor, *Encyclopedia of Educational Research*, Revised Ed. (New York, The Macmillan Co., 1952)

Mort, Paul R. and William S. Vincent, *Introduction to American Education* (New York, McGraw-Hill Book Co., Inc., 1954)

Murch, James D., *Christian Education and the Local Church* (Cincinnati, Standard Pub. Co., 1943)

Murray, A. Victor, *Education Into Religion* (New York, Harper and Bros., 1953)

Nash, Arnold S., *Protestant Thought in the Twentieth Century* (New York, Macmillan Co., 1951)

National Council of Churches of Christ in the U. S., *The Curriculum Guide for the Local Church* (Chicago, Division of Christian Education, 1950)

National Society for the Study of Education, *Modern Philosophies of Education* (Chicago, University of Chicago Press, 1955)

National Union of Christian Schools, *Course of Study for Christian Schools*, 2nd rev. ed. (Grand Rapids, Mich., Wm. B. Eerdmans Pub. Co., 1953)

Orr, James, *The Christian View of God and the World* (New York, Charles Scribner's Sons, 1897)

Park, Joe, Ed., *Selected Readings in the Philosophy of Education* (New York, Macmillan Co., 1958)

Phenix, Phillip H., "The Scientific Faith of American Scientists," *The Christian Scholar*, June, 1955, Vol. 37, No. 2)

Pierson, Arthur T., *The Bible and Spiritual Life* (New York, Gospel Pub. House, n.d.)

Redden, John D. and Francis A. Ryan, *A Catholic Philosophy of Education* (Milwaukee, Bruce Pub. Co., 1942)

Rugg, Harold and William Withers, *Social Foundations of Education* (New York, Prentice-Hall, Inc., 1955)

Sargent, S. Stansfeld, *The Basic Teachings of the Great Psychologists* (Garden City, N. J., Halcyon House, 1944)

Sherrill, Lewis J., *The Rise of Christian Education* (New York, Macmillan Co., 1953)

Smart, James D., *The Teaching Ministry of the Church* (Philadelphia, The Westminster Press, 1954)

Smith, B. Othanel, William O. Stanley, and J. Harlan Shores, *Fundamentals of Curriculum Development* (Yonkers-on-Hudson, N. Y., World Book Co., 1950)

Smith, Huston, *The Purposes of Higher Education* (New York, Harper and Bros., 1955)

Smith, H. Shelton, *Faith and Nurture* (New York, Charles Scribner's Sons, 1950)

Smith, Wilbur M., *Therefore Stand* (Boston, W. A. Wilde Co., 1945)

Spier, J. M., *An Introduction to Christian Philosophy* (Philadelphia, The Presbyterian and Reformed Pub. Co., 1954)

Spier, J. M., *What Is Calvinistic Philosophy?* (Grand Rapids, Mich., Wm. B. Eerdmans Pub. Co., 1953)

Strong, Augustus M., *Systematic Theology* (Philadelphia, Judson Press, 1907)

Swearingen, Tilford T., *The Community and Christian Education* (St. Louis, Bethany Press, 1950)

Thompson, Merritt M., *An Outline of the History of Education*, rev. ed. (New York, Barnes and Noble, Inc., 1951)

Thorpe, Louis P., and Allen M. Schmuller, *Contemporary Theories of Learning* (New York, Ronald Press Co., 1954)

Traina, Robert A., *Methodical Bible Study* (New York, Biblical Seminary of New York, 1952)

Trueblood, D. Elton, *The Predicament of Modern Man* (New York, Harper and Bros., 1944)

Vieth, Paul H., Ed., *The Church and Christian Education* (St. Louis, Bethany Press, 1947)

Voskuyl, Roger J., "A Christian Interpretation of Science," in *Modern Science and the Christian Faith* (Wheaton, Ill., Van Kampen Press, 1950)

Walker, James B., *The Philosophy of the Plan of Salvation*, 2nd Ed. (Cincinnati, Cranston and Curts, n.d.)

Walsh, Chad, *Campus Gods on Trial* (New York, The Macmillan Co., 1953)

Weaver, Henry, Jr., "A Physical Scientist Defines the Scientific Method," *Journal of American Scientific Affiliation* (Sept., 1955, Vol. 7, No. 3)

Wiley, Horton, *Christian Theology* (Kansas City, Mo., Beacon Hill Press, 1940, Vol. 1)

Witmer, John A., "A Christian Social Responsibility," *Bibliotheca Sacra* (July, 1953, Vol. 110, No. 439)

Witty, Paul A., "The Teacher Who Has Helped Me Most," *Journal of the National Education Association,* XXXVI: 386

Woodring, Paul, *Let's Talk Sense About Our Schools* (New York, Mc-Graw-Hill Book Co., Inc., 1953)

Worrell, Edward, *Restoring God to Education* (Wheaton, Ill., Van Kampen Press, 1950)

Wyckoff, D. Campbell, *The Gospel and Christian Education* (Philadelphia, The Westminster Press, 1959)

Wyckoff, D. Campbell, *The Task of Christian Education* (Philadelphia, The Westminster Press, 1955)

Wynne, John P., *Philosophies of Education* (New York, Prentice-Hall, Inc., 1947)

Young, Warren C., *A Christian Approach to Philosophy* (Wheaton, Ill., Van Kampen Press, Inc., 1954)

ADDENDA

De-Beer, John L., *Toward a Philosophy of Christian Education* (National Union of Christian Schools, 1953)

Granbard, Allen, "The Free School Movement" in *Education Yearbook,* 1973-74 (New York, Macmillan Educational Corp., 1973)

Kienel, Paul A., *The Christian School: Why It Is Right For Your Child* (Wheaton, Victor, 1971)

Lee, James, *The Flow of Religious Instruction* (Dayton, Pflaum, 1973)

Lowrie, Roy W. Jr., *Christian School Administration* (National Association of Christian Schools, 1966)

Mager, Robert F., *Goal Analysis* (Belmont, CA, Fearon, 1972)

——————, *Preparing Instructional Objectives* (Belmont, CA, Fearon, 1962)

Mager, Robert F. and Peter Pipe, *Analyzing Performance Problems* (Belmont, CA, Fearon, 1970)

Mueller, Richard J., *Principles of Classroom Learning and Perception* (New York, Praeger, 1974)

——————ed., *Readings in Classroom Learning and Perception* (New York, Praeger, 1974)

Park, Joe, ed., *Selected Readings in the Philosophy of Education,* 3rd ed. (New York, Macmillan, 1968)

Richards, Lawrence O., *A Theology of Christian Education* (Grand Rapids, Zondervan, 1975)

Silberman, Charles E., *Crisis in the Classroom* (New York, Random House, 1970)

Smith, Charles T., *Ways to Plan and Organize Your Sunday School* (Glendale, Gospel Light, 1971)

Stoop, David A., *Ways to Help Them Learn* (Glendale, Gospel Light, 1971)

Taylor, Marvin J., ed., *An Introduction to Christian Education* (Nashville, Abingdon, 1966)

GLOSSARY OF
PHILOSOPHICAL TERMINOLOGY

For Use of Classes in Philosophy and Philosophy of Education

Absolute — existing without relation to any other being; self-existent; capable of being known or conceived out of relation; uncaused

Abstract — a quality or attribute considered in isolation from the subject in which it inheres, as "whiteness," a theory considered apart from any concrete application, as "abstract truth"

Ad Hoc Hypothesis — pertains to one case alone and cannot be tested by being put into new situations. Disconnected hypothesis, unrelated to the other hypotheses in the system

Ad Hominem (to the man) — appeal to passions or prejudices rather than to the intellect

Ad Infinitum — without limit or end; carrying on forever

Aeteleological — having no purpose; opposed to teleological

A Fortiori — with stronger reason; all the more, as, if a large man can safely cross a bridge, with how much more probability can a small one

Agnosticism — the denial that ultimate reality (God) is known or knowable

Anthropomorphic — the conception of God or gods in terms of man's nature

Apology — formal vindication of a hypothesis or conviction

A Posteriori — from the latter or subsequent; from experience to general laws

A Priori — from the former or antecedent; from general laws to particular instances

Autocracy — that form of government which has a monarch of unlimited authority; an absolute, self-derived power

Axiology — the study of the general theory of values

Category — an ultimate concept or form of thought, such as time and space, cause and effect, etc.

Coherent — that condition of a philosophy of life in which the major postulates are horizontally self-consistent and vertically fit the facts; a theory of the list of truth which stresses the consistency or harmony of all our judgments

Crisis Theology — Neo-orthodoxy with emphasis on contemporary man under judgment of God

Deductive — reasoning from the general to the particular

Deism — theology which denies the immanence of God in history, while holding to the transcendence of God above history; belief in a God separate and remote from world and man; Also, belief in existence of God on evidence of reason and nature, not revelation

Demiurge — Plato's intermediary maker of the universe; assisted in creation

Democracy — that form of government in which the sovereign power resides in the people, and is exercised either directly by them or by officials or representatives elected by them

Determinism — the universe including human activity determined by fixed laws

Dialectical Theology — Neo-orthodoxy

Dialectic — the art of drawing out truth by leading hypotheses to their logical conclusion; a method of reasoning in which contradictions or opposites are overcome in a new formulation

Ding An Sich (thing in itself) — reality in itself as opposed to appearance, or the phenomenal; used by Kant

Dualism — theory which considers ultimate reality as twofold, such as mind and matter

Duty — that which a person is bound by moral obligation to do or refrain from doing

Dynamic — relating to the existence or action of some force or forces

Eclecticism — a philosophy which takes the best out of all other philosophies

Egoism — individual self-interest is motive and end of all action

Empiricism — the theory which regards experience as the only source of knowledge

Epistemology — the subdivision of philosophy which deals with the sources, nature, and validity of knowledge

Essence — the sum total of those attributes which cannot be removed from a being without destroying the being itself, as rationality in man

Ex Nihilo — describes God's act of creating the world, "Out of nothing"

Experimentalism — that branch of pragmatism which emphasizes the scientific method of problem solving

Hedonism — the doctrine that the chief good in life is composed of personal pleasure only

Humanism — a doctrine which places emphasis on man; religious and philosophical humanism abandons all concepts of the supernatural

Hypothesis — a theory which the mind tentatively holds to explain an area of reality; a guess subject to test

Idealism — the theory that regards reality as essentially spiritual or the embodiment of mind or reason

Immanent — indwelling, or operating within the process

Innate Idea — knowledge which arises from constitution of mind, first acquired by experience

Intuitionism — doctrine that moral values are immediately apprehended; that there are some self-evident truths

Materialism — the view that reality is composed of matter only

Method of Authority — the reliance upon an external source or tradition as the ground for action

Method of Inquiry — the reliance upon the scientific method as the means of solving problems

Monism — reality has a fundamental unity; one fundamental reality

Naturalism — a view of the world, and of man's relation to it, in which only the operation of natural laws and forces is assumed; all events in the cosmos are a part of the inclusiveness of nature. A world view which denies the supernatural and teleological. Universe is self-operating

Neo-Orthodoxy — a contemporary theology or religious philosophy that is dualistic and other-worldly in its approach; stress is placed on God who is transcendent and who comes to men in a "crisis," or who reveals Himself through a special revelation. Sometimes called *crisis theology* or *neo-supernaturalism*

Nominalism — the view which regards universals or abstract concepts as mere names without any corresponding realities

Pantheism — the belief or theory that God and the Universe are identical; implying a denial of the personality and transcendence of God; the doctrine that God is all and all is God

Personalism — the theory that only persons are real

Phenomenalism — the theory that phenomena are the only objects of knowledge; or the only realities of existence

Philosophy — love of wisdom; coherent organization of all knowledge
1. Metaphysics — the study of what constitutes the nature of reality and of what reality is constituted; or ultimate being, non-material being
   a. Cosmology — branch of metaphysics which deals with the cosmos; material being
   b. Ontology — branch of metaphysics which deals with the study of being as such; involves the study of God
2. Logic — study of correct thinking; science of sound reasoning
3. Epistemology — study of knowledge
4. Ethics — study of right-wrong; moral principles and practice
5. Politics — study of government
6. Aesthetics — study of beauty

Pluralism — the view that ultimate reality is not one or two, but many; hence reality has no fundamental unity

Positivism — any philosophy which repudiates the possibility of a theological or metaphysical explanation of reality and confines verifiable knowledge to a description of phenomena

Pragmatism — the philosophy which judges events in the light of their consequences; good if it works

Rational — having the faculty of reasoning; endowed with reason

Rationalism — in epistemology, the view that knowledge comes by reason

Realism — the doctrine which conceives of universals as existing outside the mind; the view which regards universals or abstract concepts as having corresponding realities

Relative — existing in relation; contingent

Science — systematically classified knowledge

Sine Qua Non — an indispensable condition; that without which a thing cannot enjoy existence. For example, a *sine qua non* for life is good

Skepticism — the point of view that all knowledge is uncertain

Static — pertaining to forces in equilibrium or to bodies at rest; opposed to dynamic

Summum Bonum — the highest or supreme good. For the Christian: the experiential knowledge of God in Christ, or the possession of God in the Holy Spirit

Tabula Rasa — the theory that the mind, before receiving impressions, is a smoothed tablet, i.e., is completely without innate ideas. From Locke

Teleological — relating to ends or final causes; dealing with design or purpose (Frequently used in respect to history, ethics, etc.)

Teleological Argument — an inductive argument from the presence of purpose in the universe to a Designer behind the universe

Theism — belief in a personal God

Theology — the study of God; a subdivision of ontology

Transcendent — existing prior to, independent of, and exalted over, the time-space universe

Universal — an abstract or general concept regarded as having an absolute, mental or nominal existence

Value — that which is worthy of esteem for its own sake; that which has intrinsic worth

Weltanschauung — world-view

World-view — a systematic philosophy of, or insight into the movement and plan of the entire universe. Philosophy of total reality

INDEX

INDEX

INDEX

INDEX

Index